The Value of Marx

D1598653

Karl Marx's writings provide a uniquely insightful explanation of the inner workings of capitalism, which other schools of thought generally have difficulty explaining. From this vantage point, Marx's works can help to explain important features and economic problems of our age, and the limits of their possible solutions. For example, the necessity and origin of money, the growth of the wage-earning class, uneven development, cycles and crises, and the relative impoverishment of the workers, leading to debt and overwork.

The Value of Marx demonstrates that:

- Capitalist production necessarily involves conflicts in production and in distribution.

- Competition is an essential feature of capitalism, but it often generates instability, crises and unemployment, showing that capitalism is not only the most productive but also the most systematically *destructive* mode of production in history.

- Capitalist economies are unstable because of the conflicting forces of extraction, realisation, and accumulation of surplus value under competitive conditions. This instability is structural, and even the best economic policies cannot avoid it completely.

The author critically reviews the methodological principles of Marx's value analysis and the best known interpretations of his value theory. He develops an interpretation of Marx focusing primarily upon the processes and relations that regulate social and economic reproduction under capitalism. When analysed from this angle, value theory is a theory of class and exploitation. The concept of value is useful, among other reasons, because it explains capitalist exploitation in spite of the predominance of voluntary market exchanges. The most important controversies in Marxian political economy are reviewed exhaustively, and new light is thrown on the meaning and significance of Marx's analysis and its relevance for contemporary capitalism.

Alfredo Saad-Filho is a lecturer in Development Economics at the School of Oriental and African Studies, the University of London.

Routledge frontiers of political economy

The Value of Marx

Political economy for contemporary capitalism

Alfredo Saad-Filho

London and New York

First published 2002
by Routledge
2 Park Square, Milton Park, Abingdon, Oxon, OX14 4RN

Simultaneously published in the USA and Canada
by Routledge
270 Madison Ave, New York NY 10016

Routledge is an imprint of the Taylor & Francis Group

Transferred to Digital Printing 2007

© 2002 Alfredo Saad-Filho

Typeset in Times New Roman by Exe Valley Dataset Ltd, Exeter

British Library Cataloguing in Publication Data
A catalogue record for this book is available
from the British Library

Library of Congress Cataloging in Publication Data
A catalog record for this book has been requested

ISBN10: 0–415–23434–4 (hbk)
ISBN10: 0–415–45926–5 (pbk)

ISBN13: 978–0–415–23434–4 (hbk)
ISBN13: 978–0–415–45926–6 (pbk)

Publisher's Note
The publisher has gone to great lengths to ensure the quality of this
reprint but points out that some imperfections in the original
may be apparent

For Rita, Lucas and Julia

Contents

Acknowledgements

I am grateful to those who have read and commented upon various drafts of this book, including Chris Arthur, Paresh Chattopadhyay, Nick Hostettler, Costas Lapavitsas, Michael Perelman, Alejandro Ramos Martinez, John Rosenthal, Simeon Scott, David Spencer, Nicola Taylor and John Weeks. I am especially indebted to Andrew Brown and Ben Fine for their valuable support and exhaustive comments, which have helped to improve every aspect of this book.

The Conference of Socialist Economists has kindly consented to the reproduction of sections of my papers 'A Note on Marx's Analysis of the Composition of Capital', *Capital & Class* 50, Summer 1993, pp. 127–146 and 'An Alternative Reading of the Transformation of Values into Prices of Production', *Capital & Class* 63, Autumn 1997, pp. 115–136. Verso and Lawrence and Wishart have kindly consented to the citation of extensive passages of, respectively, *Capital* and the *Theories of Surplus Value*, for which I am grateful.

Introduction

More than one hundred years after his death, Marx's writings continue to attract interest across the world.[1] In spite of speculation that his readership would dwindle after the collapse of the Soviet bloc, Marx's life and work have continued to attract the attention of social scientists, trade unionists, militants in anti-capitalist or environmental causes, and many others. I have been fortunate enough to witness this revival of interest in the university sector. Student demand for courses dealing with Marx's work is often overwhelming, leading to over-subscribed classes and lively debates. Marxian scholarship has also been developing strongly, as is shown by the publication of several outstanding books across the social sciences, and the continuing success of those journals open to Marxian contributions.

Although significant in themselves, these successes are a far cry from the dynamism and influence of Marxian scholarship thirty, or even twenty years ago. Today, inequity and exploitation are more heavily cloaked by 'market' ideology and by the vacuous discourse of 'globalisation' (although both have been fraying at the edges). These shifts, and changes in government policies, among them funding restrictions for education and research, have had a significant impact upon academic interests and student choices. It seems that, although much can be done to promote academic interest in Marxian themes, more significant and lasting achievements depend upon the success of social movements beyond the universities. Mass action is, obviously, urgently needed in order to constrain the erosion of the remaining social safety nets, improve the distribution of power and income across the globe, curtail the influence of financial interests and the 'sole superpower' and, more broadly, in order to preserve the possibility of life on this planet in the face of rapid environmental degradation. The positive implications of mass action for academic pluralism in general, and for Marxian research more specifically, cannot be underestimated.

Karl Marx offers no ready-made answers to the urgent problems of today. However, his writings provide a uniquely insightful explanation of the inner workings of capitalism and the articulation between distinct aspects of this economic system, and they show the enormous potential of capitalism for good and evil. From this vantage point, Marx's writings can throw light upon both the problems of our age and the limits of their possible solutions.

Three criticisms are often raised against Marx, that his writings are inconsistent, wrong or dated. This book reviews several charges of inconsistency and, within the limits of the analysis, dismisses these charges. The second criticism is not assessed directly for reasons of both space and method. However, I think that analyses inspired by Marx's writings can provide interesting answers to important questions affecting large numbers of people, and this book provides pointers for further research. Finally, the argument that Marx's works are dated because they were written in the nineteenth century is ludicrous. To the best of my knowledge, no one has been foolish enough to raise similar claims against Marx's contemporary, Charles Darwin, or against Newton, Aristotle or the Prophets, whose writings predate Marx's by centuries. The credence that this argument has received in certain circles suggests that Ronald Meek was right when he argued that:

> All too often, writers seem to assume that when dealing with Marx it is permissible to relax academic standards to a degree which they themselves would regard as quite illegitimate when dealing with any other economist.[2]

Even more puzzling than the dismissal of Marx's analysis of capitalism is the implicit recognition of the *validity* of the labour theory of value,[3] for example when the importance of labour productivity for the determination of prices, living standards and international competitivity are discussed in the press and in political circles. However, in this context Marx's name is invariably ignored.[4]

This book critically reviews selected aspects of the Marxian political economy literature, and develops it further.[5] Two issues are analysed in detail: first, the essential aspects of economic reproduction under capitalism, including what is produced and how, and the social structures underlying this mode of production, especially the structures of exploitation; second, Marxian studies are shown to explain important features of capitalism which other schools of thought, including the neoclassical, Keynesian and institutionalist, have difficulty analysing. For example, the necessity and origin of money, technical progress and the rising productivity of labour, conflicts over the intensity of labour and the length of the working-day, the growth of the wage-earning class, the inevitability of uneven development, cycles and crises, and the impoverishment of the workers – not because of declining living standards but, rather, because of the growing distance between their 'needs' and what they can afford to buy, often leading to debt and overwork.

Value plays an essential role in Marx's critique of capitalism. This is not a simple concept, and it has been interpreted in widely different ways:

'virtually every controversy within Marxist economics is at bottom a controversy concerning the nature and status of value theory.'[6]

This book develops an interpretation of value theory drawing upon a range of contributions, especially those of Ben Fine and John Weeks.[7] This interpretation is orthodox in the sense of Lukács, i.e., it follows Marx's method closely, but there is no presumption that Marx's every scribble was right, or that every silence implies disapproval. As Heller rightly put it,

> there is no such thing as an interpretation of Marx which is proof against being "contradicted" by means of quotations . . . What interests me is the main tendency (or tendencies) of his thought[8]

The main purpose of value theory is to explain the relationship between labour and exploitation in capitalism:

> the theory of value enables us to analyse capitalist exploitation in a way that overcomes the fragmentation of the experience of that exploitation . . . it enables us to grasp capitalist exploitation as a contradictory, crisis-ridden process, subject to continual change . . . [and] it builds into our understanding of how the process of exploitation works, the possibility of action to end it.[9]

Drawing upon the capitalist monopoly of the means of production, the generalisation of the wage relation and the diffusion of commodity exchanges, value theory reaches important conclusions about the structure and dynamics of capitalist accumulation, including class, conflicts, prices, distribution, credit and finance. These findings offer useful guidelines for empirical studies, and they may inform policy conclusions, although these avenues are not pursued here. This book is incomplete in other areas too. It does not discuss important aspects of value theory, including interest-bearing capital, the tendency of the rate of profit to fall and crisis theory, it ignores non-economic forms of exploitation, and it does not review many important contributions to value analysis.

In spite of these limitations, the book achieves three main objectives. First, it demonstrates that analyses inspired by Marx's theory of value can be developed cogently, and explain important features of modern capitalism. Second, it evaluates critically the trajectory of Marxian value theory in the past half century, showing that it has become increasingly sophisticated, flexible, and better able to incorporate contributions from across the social sciences. Third, it contributes to the development of this theory in several areas, described below.

This book is divided into eight chapters. Chapter 1 explains the methodological principles of Marx's analysis, and their relationship with his critique of capitalism. This chapter is inspired by the 'materialist dialectics' of the Soviet philosopher E.V. Ilyenkov, and it provides the springboard for the critique of a recent Hegelian interpretation of Marx, the 'new dialectics'.

Chapter 2 reviews critically two interpretations of Marx's value theory, the 'embodied labour' views, including 'traditional Marxism' and Sraffian approaches, and value form theories, including those associated with Rubin and the 'new interpretation'. These are the best known value analyses developed in the past half-century, and they have contributed significantly to our understanding of capitalism. However, these interpretations are found wanting for several reasons. The shortcomings of traditional Marxism have led to its stagnation and fragmentation. Sraffian analyses misconceive both value and capital, and mirror important shortcomings of neoclassical economics, among them the inability to explain money and economic dynamics satisfactorily. The Rubin tradition has recast the value debate on a new, and much more fruitful, level in the early 1970s. However, its focus upon the value relation is often at the expense of the analysis of *capital* and *capitalism*, which reduces its usefulness and is often misleading. Finally, the new interpretation offers a valuable contribution for the development of a radical critique of macroeconomic policy. Even so, this interpretation suffers from significant theoretical shortcomings, especially the tendency to conflate phenomena at different levels of abstraction and to shortcut the mediations that structure value analysis and contribute to its unique explanatory power.

Chapter 3 outlines the value analysis developed in this book. It shows that value theory focuses primarily upon the economic processes and relations that regulate social reproduction under capitalism. This analysis departs from the division of labour. On this basis relations of exploitation are defined and, subsequently, capital and capitalist exploitation are introduced. This chapter shows that capital is, on the one hand, a relation of production in which labour power, the products of labour, and goods and services more generally, become commodities. On the other hand, capital is a class relation of exploitation defined by the ability of the capitalists to compel the working class to produce more than it consumes or controls, and by the capitalist command of the surplus. In these circumstances, the products of labour generally take the value form, and economic exploitation is based upon the extraction of surplus value. When analysed from this angle, the theory of value is a theory of class and, more specifically, a theory of *exploitation*. The concept of value is useful, among other reasons, because it expresses the relations of exploitation under capitalism, and allows them to be explained in spite of the predominance of voluntary market exchanges.

Chapter 4 explains surplus value as the difference between the value produced by the workers and the value of labour power, advanced as the worker's wage; alternatively, it is that part of the social value product appropriated by the capitalists. Following the conceptualisation of capital in chapter 3, these terms are analysed as *aggregates* defined by *class* relations, rather than being merely the sum of individual subsistence needs, wages or profits. This chapter also surveys different conceptions of the value of labour power, the bundle and the share approaches, and finds them wanting on several counts. An alternative is proposed, in which the value of labour power is neither a quantity of goods nor a quantity of money; it is a quantity of *value*, the abstract labour time spent by the working class producing necessities. This value is determined at the aggregate level, through the exchange between the capitalists and the working class, and the performance of labour and exploitation in production.

Chapter 5 reviews the relationship between values and prices, through the normalisation, synchronisation and homogenisation of labour. This chapter shows that the value form of the product is due to the social division of labour, and that value creation is a social process determined by the relations of production and by society's productive capacity. Analysis of normalisation, synchronisation and homogenisation of labour explains the value-producing potential of intense and skilled labour, deskilling, intra-sectoral competition and the use of machinery and technical change, including their significance for prices, economic reproduction and crises. Finally, this chapter discusses the meaning and significance of values and prices when demand and supply do not match.

Chapter 6 discusses Marx's concept of the composition of capital, including the technical, organic and value compositions (TCC, OCC and VCC). Although the composition of capital plays an important role in Marx's analyses of the value–price relationship, technical change, the tendency of the rate of profit to fall and other processes, this chapter shows that the TCC, OCC and VCC have been generally understood only superficially and generally incorrectly. The concept of TCC is straightforward; this is the physical ratio between the material inputs and the living labour necessary to transform them into the output. The OCC and VCC are more difficult to grasp, and they are compared and contrasted in two situations, static and dynamic. The static case contrasts the value of the constant capital productively consumed per hour (VCC) with the mass of means of production processed in that time (TCC and OCC). In a dynamic context, the OCC is the *ex ante* evaluation of the constant capital technically required per hour, while the VCC is the *ex post* ratio between the new value of the circulating constant capital and the variable capital spent in the last phase of production. The static case illuminates Marx's transformation of values into prices of production, whereas the dynamic case is useful for the analysis of the tendency of the rate of profit to fall, when capital accumulation occurs simultaneously with technical change.

Chapter 7 analyses one of the most vexed issues in Marxian political economy, the transformation of values into prices of production. The literature has often explained the transformation 'problem' as the determination of prices under conditions of inter-sectoral competition, but this neoclassical perspective is misguided. In his transformation procedure, Marx is interested primarily in explaining the distribution of capital, labour and surplus value across the economy. In order to do this, a more complex form of value is necessary, which Marx calls price of production. In other words, the transformation is essentially a change in the form of value, in which case Sraffian procedures are insufficient because they conflate the levels of analysis. The approach developed in this chapter shows that, properly understood, there is no 'problem' in Marx's transformation, and no inconsistency in his analysis. His theory is valuable because it explains the meaning and significance of prices. Calculation of the price vector is elementary in this context.

Finally, chapter 8 summarises the value analysis developed previously, through a critical review of Marxian and other radical contributions to the theory of money, credit and inflation. Marx's theory of money has often been examined as if it were significant only because of his derivation of money from the commodity. This chapter argues that this viewpoint is infertile, and that this theory can be developed in important ways, including the explanation of inconvertible money and inflation. The former is important because it shows that Marx's approach is internally consistent and it can accommodate important aspects of modern capitalism. The latter is a significant current problem, and analysing it is relevant both theoretically and politically.

Applications such as these demonstrate the vitality and contemporary relevance of Marxian political economy, and indicate its potential usefulness both as an analytical and critical policy instrument.

1 Materialist dialectics

Marx's method, especially in *Capital*, is difficult to summarise. Widely different interpretations of his method derive from distinct views of the role and objectives of his theory and from the scope and incompleteness of Marx's published works.[1] These methodological controversies have played a significant role in the development of Marxian political economy. However, it is unlikely that they would have become as far-reaching, and developed such importance, if Marx had been less cryptic himself on method. In the postface to the second edition of *Capital 1*, Marx concludes that 'the method employed in *Capital* has been little understood [as] is shown by the various mutually contradictory conceptions that have been formed of it'.[2] In spite of this, Marx never explained his own method fully.

Marx's reticence can be explained in at least three different ways. For Tony Smith,[3] Marx downplayed the method of *Capital* primarily in order to make the book more accessible to his working class readers, 'a consideration which to me outweighs everything else.'[4] This hypothesis is supported by Marx's statement that *Capital* 'will ... be much more popular and the method will be much more hidden than in [the *Contribution*].'[5] Smith reasonably conjectures that the tension between the complexity of the book and Marx's desire to find an attractive form of exposition led him to downplay the methodological aspects of *Capital*. However, this is insufficient explanation, because Marx repeatedly stated that he would never 'dumb down' his work merely in order to increase its appeal:

> the method of analysis which I have employed, and which had not previously been applied to economic subjects, makes the reading of the first chapters rather arduous ... This is a disadvantage I am powerless to overcome, unless it be by forewarning and forearming those readers who zealously seek the truth. There is no royal road to science, and only those who do not dread the fatiguing climb of its steep paths have a chance of gaining its luminous summits.[6]

Chris Arthur offers a different explanation. He argues that Marx never explained his own method adequately because he was uncertain himself, especially about its relationship with Hegel's method:

> I have concluded that Marx himself was confused about the relevance of Hegel's logic. Accordingly, I believe it is necessary to *reconstruct* the critique of capital . . . more consistently and explicitly than Marx.[7]

Arthur's claim has potentially far-reaching implications that cannot be pursued here.[8] However, it is possible to interpret the evidence in another way. This chapter argues that Marx was aware of the meaning and significance of his own method and did not downplay its importance merely in order to broaden the appeal of his work. Marx avoided a detailed explanation because, with few exceptions, his work is not primarily about methodology (or even philosophy). It is, rather, a *critique* of capitalism and its apologists. In his work, method generally plays an important but secondary role, and it is generally submerged within the argument.[9] In the light of Marx's works and the ensuing controversies, this chapter identifies Marx's methodological principles and their relationship with his analysis of capitalism.

This chapter is divided into three sections. The first summarises the principles of the 'materialist dialectic' interpretation of Marx's method in *Capital*, and reviews the implications of this interpretation of Marx's work. The second critically analyses a recent Hegelian interpretation of Marx, the 'new dialectics'. The third section concludes this chapter.

1.1 Real abstractions and mental generalisations

Lenin famously argued that:

> If Marx did not leave behind him a "*Logic*" (with a capital letter), he did leave the *logic* of *Capital* . . . In *Capital*, Marx applied to a single science logic, dialectics and the theory of knowledge of materialism . . . which has taken everything valuable in Hegel and developed it further.[10]

This section develops Lenin's claim in the light of the 'materialist dialectics' outlined by the Soviet philosopher E.V. Ilyenkov.[11] Materialist dialectics presumes, first, that the concrete analysed in *Capital*, the capitalist economy, is integral and whole, and that this organic system of mutually conditioning things or phenomena is determining with regard to its parts, or moments.[12] Second, in order to reconstruct the concrete in thought, analysis ought to mirror the structure of the concrete; in other words, it should start from the whole rather than from its parts.

In contrast, metaphysical approaches, including formal logic, tend to view the concrete as an agglomeration of ontologically independent elements linked only externally and more or less contingently.[13] Metaphysical approaches are generally structured around mental generalisations. For philosophers in the tradition of Locke, Kant and Mill, this is the only legitimate procedure for conceptual development.[14] Mental generalisations are based upon the arbitrary selection of certain relations or common properties for further analysis, for example, in economics, 'labour', 'demand', 'market' or 'utility'.

Mental generalisations are necessary for scientific analysis because they assist the essential tasks of identification and classification. However, they have little explanatory value for three reasons. First, they are tautological; mental generalisations identify certain elements present in everything because only things with these attributes are included in the analysis. Second, mental generalisations are external to the objects. They may express either objective facts or merely subjective fictions, and it can be difficult to distinguish between the two. Third, the properties which they identify may have widely distinct levels of complexity and may represent very different aspects of the phenomena of interest, in which case their relationship with the concrete is left unclear.[15] Because of these limitations, conclusions reached through mental generalisation lack general validity.

These insufficiencies can be overcome if the analysis is based, instead, upon real or concrete abstractions.[16] This approach was originally outlined by Spinoza, who argued for the 'deduction of the particular properties from the actual universal cause', rather than the 'deduction of the properties of things according to the formal rules of syllogistics.'[17] Hegel developed Spinoza's insight. He claimed that truth cannot be grasped through contemplation, but only through the ascent from sensual contemplation to the abstract expression of the concrete in the concept, which brings out its content and meaning (see section 1.2). Marx modified and applied this approach in his value theory and elsewhere.

Whereas mental generalisations are based upon external relations selected by the observer, real abstractions are based upon material reality, and they disclose concrete universals that include the *essence* of the particulars. In other words, and very simply, enquiries based upon mental generalisations can start from any feature of the concrete. In contrast, materialist dialectics selects the most important feature of the concrete, and reconstructs the other features systematically on the basis of this essence.[18] The essence is the objectively most general feature of the particulars, or their 'internal law-governed structure'; in other words, the essence comprises the logically and historically determinant features of the particulars, and it is the key to their internal relations.[19] Consequently, the essence is, first, a logical category that supplies the basic mediations for the reconstruction of the concrete in thought. Second, it is the actual (rather than merely theoretical or ideal) source from which the particulars spring. Third, it is a historically emerging result.[20] The essence arises as an exception from the rule, and it gradually displaces previous concrete universals to become the essence of a new set of phenomena through historical processes that can be analysed only concretely (see below, the examples of abstract labour, value and capital).[21]

This does *not* imply that the essence is always a separate entity lying either behind or underneath the phenomena, in which case its identification would require 'unveiling' or, alternatively, 'piercing through' the appearances in order to find something which, at least theoretically, can be mapped to the particulars. Rather, the essence generally exists only *in and through* the phenomena, and the latter are not merely the form of manifestation of the essence but, more strongly, its *mode of existence*.[22] For example, there is no actual 'fruit' which is the essence of all apples, plums and oranges. There are only individual fruits whose essence, or common biological and historical traits, can be revealed analytically.

In sum, materialist dialectics examines the concrete in order to identify the material structures of determination of reality, especially the essence of the phenomena under investigation and the mediations between them. Systematic analysis of the essence and its development illuminates the links between the particulars and allows the introduction of concepts expressing these relations, which are necessary for the reconstruction of the concrete in thought.[23] Eventually, this procedure outlines

> a criss-crossing field of mediations which amounts to a totality: no term in the field stands as its own . . . [T]otalising theory requires the notion of determinate [real] abstraction. Minus the notion, the conception of a "mutual interaction" taking place between "different moments", as is the case with "every organic whole" . . . amounts to banality: everything somehow affects everything else . . . To put bones into the flesh of totality we need to understand how terms can form and reform, or constitute and reconstitute, other terms: how one term's mode of existence can be another term, without remainder. This logically stronger conception redeems totality, and "dialectics", from the vague notion of mere reciprocal interaction.[24]

Let us discuss briefly three examples, which illustrate materialist dialectics and its differences from formal logic. The first example substantiates the claim that abstract labour is the essence of labour under capitalism. The second shows why abstract labour is the substance of value. The third explains the relationship between money, value and capital (see chapters 2 and 3).

Abstract labour

Labour is the purposeful expenditure of human energy in order to transform given natural and social conditions in a predetermined manner (see section 3.1). Therefore, labour mediates the metabolism between societies and their surrounding environment.[25] This 'physiological' definition derives from a mental generalisation across all types of concrete labour. Although simple and often adequate, it may be insufficient for two reasons. First, it is excessively general; several forms of purposeful energy expenditure are not generally considered labour, for example those activities directly related to the upkeep and reproduction of the individual and the household, leisure and self-expression, and the arts. Second, this transhistorical definition is analytically sterile. Inspection of reality shows that certain types of labour, for example cooking, design, management, or personal services, can vary significantly over time and place in terms of the work process and the circumstances in which these activities are performed. In spite of the importance of these features of human labour, the physiological definition of labour cannot be developed systematically in order to explain them.

Analysis of the meaning and significance of labour under capitalism is potentially more fruitful if one departs from its essence, *abstract labour*. Abstract labour can be defined simply as labour performed by wage workers directly engaged in the production of surplus value (see section 3.2). This is the essence of labour under capitalism for three reasons. First, the employment of wage labour in order to produce surplus value is typical of, and defines, capitalist relations. Second, the diffusion of capitalism gradually dislocates non-capitalist production. Non-wage forms of labour tend to be marginalised, and the employment of wage workers becomes contingent upon the production of surplus value.[26] Third, systematic analysis of abstract labour allows the introduction of other categories explaining the structures and social relations in capitalism, which is the guiding thread through *Capital*.

Under capitalism, labour generally has a double determination, it is both concrete and abstract. As concrete labour, work is a transformative activity; as abstract labour, work is subsumed by, or exists in and through, a specific social form. Abstract labour predominates over concrete labour because the performance of concrete labour generally depends upon the extraction of surplus value rather than, for example, need for the output.

This example highlights four important features of materialist dialectics. First, real abstractions reveal the essence of the phenomena under analysis, but the essence may not manifest itself in every particular.[27] In the example above, abstract labour is the essence of labour under capitalism even though some labours are unpaid (e.g., voluntary work), some unpaid workers can produce surplus value (e.g., prisoners subcontracted by private firms), and some wage workers do not produce surplus value (e.g., civil servants).

Second, in contrast with mental generalisations, the meaning and significance of concepts determined through real abstraction cannot be discovered unproblematically on inspection. In other words, materialist dialectics (based upon real abstractions) and formal logic (based upon mental generalisations) are mutually exclusive points of departure for scientific analysis.

Third, materialist dialectics may lose validity if pushed beyond its logical and historical limits.[28] For example, there is no direct correspondence between the stature of labour under capitalism and in other modes of production. In *Capital*, Marx addresses the structures and processes of social and economic reproduction under *capitalism*. Only a small part of the book refers to other modes of production, and there can be no presumption that Marx's analysis can encompass them unproblematically.[29]

Fourth, the validation of materialist dialectic analyses includes three separate stages: determination of the meaning and significance of the concepts and their internal relationship through logical and historical investigation; the explanation of phenomena that apparently contradict the 'internal law-governed structure'; and verification of the correspondence between the concrete and its theoretical representation.[30]

Value

Value analysis is critically important for Marx, and its meaning and validity have been the subject of considerable debate.[31] This example discusses Marx's identification of abstract labour as the substance of value. Marx's argument was famously criticised by the Austrian economist Eugen von Böhm-Bawerk, for whom Marx derives the

> "common factor" which is the characteristic of exchange value . . . [by] exclusion . . . [However] he limits from the outset the field of his search . . . to products of labor as against gifts of nature . . . To exclude the exchangeable goods which are not products of labor in the search for the common factor which lies at the root of exchange value is . . . a great error of method.[32]

Böhm-Bawerk presumes that the determination of the substance of value should be based upon a mental generalisation and the application of the rules of formal logic.[33] However, this critique is invalid. Marx's analysis does not depart from the exchange of two arbitrary commodities in given quantities, $xA=yB$, labour being the third or common element, and it does not follow the rules of formal logic.[34] Rather, his analysis is based upon real abstraction and it follows the principles of materialist dialectics.

The claim that abstract labour is the substance of value is based upon three premises. First, as argued above, labour is a transhistorical condition for social and economic reproduction. Second, abstract labour is the typically capitalist form of labour, and it predominates over concrete labour. Third, value (or commodity) relations are the general form of human intercourse under capitalism, and in this mode of production value relations mediate social and economic reproduction.[35] Capitalism developed historically through the generalisation of value relations, among them the monopoly of the means of production by a class of capitalists, the diffusion of commodity production through wage labour, the growth of commodity exchange, and the subordination of production by the profit motive. These value relations have established historically the predominance of abstract labour; conversely, the diffusion of abstract labour reinforces the commodification of human relations and production for profit.[36] Logically, systematic development of Marx's value analysis, founded upon abstract labour, can explain several important aspects of reality at distinct levels of complexity, including the capital relation, surplus value, competition, the distribution of labour and its products, the commodity form of non-products of labour (e.g., virgin land and pollution rights), interest-bearing capital, and so on.[37]

Capital

The transition between Marx's presentation of simple commodity circulation, represented by C–M–C' (commodity, money, another commodity), and the circuit of capital, M–C–M' (money–commodity–more money), is often presented as a purely logical step. For example, Patrick Murray claims that:

> Within simple commodity circulation . . . money that seeks to preserve itself as money seems to have no choice but to abstain from circulation . . . If money cannot preserve itself through isolation from circulation, it must preserve itself in the very act of circulating. This is precisely what the transition of money as such into money as capital effects . . . Hoarded away and secure from the risks of circulation, money always exists in a definite, finite amount, a fact which contradicts its logical determination as the embodiment of universal wealth . . . Capital, on the other hand, resolves the stagnating contradiction of money as such by positing itself as the process of valorization—the process of money going beyond its quantitative barrier, i.e., by increasing itself through circulation.[38]

Murray's view, inspired by Hegel's dialectics, is misguided, misleading and wrong (see section 1.2). It is misguided because it presumes that the concepts of money and capital are self-acting subjects which somehow actualise themselves historically because of purely logical imperatives. It is misleading because Murray's neglect of the social, economic and historical context in which commodities, money and capital exist obscures and devalues human agency. Finally, it is wrong because Murray confuses the fact that money is qualitatively *general* with the presumption that it ought to become quantitatively *unlimited*.[39]

In chapter 4 of *Capital 1* Marx does not 'derive' the concept of capital from the concept of commodity, or the capital circuit from simple commodity circulation. He merely *contrasts* the circuits C–M–C, M–C–M and M–C–M' in order to demonstrate that commodity circulation cannot systematically add value, in which case exchange or 'profit upon alienation' cannot be the source of surplus value. In other words, although some may profit at the expense of their customers, this is not possible for all the sellers, and 'profit upon alienation' cannot explain social and economic reproduction under capitalism. This conclusion lends support to Marx's argument that only the systematic exploitation of wage workers by the capitalist class can explain the valorisation of capital (see section 4.1).[40] In short, Marx's theory is not based upon conceptual developments. He uses materialist dialectics to investigate

> *a real fact*—the fact that money put in *capitalist* circulation, passing through all of its metamorphoses, brings a return—surplus-value. Then one has to go back to establish the conditions which make this fact possible.[41]

Let us summarise the principles of materialist dialectics. This approach presumes that the phenomena (the particulars that make up concrete reality) are conditioned by, and generally the mode of existence of, common essences. The relationship between essence and phenomenon is determined by a range of mediations, including social structures, laws, tendencies, counter-tendencies and contingency, operating at distinct levels of complexity. Theoretical understanding of the concrete should depart from the essence and gradually reveal the mediations that establish the meaning and significance of each part within the whole. By the same token, historical studies help to identify the real (rather than merely conceptual) structures and contradictions of the concrete, whose development shapes the material reality.[42] This systematic procedure allows the reconstruction of reality as the mental expression of the real articulation of the phenomena.[43]

Whereas formal logic builds theories using connected but ontologically independent concepts, as if they were Lego blocks, materialist dialectic theories are integrated wholes. This is attractive, because capitalism is an organic system.[44] However, this approach complicates the introduction of new concepts. It is no longer possible merely to add categories and simply replace those that no longer 'fit'. New concepts have to be developed from previously existing categories, and their introduction often sublates or, at least, demands refinement in the previous categories.[45] As Engels put it, it would be wrong to

> look in Marx for fixed, cut-and-dried definitions that are valid for all time. It should go without saying that where things and their mutual relations are conceived not as fixed but rather as changing, their mental images, too, i.e. concepts, are also subject to change and reformulation; that they are not to be encapsulated in rigid definitions, but rather developed in their process of historical or logical formation.[46]

More specifically, Arthur shows that:

> In a dialectical argument the meanings of concepts undergo shifts because . . . the significance of any element in the total picture [cannot] be defined for good at the outset . . . As the presentation of the system advances to more complex, and concrete, relationships the originating definition of a concept shifts accordingly, normally towards greater

definiteness, although sometimes new and broader applications of the concept come into view. Thus the dialectical method remains open to fundamental reorganisations of the material so far appropriated, as it gets closer to the truth of things.[47]

In sum, concepts at distinct levels of abstraction necessarily coexist in dialectical theories. Analytical progress includes the introduction of new concepts and the refinement and reproduction of the existing concepts at greater levels of complexity. Consequently, the meaning and significance of Marx's concepts depends upon the *level* of analysis.[48]

Let us see two examples of the sublation of a relatively simple form of a concept by a more complex form. First, Marx's concept of commodity shifts between pre-capitalist and capitalist production (see section 3.2):

> The commodity as it emerges in capitalist production, is *different* from the commodity taken as the element, the starting point of capitalist production. We are no longer faced with the individual commodity, the individual product. The individual commodity, the individual product, manifests itself not only as a real product but also as a commodity, as a part both really and conceptually of production as a whole. Each individual commodity represents a definite portion of capital and the surplus value created by it.[49]

Second, the concepts of price of production and general rate of profit shift when Marx introduces the concept of commercial capital (see chapter 7):

> Commercial capital . . . contributes to the formation of the general rate of profit according to the proportion it forms in the total capital . . . We thus obtain a *stricter and more accurate definition* of the production price. By price of production we still understand, as before, the price of the commodity as equal to its cost . . . plus the average profit . . . But this average profit is now determined differently. It is determined by the . . . total productive and commercial capital together . . . The price of production . . . [is] less than the real production price of the commodity; or, if we consider all commodities together, the price at which the industrial capitalist class sells them is less than their value . . . *In future we shall keep the expression "price of production" for the more exact sense just developed.*[50]

1.2 Marx, Hegel and 'new dialectics'

A Hegelian interpretation of Marx's method, the 'new dialectics', has gained popularity recently among scholars.[51] This section critically reviews this interpretation, in the light of the materialist dialectics explained in section 1.1.

New dialectics is not a school of thought but, rather, a Hegelian stand-point from which Marx's work is interpreted. This approach is inspired by Lenin's aphorism:

> It is impossible completely to understand Marx's *Capital*, and especially its first chapter, without having thoroughly studied and understood the *whole* of Hegel's *Logic*. Consequently, half a century later none of the Marxists understood Marx!![52]

New dialectics is structured by two principles. First, Hegel and Marx shared a similar method; however, where these methods lack correspondence, Marx's work should be reconstructed along Hegelian lines.[53] Second, *Capital* is, or should be, structured as an organised system of categories. In these systems the exposition begins with the starting category, or

> the simplest and most abstract category, one from which the remaining categories of the theory can be derived . . . [it] must be the most abstract and simplest determination immanent to that object.[54]

Systematic development of the contradictions and insufficiencies in the starting category objectively 'call' into the system other concepts and categories, at increasingly complex levels of analysis. Every concept or category should be derived through this procedure, and any extraneous assumption with respect to the structure of the inquiry, the role of each concept in it or the relations between concepts, must be grounded eventually.[55] In other words, the presentation is structured purely by logical criteria, and its architecture is determined by the categorial sequence:

> Generally the presentation is one of gradual transcendence of abstract determination in a movement towards concrete determination, that is of concretisation. The presentation moves forward by the transcendence of contradiction and by providing the ever more concrete *grounds*—the conditions of existence—of the earlier abstract determination.[56]

Repetition of this procedure leads to the reconstruction of the concrete in thought:

> The presentation ends when all the conditions of existence needing to be addressed are comprehended by the entire system of categories developed. The forms incorporate within themselves, and produce through their own effectivity, these conditions . . . [T]he totality so grounded is judged self-sufficient.[57]

New dialectics denies that study of the historical development of the concrete can contribute to its reconstruction in thought, in which case differences between the mode of presentation and the historical development of the concrete are irrelevant.[58] Therefore, the sections of *Capital* that review the history of capitalism allegedly include illustrative material only. Although these sections may help to substantiate the categorial analysis, they play no essential role in the book.

This approach is elegant and appealing, and it was shown in section 1.1 that Marx employs a similar procedure in *Capital* and elsewhere. However, although new dialectics has much to add to previous analyses of the structure and content of Marx's work, it is marked by four weaknesses, which make this interpretation of Marx's method insufficient and, at times, potentially misleading.

Necessity

New dialectics has not demonstrated that the unfolding of two distinct concepts, when used as alternative starting points, *necessarily* leads to substantially different outcomes, of which at least one is analytically unacceptable. In the context of *Capital*, if the unfolding of another concept rather than the commodity also led to the reconstruction of capitalism in thought there would be no immanent reason to select the commodity as the starting point of the book. In this case, the presumption that *Capital* is the product of systematic dialectical derivation would become open to question.[59]

Sufficiency

The argument that the choice of the correct starting point and the systematic derivation of categories are *sufficient* to reconstruct the concrete has never been substantiated. This difficulty may be expressed as follows. If the unfolding of a relatively abstract concept, for example the 'correct' starting point, does not lead to the introduction of the concepts necessary for the analysis, or if the presentation requires the periodical incorporation of social and historical elements that cannot be derived from within the logical structure, some of the central claims of new dialectics would be seriously weakened. This limitation of new dialectics can be illustrated by three examples. First, it is *impossible* to derive the contemporary predominance of inconvertible paper money purely logically from the value forms presented in the first chapter of *Capital 1* (see section 8.2). Second, the state derivation debate has shown that it is *impossible* to conceptualise the capitalist state in a strictly logical framework drawing from the contradictions in the commodity, at least if functionalism or reductionism are to be avoided.[60] Third, it is *impossible* to understand the (changing) limits of state intervention in the economy purely through the analysis of the logic of capital.

Structure and context

Attempts to reconstruct the concrete simply through the derivation of relatively concrete categories from more abstract categories are limited because systematic analyses are context-independent, whereas the concrete is determined partly by structure and tendency, and partly by agency, counter-tendencies, context and contingency.[61] Whereas tendencies arise systematically from the structure of the system, the counter-tendencies can arise at any level of abstraction, and they can shift the meaning of categories at any level.[62] Therefore, even if the critiques above did not hold, and if new dialectics could capture the structural determinants of capitalism, its neglect of the historical determinations of the concrete would prevent the explanation of the counter-tendencies and the context in which they interact with the tendencies.[63] This is possible only through the regular incorporation of historical material from outside the categorial system, which new dialectics is generally unwilling or unable to do. Consequently, new dialectics often cannot explain the structure of capitalism precisely enough to inform empirical analysis.[64]

Idealism

New dialectics is idealist because it focuses primarily upon logical constructs rather than the material structures of determination of the concrete. This Hegelian approach is analytically unsound and potentially misleading because it 'substantializes the logical or, what amounts to the same thing, *logicizes* the empirical':[65]

> It has become something of a minor vogue . . . to attempt to "reconstruct" *Capital* as an unbroken series of intertwining "dialectical syllogisms" as if the discourse of proof in *Capital* would be incomplete and insufficient without appeal to some "logic" which is not to be found precisely in that discourse itself, and as if Marx's analysis were constrained to follow a conceptual ordering determined by the requirements of this "logic", rather than the conceptual ordering proper to the analysis . . . being determined by the requirements for grasping its specific subject-matter. The intellectual poverty of such exercises lies in just that sort of formalistic ordering of pre-given materials which, ironically . . . inspired Marx's explicit rejection of Hegelian philosophy in the first place.[66]

Hegel was one of the founding fathers of dialectics, and Marx 'openly avowed . . . [himself] the pupil of that mighty thinker'.[67] However, in spite of his admiration Marx was also heavily critical of Hegel:

> My dialectical method is, in its foundations, not only different from the Hegelian, but exactly the opposite to it. For Hegel, the process of thinking, which he even transforms into an independent subject, under the name of "the Idea", is the creator of the real world, and the real world is only the external appearance of the idea. With me the reverse is

true: the ideal is nothing but the material world reflected in the mind of man, and translated into forms of thought . . . With him [the dialectics] is standing on its head. It must be inverted, in order to discover the rational kernel within its mystical shell.[68]

Hegel's system is idealist, first, because for him concepts exist independently of the material circumstances or the real relations in the concrete. The concrete universal, in particular,

> exists . . . only as a concept, only in the ether of pure thought, by no means in the sphere of "external reality". That was . . . the reason why Hegel believed materialism to be impossible as philosophy (for philosophy is a science of the universal, and [for Hegel] the universal is thought and nothing but thought).[69]

Second, Hegel believes that '[t]he concrete is in the final analysis . . . the product of thought.'[70] In contrast, for materialist dialectics conceptual derivation involves the identification of actually existing essences, concepts and mediations, in order to reconstruct in the mind the structures of determination of material reality (see section 1.1):

> the process of theoretical abstraction must be founded on historical observations and must find its justification in terms of its power to understand and interpret historical experience.[71]

In conclusion, Marx's method is not based on conceptual derivations. For example, Marx stated unambiguously that:

> I do not proceed from "concepts", hence neither from the "concept of value" . . . What I proceed from is the simplest social form in which the product of labour presents itself in contemporary society, and this is the "commodity". This I analyse, initially in the form in which it appears. Here I find that on the one hand in its natural form it is a thing for use, alias a use-value; on the other hand, a bearer of exchange-value, and from this point of view it is itself an "exchange-value". Further analysis of the latter shows me that exchange-value is merely a "form of expression", an independent way of presenting the value contained in the commodity, and then I start on the analysis of the latter.[72]

Purely conceptual reasoning is limited because it is impossible to explain why relations that hold in the analyst's head must also hold in the real world. More broadly, new dialectics is insufficient and potentially misleading because it aspires to reconstruct the reality purely through concepts, even though the concrete is historically grounded and, therefore, irreducibly contingent. The concrete can be analysed theoretically only if historical analysis belongs *within* the method of exposition. By eschewing this link new dialectics becomes unable to explain the concrete other than as the manifestation of conceptual necessity.[73] In other words, the most important shortcoming of new dialectics is the failure to appreciate that the requirement that complex concepts should be derived from the contradictions in simpler ones is not the only let alone the most important feature of Marx's method. Rather, what matters most is why, how and when new concepts and new material should be incorporated into the analysis, such that it becomes richer, more solid, and better able to reconstruct the concrete.

In spite of the substantial contribution that the new dialectics has given to the understanding of Marx's method and the content of his works, this perspective remains insufficient to capture either the wealth of the concrete or the wealth of *Capital*.

1.3 Conclusion

This chapter has interpreted Marx's method in *Capital* and elsewhere through the principles of materialist dialectics. This approach uses dialectics to identify the essential features of the concrete and their real contradictions, in order to explain the reality and the potential sources of historical change. For materialist dialectics, recognition of the fact that history and logic are inseparable is not a concession to empiricism but, rather, a consequence of the fact that reality cannot be reduced to concepts. This view was contrasted to a Hegelian alternative, the new dialectics, that interprets Marx's method as a mechanical if dialectical set of thought processes, whose movement is largely independent of the real structures of determination of the concrete.

However, Marx's method is primarily a flexible investigative tool, and it does not exist in the rarified domain of new dialectics. Scott rightly argues that the attempt to reduce Marx's method

> to a number of rules, as in books on formal logic, is . . . inappropriate since it reduces specific content to empty form . . . [T]he form and content of the dialectic is . . . inseparable from social being in general, and specific social struggles in particular . . . [T]he dialectic is employed only in the "method of presentation" and, unlike Engels, Marx did not . . . accept the idea of a universal and immanent dialectic.[74]

Materialist dialectics provides a context-specific platform for the analysis of capitalism, in two senses. First, it is historically limited because the phenomena and their essences change over time. Second, the analysis progresses through logical derivations *and* the regular incorporation of historical material. Materialist dialectics recognises that scientific investigation requires not only familiarisation with the subject as a historically existing entity, but also application of the method of analysis in such a way as to reveal most effectively the structures, tendencies and counter-tendencies associated with reality.[75]

2   Interpretations of Marx's value theory

This chapter reviews critically two interpretations of Marx's value theory, the 'embodied labour' views, including 'traditional' Marxism and Sraffian approaches, and value form theories, including those associated with Rubin and the 'new interpretation' developed by Duménil and Foley.

Differences between these interpretations are largely due to distinct understandings of the value relation. Whereas the former claims that value is the average labour time embodied in the commodities, the latter argues that value is the command over social labour represented by money. Different perceptions of the value relation, distinct interpretations of the role, meaning and significance of value analysis and, more broadly, divergent views about the nature and legitimacy of capitalism, help to explain why Marx's theory has been hotly debated for over one hundred years.

This chapter does not include a comprehensive survey of interpretations of Marx's theory of value.[1] Its aim is merely to outline the two most influential interpretations, and their best-known offshoots, and critically examine their contribution for the development of Marxian political economy. This chapter is divided into three sections. Section 1 reviews, respectively, the traditional and Sraffian interpretations of Marx. Section 2 analyses value form theories, including the Rubin tradition and the new interpretation. Section 3 draws the main conclusions from the analysis.

2.1 Embodied labour approaches

Some of the most influential readings of Marx hold that value is the labour embodied in commodities during production. These readings define abstract labour in opposition to concrete labour; it is labour in general, abstracted from the form of the activity.[2] Two such views are considered in this section, the traditional and the Sraffian.

2.1.1 Traditional Marxism

According to the 'traditional' interpretation, Marx's theory of value is not essentially different from Ricardo's. It may be summarised as follows:[3]

(a)   The main subject of the theory of value is the analysis of capitalist exploitation. The categories developed in the first three chapters of *Capital 1* (commodity, value and money) are only indirectly related to this issue, because they belong to a broader set of modes of production, especially simple commodity production, where capitalist exploitation does not necessarily exist.

(b)   The concept of value is necessary for the determination of the rate of exploitation. This reading focuses upon the magnitude of value, defined as the quantity of abstract labour embodied in each commodity. The substance and form of value and the links between value and money are largely neglected.

(c)   The analysis of profit requires the determination of commodity prices, including labour power. This is done through a set of assumptions that usually includes general equilibrium (simple reproduction). Consequently, prices are only relative to a *numéraire*. It follows that a theory of money is unnecessary, and money is effectively a veil.

(d)   The determination of relative prices has two stages. First, it is assumed that all capitals have equal value compositions (see chapter 6), in which case the exchange ratios are determined by embodied labour alone. Second, the value compositions are allowed to vary; in this case, relative prices differ from the embodied labour ratios, but it is presumed that the latter determine the former algebraically.

(e)   The conceptual apparatus is elementary. Commodities are use values put out for sale; value is often conflated with exchange value, and the articulation between value and price is left unclear (even though they are presumed to be quantitatively comparable).

(f)   There is little concern with the distinction between levels of analysis and the interaction between tendencies, counter-tendencies and contingency. Theory arguably captures the basic tendencies of capitalism, and expects them to be translated unproblematically into empirical outcomes.

The traditional approach has important virtues, especially the focus on the mode of exploitation. This emphasis concurs with Marx's own concerns, and it highlights some of his most distinctive contributions; it is also conducive to the critique of the structures of circulation and distribution, such as private property and the market. However, traditional Marxism suffers from two significant shortcomings. First, it disconnects the analysis of the mode of production from the circulation and distribution of the output, which grossly exaggerates their independence.[4] Second, traditional Marxism wrongly claims that Marx's analysis of commodities, value and money addresses a broad set of commodity modes of production, especially simple commodity production (SCP), and that his analysis of capitalism proper starts only in chapter 4 of *Capital 1* (see sections 2.2.1 and 3.1 below). In this case, two sets of relative prices exist. One is based on embodied labour, and it rules pre-capitalist exchange, while the other is based on equal profitability, and it regulates capitalist exchanges (see chapter 7):

Under certain conditions which prevailed between independent small producers in pre-capitalist societies (what Marx calls "simple commodity production") exchange of equal values was the rule. If under capitalist conditions there are other more complicated relations determining the quantitative exchange relations, this does not make an economic theory based on the determination of value by socially necessary labour inconsistent, provided there is a clear and consistent method of deriving prices from values.[5]

Presumably, the transition between these stages is a historical process, in which case the transformation between the two types of relative prices (values and prices of production) can be analysed historically as well as algebraically.[6] This approach is wrong both logically and historically. Generalised exchange at value has never existed because, in general, products become commodities only under capitalism. Moreover, it was shown in section 1.1 that, although Marx often draws on historical studies in order to explain difficult points or trace the evolution of important categories, the only mode of production that he analyses systematically in *Capital* is *capitalism*. Hence, although commodities, value and money may have existed for millennia, *Capital* focuses upon their capitalist determinations only, and no systematic inferences may be drawn about their meaning and significance in other modes of production.[7]

Misperceptions such as these have contributed to the transformation of traditional Marxism into a 'Ricardian Marxism'. However, this position is untenable (see section 8.1).[8] Marx was at pains to distinguish his views from Ricardo's and, in large chunks of his writings, Marx excoriates Ricardo's methodological and other errors. In particular, Marx argues that Ricardo's approach is insufficient because it fails to explain the relationship between money and commodities and between abstract labour and value, as well as the mode of labour and the relations of exploitation under capitalism.[9]

2.1.2 Sraffian analyses

Dissatisfaction with the shortcomings of traditional Marxism led to the development of two alternative approaches: the Sraffian (or neo-Ricardian) and value form theory (see section 2.2). The Sraffian approach is developed and explained by, among others, Pasinetti and Steedman, drawing upon works by Bortkiewicz, Dmitriev, Seton, Sraffa and Tugan-Baranowsky.[10] Sraffians attempt to develop the traditional model, focusing upon the articulation between the value and the price systems.[11] The main features of the Sraffian approach are the following:

(a) Only the magnitude of value is discussed in detail; its substance and form are almost completely disregarded. The analysis usually involves two sets of equations; one represents the value system, and the other the price system.

(b)   The value system is described by $\lambda=\lambda A+l=l(I-A)^{-1}$, where λ is the $(1 \times n)$ vector of commodity values, A is the $(n \times n)$ technical matrix and l is the $(1 \times n)$ vector of direct labour.

(c)   The price system is described by $p=(pA+wl)(1+r)$, where p is the $(1 \times n)$ price vector, w is the wage rate, and r is the profit rate.

(d)   As the analysis is primarily concerned with the relationship between the value and price systems, money has no autonomous role and, when considered at all, it is merely a *numéraire*.[12]

(e)   These definitions of value and price are the basis for a wide-ranging critique of alleged inconsistencies in Marx, which leads to the conclusion that the traditional Marxist project of determining value from embodied labour is flawed. Very briefly, first, the price system has two degrees of freedom, because it has n equations, one for each commodity, but $n+2$ unknowns, the n prices and the wage and profit rates. Therefore, while the value system can usually be solved (provided that the matrix A is well behaved), the price system can be solved only if additional restrictions are introduced, for example the identity of the value of labour power with the value of a bundle of goods (the wage is the price of this bundle; see section 4.2), and a normalisation condition such as one of Marx's aggregate equalities (*either* total prices equal total values, *or* total profits equal total surplus value; see chapter 7). However, the other aggregate equality is not generally possible, which is allegedly destructive for Marx's analysis.[13] Second, the Sraffian representation of Marx cannot distinguish labour from other inputs, in which case it cannot be argued that labour creates value and is exploited, rather than any other input, e.g., corn, iron or energy.[14] Third, even if labour does create value and is exploited, the only meaningful relationship between labour and prices is through the proposition that a positive rate of exploitation is necessary and sufficient for positive profits, which has little empirical significance.[15]

Sraffian analyses have contributed significantly, if indirectly, to Marxian studies of the relationship between the mode of production and the structures of distribution. However, the Sraffian approach is insufficient in several respects, and its critique of Marx has been rebutted convincingly.[16] In what follows, two aspects of the Sraffian critique of Marx are briefly assessed: the shortcomings of the value equation and the Sraffian inability to represent capitalist relations of production satisfactorily.

The value equation, $\lambda=\lambda A+l$, states that commodity values are equal to the input values (λA) plus the living labour necessary to process them (l). Although this equation represents correctly Marx's *definition* of value (see chapter 5), it is unsuitable for the *calculation* of commodity values. Let us see why.

For simplicity, suppose that the matrix A represents the average production technologies, however they may be determined. Suppose, also, that the vector *l* represents the average number of *concrete* labour-hours (printing, construction, assembly, etc.) necessary to transform the inputs into the output. Even under these generous assumptions, the vector *l* cannot be directly used to calculate the value produced because this vector measures concrete rather than abstract labour. Since these labours are qualitatively distinct, any operation across them is meaningless.[17] By the same token, labour employed in distinct activities, whether or not vertically integrated, may produce distinct quantities of value per hour because of training and other differences, for example, designing and painting cars, or building and decorating new homes (see section 5.3).

Suppose, instead, that *l* is a vector of *abstract* labour.[18] Although this would avoid the problems outlined above, it would still not allow the value vector to be *calculated*. For this assumption implies that, in order to calculate the abstract labour necessary to produce each commodity (λ), one needs to know how many hours of abstract labour are necessary to produce each commodity (*l*). Because it involves a tautology, the assumption that *l* is abstract labour does not allow the quantitative determination of value.[19]

These shortcomings are symptomatic of the Sraffian inability to grasp the essence of capitalist relations of production and the specific features of this mode of production (see section 1.1 and chapter 3).[20] The Sraffian system is such that production resembles a purely technical process, not necessarily capitalist, in which case, first, capital is merely a collection of use values rather than a social relation of production. Second, the substance of value, abstract labour, is undistinguishable from average units of concrete labour time. Finally, the social aspect of production is either assumed away or projected upon the sphere of distribution, through the rate of exploitation. In sum, a 'social process is replaced by technical coefficients and social relations by the distribution of the product between the social classes.'[21]

The Sraffian model is not even internally consistent. It presumes that the technical relations of production are given independently of the value and price systems, and implies that, for Marx, calculation of the price vector would necessitate value magnitudes, but not the converse. Since this is not the case, value analysis is allegedly redundant. This is wrong because, first, it misrepresents Marx's argument (see chapter 7). Second, the production structure is socially, rather than technically, determined. Under capitalism, competition determines the allocation of labour and means of production, the quantities produced and the technologies, in which case value relations are *causally determinant* vis-à-vis technologies and prices.[22] Consequently, 'the labour theory of value is not redundant, but rather provides the explanation of price lacking in Sraffa's own account.'[23] In sum, Sraffian analyses cannot distinguish capitalism from other societies that equalise rates of return. As a result, they cannot explain capitalist social relations, exploitation, the distribution of income, the sources of economic data, the process of competition and, most damagingly, the price form.[24]

2.2 Value form theories

Value form theories (VFT) were developed primarily in the 1970s, partly as a
reaction against the insufficiencies of traditional Marxism and the excesses
of Sraffianism.[25] The development of VFT was aided by the rediscovery of
the works of the Soviet economist Isaak Illich Rubin (1896–1937) in the
West in the early 1970s. In what follows, VFT is analysed critically through
Rubin's work. Subsequently, a contemporary approach drawing upon VFT is
examined, the 'new interpretation' of Marx's value theory.

2.2.1 The Rubin tradition

This interpretation of Marx's value theory is inspired by the Soviet
economist I.I. Rubin and by independent contributions from, among others,
Louis Althusser, Hans-Georg Backhaus and Suzanne de Brunhoff.[26] This
approach generally starts from the social division of labour. It claims that
the essential feature of the capitalist division of labour is the commodity
relation, or the production of commodities by 'separate', or independent,
producers:

> The value-form of the product of labor is not only the most abstract,
> but is also the most universal form, taken by the product in bourgeois
> production, and stamps that production as a particular species of social
> production, and thereby gives it its special historical character ... Thus
> the "value form" is the most general form of the commodity economy.[27]

The commodity features of capitalism are so important that Rubin often
refers to the subject of his analysis as the 'commodity-capitalist' economy.[28]
The counterpart to the independence of the producers is the need to produce
a socially useful commodity or, in other words, one that is sold (the
imperative to sell has been called the 'monetary constraint').[29] Because of
separation and the monetary constraint, this tradition argues that commodities are produced by private and concrete labours that, at best, are
potentially or only ideally abstract and social. Private and concrete labour
is converted into social and abstract labour if and when its product is
exchanged for money:

> In a commodity economy, the labour of a separate individual, of a
> separate, private commodity producer, is not directly regulated by
> society. As such, in its concrete form, labour does not yet directly enter
> the social economy. Labour becomes social in a commodity economy
> only when it acquires the form of socially equalized labour, namely, the
> labour of every commodity producer becomes social only because his
> product is equalized with the products of all other producers ...
> [A]bstract labour ... [is] labour which was made equal through the all
> round equation of all the products of labour, but the equation of all the

products of labour is not possible except through the assimilation of each one of them with a universal equivalent . . . [The] equalization of labour may take place, but only mentally and in anticipation, in the process of direct production, *before* the act of exchange. But in reality, it takes place through the act of exchange, through the equalization (even though it is mentally anticipated) of the product of the given labour with a definite sum of money.[30]

The Rubin tradition has contributed in at least two important ways to the development of Marxian value analysis. First, the claim that abstract labour is social labour indirectly formed through sale is applicable to commodity economies only, and it provides the springboard for a forceful critique of ahistorical embodied labour views (see section 2.1). This critique has helped to shift the focus of Marxian studies away from the calculation of values and prices and towards the analysis of the social relations of production and their forms of appearance.

Second, this tradition has emphasised the importance of money for value analysis, because value appears only in and through price. Since money plays an essential role in commodity economies, non-monetary or general equilibrium interpretations of Marx's theory are fundamentally wrong, the search for an unmediated expression of abstract labour is futile, and attempts to calculate embodied labour coefficients are rarely meaningful (see section 5.4).[31] Emphasis on the importance of money has facilitated the resurgence of interest in Marxian monetary analysis (see chapter 8), and the critique of embodied labour views has opened avenues for the development of more cogent interpretations of Marx.

However, the claim that separation is the essential feature of commodity production has led the Rubin tradition to subsume capitalist relations of production under simple value relations. Consequently, in spite of its significant contribution to the analysis of value, this tradition has added little to our understanding of *capital* and *capitalism*.

Focus on the value relation implies that commodity economies are essentially a congregation of producers that, in principle, do not belong in the social division of labour. Because of separation and specialisation, the producers must sell their own goods or services in order to claim a share of the social product for their own consumption. In other words, in this type of society production is essentially for consumption, and private and concrete labour is analytically prior to social and abstract labour, which exist only ideally before sale. The equalisation, abstraction and socialisation of labour are contingent upon sale, and commodity values are determined by the value of the money for which they are exchanged. The inability to sell shows that the decision to produce was wrong, the good is useless, and the labour did not create value.[32]

In contrast, in capitalist economies the *essential* separation is between the wage workers and the means of production, monopolised by the class of capitalists (see section 3.2).[33] Production takes place when capitalists hire workers in order to supply goods for profit. Since the performance of labour is conditioned by this social form, the output is necessarily a commodity; it *has* a use value, and it *is* a value (if the commodity is not sold its use value is not realised, and its value is destroyed; see section 5.3).[34] In sum, whereas the labour of independent commodity producers is relatively free of social determinations and its social character is contingent upon *exchange*, under capitalism the *mode of labour* is socially determined (see chapter 5):

> Capitalism throws workers together into workplaces in increasing numbers, where their labor is *collective* labor. The work of a laborer employed in a plant with a thousand other workers can in no sense be described as private, nor as individual . . . capitalist production involves collective, cooperative labor, *directly* social, consciously directed and controlled—the collective and cooperative power of the working class dominated and subsumed under the authority of capital. That which is private is not labor-in-production, but the commodity that is the result of the production process.[35]

These limitations of the Rubin tradition are largely due to the conflation between capitalist production (the systematic production of commodities for profit) with simple commodity production (the socially unregulated production of commodities by independent producers).[36] This is flawed both historically and theoretically:

> [in] the case of individual producers who own their own means of production and . . . where none of the inputs used in production is bought, but all are produced within a self-contained labor process . . . only the final product of the labor process is a commodity. Each article of the means of production is produced in social isolation by each producer, never facing the discipline of competition. There is no social mechanism for bringing about a normal expenditure of labor time in the products that are the means of production. In such a situation, competition's only function is to impose the rule of a uniform selling price in the market place . . . The only objective necessity is that his or her total labor expenditure . . . be sufficient to allow for the reproduction of the family. Should some producers be able to deliver their commodities with less expenditure of effort than others, the more "efficient" producers will enjoy a higher standard of living. *This higher standard of living of some in no way pressures the less efficient to raise their efficiency.*[37]

The Rubin tradition's sharp focus upon the value relation has contributed to important advances in Marxian value analysis. However, neglect of the wage relation and the mode of labour have limited its ability to distinguish capitalism from other modes of production. The Rubin tradition wrongly presumes that commodity exchange is the determinant aspect of capitalism, conflates money with the substance of value, and eschews the mediations that structure Marx's value analysis. Lack of analytical depth explains its failure to illuminate important real relations identified by Marx, for example the capitalist monopoly of the means of production, the subordination of the workers in production, the social regulation of production through competition, mechanisation and deskilling, and the mediations between value and price (see chapters 5 and 7). Because of these limitations, the Rubin tradition is poorly equipped to explain the main features of capitalism and to analyse their social, economic and political consequences empirically.

2.2.2 The 'new interpretation'

In the early 1980s Gérard Duménil and Duncan Foley independently outlined a 'new interpretation' (NI) of Marx's value theory,[38] drawing upon works by Aglietta and Rubin.[39] The growing popularity of the NI among Marxists in the past two decades has helped to shift the value debate away from the relatively sterile polemics against the Sraffian critics of Marx and the highly abstract analyses of the Rubin tradition, and into more substantive issues. The contribution of the NI is largely based upon its emphasis on the net rather than gross product, and its distinctive definitions of value of money and value of labour power (see below). Drawing upon these concepts, the NI argues, first, that empirical analyses employing Marxian categories are both possible and interesting[40] and, second, that the 'transformation problem' is irrelevant (see chapter 7).

The NI stems from a value form interpretation of Marx, whence labour becomes abstract, and is socialised, through sales.[41] Two implications follow: first, money is the immediate and exclusive expression of abstract labour and, second, the value created by (productive) labour is measured by the quantity of money for which the output is sold. This interpretation bypasses the conceptual difficulties in the relationship between individual prices and values (see chapter 5), and the pitfalls associated with the transformation problem, by remaining at the aggregate or macroeconomic level. At this level, money is essentially command over the newly performed abstract labour. There is no necessary relationship between individual prices and values, and this theory cannot discriminate between alternative price systems. This allegedly increases its generality in the light of potentially pervasive imperfect market structures.

Algebraically, the total (abstract) labour performed, lx, creates the gross product, x, but only the value of the net product, $y = x - Ax$, where A is the $(n \times n)$ technical matrix, l is the $(1 \times n)$ vector of unit labour requirements, x is the $(n \times 1)$ gross output vector, and y the $(n \times 1)$ net output vector. The value of money, λ^m, is the ratio between the total labour performed and the price of the net product:

$$\lambda^m = \frac{lx}{py} \tag{1}$$

The value of money measures the quantity of labour represented by the unit of money, or the abstract labour time that adds one pound sterling (or dollar or whatever) to the value of the product.[42] For the NI, equation (1) represents Marx's equality between total value and total price. The newly produced money-value is allocated across the net product as the price of these commodities.

The value of labour power, V, is defined as the wage share of the national income,[43] and surplus value, S, is the residual (see section 4.1). If w is the hourly wage rate and wlx is the wage mass, V is the wage rate times the value of money:[44]

$$V \equiv \frac{wlx}{py} = w\lambda^m$$

It follows that:

$$S = 1 - V = 1 - \frac{wlx}{py} = \Pi$$

where Π is total profit, in which case Marx's equality between total surplus value and total profit also holds by definition.[45] Finally, the rate of surplus value is:

$$e = \frac{S}{V} = \frac{\Pi}{W}$$

This ratio is determined when commodities are priced and wages are paid. It is unaffected by the use of wage revenues, which may include the consumption of necessities or luxuries, saving or hoarding. For the NI, this relationship shows that profit is merely redistributed surplus value (see section 4.2).

Let us consider the contribution of the NI more closely, starting with the operation in the **net** product. There are two ways to conceptualise the economy's net product. In use value terms, it comprises the means of consumption and net investment, or that part of the gross output over and above that necessary to maintain the productive system, or to repeat the same pattern and level of production. In value terms, it is identical with the newly performed labour. This raises the problem of the value of the gross product, since labour creates the entire gross product but only part of its value.

The NI implies that the conventional definition of Marx's equalities in the gross product is inconsistent because the value of the means of production is counted twice in the value of the gross product. It counts, first, as the value of the newly produced means of production and, again, as the new value of the means of production used up (see section 5.2). However, the latter does not correspond to labour actually performed either in the current period or previously; this is merely a reflection of labour carried out and value created elsewhere.[46] These insights are persuasive. However, focus on the net product may be misleading, for two reasons. First, empirically, the net product is defined over a

> time period other than the turnover period of capital. Net national product, for example, is defined for a year or a quarter. In consequence, the two components of net capital value (variable capital and surplus value) are aggregated over several turnovers, and conceptually one loses sight of the fundamental aspect of circulation, which is the recapture of capital advanced through sale of commodities and the replacement of the material components of production.[47]

Second, and more importantly, focus on the net product eliminates the production of the means of production (other than that required for expanded reproduction). As a result, a significant proportion of current production is rendered invisible as if it were redundant, and the largest proportion of commodity exchanges, those between the producers, vanishes as if it were inconsequential. Therefore, the use of money as capital and as means of payment, and the role of the credit system, are significantly restricted (see section 8.3).

Because of double counting of the input values in the value of the gross output, the NI defines the value of money on the net rather than the gross product. This definition of value of money is seductive for three reasons: first, it avoids the simplifying assumptions that encumber the traditional and Sraffian approaches; second, it appeals to the contemporary experience with inconvertible paper currencies and the perceived importance of the macroeconomic determinants of the value of money, especially through fiscal and monetary policy; third, it facilitates the analysis of imperfect market structures and monopoly power, which can hardly be achieved by the traditional approach.

In spite of these significant advantages, this concept of value of money is limited in two important ways. First, it is merely the *ex post* reflex of the relationship between (abstract, productive) labour performed and the money-value added in the period. It is known only *after* labour is performed, commodities are produced and priced, and the technologies are determined. In this respect, it is unrelated to the Marxian concept of value of the money-commodity, that is determined prior to circulation (see section 8.1). Second, the value of money is unable to reflect the distinct levels of complexity of the value relation, including the social relations of production and distribution, the labour performed, the relations between supply and demand, monopoly power, the quantity and velocity of money, and the credit system. Each of these factors can affect the price system in different ways, but the NI is unable to distinguish systematically between them, or to ground them analytically and explain their implications.

In short, the value of money short-circuits the real structures and relations between social labour and its representation in money in order to address the extant macroeconomic relationships. Unfortunately for the NI, these mediations inherently contain the possibility of disequilibrium and crisis. To collapse the mediated expression of value as price into the simple division of the total hours worked over the price of the total net product is to set aside the complexity of the real processes involved and to obscure the inherent potential for disequilibrium in the economy, which weakens the theory's ability to address the very relations which it should wish to confront.[48]

The NI concept of value of labour power suffers from similar short-comings (see section 4.2). For the NI, the value of labour power is the workers' share of the national income, which is determined by class struggle.[49] However, this definition of the value of labour power does not extend beyond one of the effects of exploitation, the inability of the workers to purchase the entire net product. This was the same aspect of exploitation which the 'Ricardian socialist' economists emphasised in the early nineteenth century, and this is the only aspect of exploitation considered in Sraffian analyses.[50]

This notion of value of labour power can be misleading. First, it can dilute the ability of theory to explain the primary form of class conflict in capitalism, which takes place in production rather than distribution. Second, it may create the illusion that the net product is 'shared' between workers and capitalists at the end of each production period, or that exploitation is due to the unfair distribution of income (see chapter 4). Third, it may support the classical dichotomy between ordinary commodity values, determined by labour embodied, and the value of labour power, given by supply and demand.

In sum, there are two distinct aspects to the contribution of the NI for the development of value analysis. On the one hand, it bypasses the transformation problem (especially the spurious debate about the 'correct' normalisation condition), and it rightly rejects the equilibrium framework in which value theory, and the transformation in particular, was discussed in the past. These important contributions are part of a broader reconsideration of Marx's value theory, providing the foundation for a new, critical macroeconomics. These achievements are important, and the objective is worthwhile.

On the other hand, the NI is open to criticism on several grounds. This approach has been developed in order to address the appearances directly, through a 'Marxian macroeconomics'. However, this important objective exacts a heavy toll. The NI has little analytical 'depth', emphasises exchange and distribution at the expense of production, and it eliminates the mediations and the complex relationship between value and price and surplus value and profit, treating them as if they were identical. As a result, the NI becomes unable to incorporate some of Marx's most important insights into the analysis, including technical change, accumulation, the credit system and crises, other than as exogenous accretions. These limitations are due to the internal structure of the NI, and they explain why it has been accused of tautology (because of the way in which it validates Marx's equalities) and empiricism (because it does not highlight the structures whose development underlies value analysis).[51] Therefore, it is difficult to develop the NI further without making use of arbitrariness in the choice of phenomena to be explained, the judgement of their importance and their relationship with the other features of reality.

2.3 Conclusion

The capitalist division of labour can be approached in two different ways. Most neoclassical economists and some Marxists usually adopt the point of view of circulation (exchange). From this viewpoint, the capitalist economy appears as an unco-ordinated collection of competing activities, distinguished from one another by the commodities produced in each firm and their possibly distinct technologies. This approach tends to emphasise the processes that bring coherence to decentralised economies and ensure that needs are satisfied, subject to constraints. In this context, relative prices and the distribution of labour and income are highly important. The inquiry may be extended subsequently into why the 'invisible hand' can fail, in which case there are disproportions and crisis. These issues are worthy of detailed study and bring to light important aspects of capitalism. Unfortunately, however, they are not conducive to the analysis of the mode of *production*. This is a severe limitation, because the essential differences between capitalism and other modes of production stem from the relationship between the workers and the owners of means of production and the mode of labour associated with it. One of Marx's most important claims is that, if the analysis is restricted to circulation or distribution and ignores the sphere of production, some of the most important features of capitalism remain hidden (see chapter 3).

In contrast, analyses that emphasise production at the expense of exchange sometimes impose equilibrium conditions arbitrarily, in order to focus upon the technologies of production. In this case, it becomes difficult to grasp the significance of money and the relationship between concrete and abstract labour and, more broadly, the historical limits of value analysis. The meaning of competition, technical change and capital migration, and the conflict-ridden relationship between the social classes, are correspondingly blurred (see chapter 5).

These shortcomings show that value analysis ought to consider both production and exchange, the mediations between these spheres and the different levels of analysis. It is sometimes appropriate to short-circuit certain mediations in order to focus upon certain aspects of capitalism rather than others, but this can be risky because it may become difficult to know where and how to introduce important structures or tendencies into the analysis. In this case, it may be necessary to resort to arbitrariness, or to plug into value analysis unrelated studies uncritically, which smacks of eclecticism and is rarely fruitful.

3 Value and capital

In his theory of value, Marx analyses critically the economic processes and relations that regulate social reproduction under capitalism.[1] This chapter interprets the meaning and significance of Marx's value analysis in the light of the materialist dialectics developed in chapter 1. This is achieved in three sections. The first analyses the relationship between the division of labour, exploitation and the value relation. Although Marx's analysis is valid for capitalism only (see section 1.1), its background is broader: the need to divide labour in order to reproduce human society. This can be achieved in potentially very different ways, one of which is capitalism.[2]

Section 2 discusses the capital relation. It shows that, on the one hand, capital is a relation of production in which labour power, the products of labour, and goods and services more generally, tend to become commodities. On the other hand, capital is a class relation of exploitation defined by the ability of the capitalists to compel the working class to produce more than it consumes or controls, and by the capitalist command of the surplus. Section 3 draws the main conclusions of this chapter.

3.1 Division of labour, exploitation and value

The concept of value cannot be grasped immediately.[3] In order to explain value and its significance under capitalism, Marx departs from human labour in general. Labour is the process of transformation of given natural and social conditions in order to achieve predetermined outcomes, the goods and services necessary for social reproduction, that Marx calls use values:[4]

> Labour, then, as the creator of use-values, as useful labour, is a condition of human existence which is independent of all forms of society; it is an eternal natural necessity which mediates the metabolism between man and nature, and therefore human life itself.[5]

In every society the social labour power (the capacity to work of all individuals, including their knowledge, ability and experience)[6] is a community

resource employed according to cultural, natural and technological constraints.[7] Labour is everywhere divided according to gender, age, lineage or
class, and the product of social labour must be similarly divided. In addition
to this, in most societies, groups or classes of non-producers live off transfers
due to the exploitation of the producers.[8]

Class relations of exploitation are determined by the form of extraction
of surplus labour from the direct producers (see section 3.2 and chapter 4).[9]
These relations include the structures and processes that compel the producers to produce more than they consume or control, and the mechanisms
of appropriation of the surplus by the exploiters. Even when narrowly
defined in purely economic terms exploitation is a totality, including several
aspects of social life, among them the property relations, the distribution of
labour, control over the production process, and the distribution of the
output.

The defining characteristic of capitalism is the exploitation of the wage
workers by the capitalists through the extraction of surplus value (see
below).[10] In order to explain this mode of exploitation, Marx starts from
its most abstract feature, the value relation. For Marx, the value relation
and its grounding upon the social division of labour do not need to be
demonstrated; they are indisputable *facts*:

> even if there were no chapter on "value" at all in my book, the analysis I
> give of the real relations would contain the proof and demonstration of
> the real value relation. The chatter about the need to prove the concept
> of value arises only from complete ignorance both of the subject under
> discussion and of the method of science. Every child knows that any
> nation that stopped working, not for a year, but let us say, just for a few
> weeks, would perish. And every child knows, too, that the amounts of
> products corresponding to the differing amounts of needs demand
> differing and quantitatively determined amounts of society's aggregate
> labour . . . And the form in which this proportional distribution of
> labour asserts itself in a state of society in which the interconnection of
> social labour expresses itself as the private exchange of the individual
> products of labour, is precisely the exchange value of these products.[11]

The value relation can be analysed at distinct levels. At a relatively abstract
level, or in non-capitalist societies where commodity production and
exchange are marginal, value is significant only as exchange value, a mental
generalisation that expresses the rate of exchange of one commodity for
another. In this case,

> The "value-form", whose final shape is the money-form, is completely
> without content. The category of exchange-value leads an "antediluvian
> existence". One can find exchange-values in ancient Rome, in the Middle
> Ages and in capitalism; but different contents are hidden behind each of

these forms of exchange-value. Marx stresses that "exchange-value" detached from the concrete relations under which it has arisen is an unreal abstraction, as exchange-value "can never exist except as an abstract, one-sided relation to an already given concrete and living whole"[12]

At this level of analysis, abstract labour is also a mental generalisation because, first, production aims primarily at the creation of specific use values, rather than the valorisation of capital.[13] Second, the labour markets are thin, highly fragmented and often absent.[14] Third, the division of labour across society and within the workplace remains relatively undeveloped.[15] Fourth, the exchange values are highly dependent upon non-market relations, rather than being determined primarily by the forces of production and competition.[16] In this case, the labour process has few social determinations, products take the commodity form only if they find their way into exchange, and the abstraction of labour is contingent upon sale.

In contrast, in capitalist societies wage labour is the form of social labour, and the products, other assets and social relations generally have the commodity form. In these societies labour is essentially abstract, and exchange value is the form of expression of the value relation:

> For Marx the value of a commodity expresses the particular historical form that the social character of labour has under capitalism . . . This suggests first, that the generalisation of the commodity form of human labour is quite specific to capitalism and that value as a concept of analysis is similarly so specific. Secondly, it suggests that value is not just a concept with a mental existence; it has a real existence, value relations being the particular form taken by capitalist social relations.[17]

The abstraction of labour and the commodification of the social product can be analysed at two levels. First, in production, wage workers are typically hired on the labour market and compelled to work in order to produce goods and services primarily for profit (surplus value) rather than need (use value), using commercially available inputs. Consequently, the products are commodities since their inception, and abstract labour predominates logically over concrete labour (see sections 1.1 and 2.2.1 and chapter 5).[18] Second, the exchangeability of the products demonstrates, in the sphere of exchange, the substantive identity of all types of labour. Marx contrasts the determinations of labour in simple commodity exchange and in capitalism as follows:

> what is it that forms the bond between the independent labours of the cattle-breeder, the tanner and the shoemaker? It is the fact that their respective products are commodities. What, on the other hand, characterizes the division of labour in manufacture? The fact that the

specialized worker produces no commodities. It is only the common product of all the specialized workers that becomes a commodity . . . The division of labour within manufacture presupposes a concentration of the means of production in the hands of one capitalist; the division of labour within society presupposes a dispersion of those means among many independent producers of commodities . . . Division of labour within the workshop implies the undisputed authority of the capitalist over men, who are merely the members of a total mechanism which belongs to him. The division of labour within society brings into contact independent producers of commodities, who acknowledge no authority other than that of competition.[19]

3.2 Capital

Marx opens his best known book with the following statement:

The wealth of societies in which the capitalist mode of production prevails appears as an "immense collection of commodities"; the individual commodity appears as its elementary form. Our investigation therefore begins with the analysis of the commodity.[20]

The expression 'in which the capitalist mode of production prevails' is essential, because it situates the subject of Marx's analysis and the historical limits of its validity.[21] Although commodities have been produced for thousands of years, and their production and exchange are historical premises of capitalism, commodities produced under capitalism are essentially *distinct* from those produced in other modes of production. This difference arises because, under capitalism, the social output typically takes the commodity form and, more importantly, labour power also takes this form:

Two characteristic traits mark the capitalist mode of production right from the start . . . *Firstly.* It produces its products as commodities. The fact that it produces commodities does not in itself distinguish it from other modes of production; but that the dominant and determining character of its product is that it is a commodity certainly does so. This means, first of all, that the worker himself appears only as a seller of commodities, and hence as a free wage-labourer – i.e., labour generally appears as wage-labour . . . [T]he relationship of capital and wage-labour determines the whole character of the mode of production . . . The *second* thing that particularly marks the capitalist mode of production is the production of surplus-value as the direct objective and decisive motive of production. Capital essentially produces capital, and does this only as long as it produces surplus-value.[22]

Marx's view of capital and capitalism has four important implications for value analysis:

What is capital

Capital is often defined as an ensemble of things, including means of production, money and financial assets. More recently, individual or social attributes have been defined as forms of capital, for example human, cultural or social capital.[23] These definitions are wrong, because the existence of those assets or attributes does not imply that capital also exists. Some (e.g., instruments of production, knowledge and social relations) have existed since the dawn of humanity, while others (e.g., money) predate capitalism by many generations. It is historically misguided and analytically vacuous to extend the concept of capital where it does not belong, as if it were universally valid.[24] More specifically, an axe, draught animal, or even one million dollars may or may not be capital; that depends upon the context in which they are used. If they are engaged in production for profit through the (possibly indirect) employment of wage labour, they are capital; otherwise, they are simply tools, traction animals, or banknotes.

Capital is a social relation between two classes, capitalists and workers, that takes the form of things. This social relation is established when the means of production, including the buildings, machinery, tools, vehicles, land and so on, are monopolised by a class, the capitalists, that employs wage workers in production for profit. The workers must sell their labour power regularly and continually because they do not own means of production, cannot produce independently and, in commodity societies, need money in order to purchase the use values that they covet. Once this class relation of production is posited, capital exists *in and through* the means of production, commodities and money employed in the process of self-expansion of value, that Marx called valorisation:

> Capital is not a *thing*, any more than money is a *thing*. In capital, as in money, certain *specific social relations of production between people* appear as *relations of things to people*, or else certain social relations appear as the *natural properties of things in society* . . . Capital and wage-labour . . . only express two aspects of the self-same relationship. Money cannot become capital unless it is exchanged for labour-power . . . Conversely, work can only be wage-labour when its *own* material conditions confront it as autonomous powers, alien property, value existing for itself and maintaining itself, in short as capital . . . Thus wage-labour, the wages system, is a social form of work indispensable to capitalist production, just as capital, i.e. potentiated value, is an indispensable social form which must be assumed by the material conditions of labour in order for the latter to be wage-labour. Wage-

labour is then a necessary condition for the formation of capital and remains the essential prerequisite of capitalist production.[25]

Capital is a totality

Capital is a relation between two classes, the capitalists and the working class, which ultimately determines how goods and services are produced and distributed across society.[26] As a totality engaged in self-expansion through the employment of wage labour, capital is primarily *capital in general*. This is the general form of capital.[27]

Capital in general is best represented by the circuit of industrial capital, M–C–M', where M is the money advanced to buy commodities (means of production and labour power), C, for processing and, later, sale for more money M'. The difference M'−M is the surplus value, which is the foundation of industrial and commercial profit and other forms of profit, including interest and rent. The circuit of industrial capital represents the essence of capital, valorisation through the production of commodities by wage labour.[28] In this circuit, capital shifts between different forms, money, productive and commodity capital, as it moves between the spheres of exchange, production and, upon its completion, exchange. Although this movement is critical for the process of valorisation, profit is due to the surplus labour performed in production only.[29] However, profit is not the only thing that capital produces: the social outcome of its circuit is the *expanded reproduction* of capital, the renewal of the separation between capitalists and wage workers. In this sense, 'Accumulation of capital is . . . multiplication of the proletariat.'[30]

One word of caution. Capital in general has been described by some, drawing on the work of Roman Rosdolsky, as the sum total of the existing capitals. This macroeconomic aggregate is allegedly the subject of analysis in *Capital 1* and *2*, whereas 'many capitals', analysed in *Capital 3*, includes rival capitals in competition (see chapter 7).[31] Rosdolsky's approach is valuable and it has contributed decisively to the appreciation of the distinct levels of analysis in *Capital*. However, the presumption that *Capital 1* is concerned with the total social capital and *Capital 3* with many capitals in competition is incorrect for two reasons. First, capital exists *only* as a myriad of capitals in competition, and it is nonsensical to presume that it could exist otherwise:

> Conceptually, *competition* is nothing other than the inner *nature of capital*, its essential character, appearing in and realized as the reciprocal interaction of many capitals with one another, the inner tendency as external necessity . . . Capital exists and can only exist as many capitals, and its self-determination therefore appears as their reciprocal interaction with one another.[32]

Second, Marx distinguishes between two types of competition, between capitals in the same branch of industry and capitals in different branches. The former is examined in *Capital 1*,[33] and it explains the sources of technical change, the tendency towards the *differentiation* of the profit rates of capitals producing similar goods with distinct technologies, and the possibility of crisis of disproportion and overproduction. The latter is examined in *Capital 3*;[34] it explains the possibility of migration, the tendency towards the *equalisation* of the profit rates of competing capitals, and other equilibrating structures and processes associated with competition (see chapters 5 and 7). The former is relatively more important than the latter because, first, profit must exist before it can be distributed and tendentially equalised and, second, although migration can raise the profit rate of individual capitals, only technical progress can increase systematically the profitability of capital as a whole. In spite of the considerable merits of his analysis, Rosdolsky fails to appreciate the differences between these two forms of competition, and analyses explicitly only the latter, as if the more abstract form of competition did not exist.[35]

Capital and exploitation

The capital relation implies that the means of production have been monopolised by a relatively small number of people.[36] In contrast, the majority are forced to sell their labour power in order to purchase commodities which, as a class, they have produced previously (see chapter 4):

> The process [of production] only becomes a capitalist process, and money is converted into capital, only: 1) if *commodity production*, i.e., the production of products in the form of commodities, becomes the general mode of production; 2) if the commodity (money) is exchanged against labour-power (that is, actually against labour) as a commodity, and consequently if labour is wage-labour; 3) this is the case however only when the objective conditions, that is (considering the production process as a whole), the products, confront labour as independent forces, not as the property of labour but as the property of someone else, and thus in the form of *capital*.[37]

It follows that, first, there is a relationship of mutual implication between capitalism as the mode of social production, wage labour as the form of social labour, and the commodity as the typical form of the output.[38] Second, capital is a *class relation of exploitation* which allows capitalists to live off the surplus value extracted from the working class.[39] In this sense,

> The capital-labour relation is itself a contradiction which forms the fount of class struggle, while the reproduction of both capital and

labour incorporate a contradiction between individuality and collective class action.[40]

Productive and unproductive labour

Wage labour employed by capital in commodity production for profit performs both concrete and abstract labour, and produces surplus value. This type of labour is *productive*:

> productive labour in a capitalist economy . . . [is] all wage labour hired out of capital that both produces use values in the form of commodities and, in so doing, directly produces surplus value for capital. Thus, productive labour contributes to the commodity both in some physically determinate effect and in surplus value. This holds true for both 'mental' and 'manual' labour, labour producing luxury commodities, and labour producing both 'goods' and 'services' as commodities. Unproductive labour, which is all wage labour that is not productive labour, includes all labour hired out of revenue and two types of labour hired out of capital: labour expended in the genuine costs of circulation and labour expended in the exploitative managerial functions of capital.[41]

In contrast, workers employed in circulation activities, for example those involved in the transformation of commodity capital into money capital, or the latter into productive capital, are unproductive:

> Marx distinguishes labor hired by "productive" capital, or more precisely by capital in the *phase of production*, from labor which is hired by commodity or money capital, or more precisely capital in the *phase of circulation*. Only the first type of labor is "productive", not because it produces material goods, but because it is hired by "productive" capital . . . The productive character of labor is an expression of the productive character of capital.[42]

The distinction between productive and unproductive labour, and between these types of labour and other activities that are not generally considered labour (e.g., non-commercial activities including housework, gardening, childcare and leisure, see section 1.1), underpins the concept of surplus value. This distinction is historically specific, and it has no bearing upon the usefulness of the activities or the significance of their outcome. It is merely a reflex of the social relations under which these activities are performed.

3.3 Conclusion

Marx's value theory departs from the ontological principle that human societies reproduce themselves, and change, through labour. Labour and its products are socially divided and, under capitalism, these processes and their outcomes are determined by the monopoly of the means of production by the class of capitalists, the commodification of labour power and the commodity form of the products of labour. In these circumstances, the products of labour generally take the value form, and economic exploitation is based upon the extraction of surplus value. In other words, the capital relation includes the monopoly of the means of production, wage labour, and the continuous reproduction of the two large and mutually conditioning social classes, the capitalists and the workers.[43]

When analysed from this angle, the theory of value is a theory of class, of class relations and, more specifically, a theory of *exploitation*. The concept of value is useful because it expresses the relations of exploitation under capitalism and allows them to be explained in spite of the deceptive appearances created by the predominance of voluntary market exchanges.

4   Wages and exploitation

Marx's theory of surplus value is one of the most important and hotly disputed aspects of his value analysis. It was shown in section 3.2 that surplus value is that part of the social value product appropriated by the capitalists. The surplus value is the difference between the value produced by the workers and the value of labour power.

This chapter analyses two essential aspects of capitalist exploitation, the wages system and the value of labour power, in three sections. The first explains capitalist exploitation in detail. The second analyses the value of labour power and briefly reviews alternative interpretations of this concept. The third section draws the main conclusions of the study.

4.1 Wage labour and exploitation

From the point of view of distribution, capitalist exploitation can be conceptualised and measured at three levels, the physical, macro-monetary and value levels.[1]

The physical level was discussed in sections 2.1.2 and 3.2. Very briefly, there is exploitation if part of the social product is appropriated by a class of non-producers by custom or law, or under the threat or use of force, or because refusal to comply might disorganise the social reproduction. These conditions often are mutually reinforcing. For example, in antiquity, slavery was sanctioned by custom and by law. Its viability depended upon the regular use of force including, even in the most paternalistic systems, the torture, mutilation and death of recalcitrant slaves. Finally, slave rebellions would tend to disable the largest and most efficient production units, generate widespread social instability and throw into question the legitimacy of the state, leading to economic hardship and, potentially, to civil war.

The physical or surplus analysis is not wrong but it is transhistorical and, therefore, excessively general. It applies whenever the producers, as a class, are compelled to produce more than they themselves consume or control, the residual being appropriated by their masters, lords or employers. This level of analysis is important because it highlights the similarities between different modes of exploitation. However, its generality is also a source of weakness, because the analysis is unable to distinguish between modes of exploitation, or show how the surplus is pumped from the producers in each case.[2]

At the macro-monetary level of analysis, capitalist exploitation is revealed by the existence of profits, including interest, rent and other forms of profit. The rate of exploitation is measured by the profit–wage ratio.[3] With their share of the national income, the capitalists appropriate part of the national product, including the investment and luxury goods.[4] The existence of profits is a symptom of exploitation, but the profit–wage ratio is an imprecise measure of exploitation for three reasons. First, profits and wages are originally assessed at the firm level, then aggregated for the entire economy. This does not correspond to the actual process of exploitation, that is determined by the class structure of society, the mode of production that corresponds to it, and the appropriation of part of the social product by the capitalist class (see below). In other words, exploitation takes place at the level of capital in general and it is mediated by generalised commodity relations, in which case wage workers are exploited *qua* workers, regardless of the profitability of the firms where they are currently employed:

> exploitation is a social (society-wide) phenomenon . . . Thus the quantity and rate of surplus value are in the first instance social or society-wide, not the result of an aggregation of quantities and rates prevailing in each workplace . . . To establish a general rate of surplus value by beginning with the relationship between wages and profits in each industry . . . negates the socialized nature of capitalist production and its complex division of labor. In effect, it assumes that each worker produces his own means of subsistence in isolation. In reality, each worker labors and receives a claim on the total value produced in society. He then exchanges this claim against a collection of use values that is the result of the combined, cooperative labor of all workers.[5]

Second, transfers create systematic discrepancies between commodity prices and values. As a result, the profit–wage ratio may be different from the ratio between the abstract labour required to produce the necessities and the surplus, which Marx called necessary and surplus labour time (see below). Third, wages, prices and profits are determined at market prices, and they can fluctuate widely regardless of changes in the conditions of production, especially after the development of the credit system.

In sum, analysis of exploitation at the physical level shows what distinct modes of exploitation have in common, but it cannot pinpoint the specificities of each mode. In contrast, analysis of the macroeconomic implications of capitalist exploitation is useful because it lends itself to empirical studies. However, it focuses upon one of the consequences (rather than the cause) of exploitation, the inability of the workers to command the entire net product, and it is potentially misleading because the profit–wage ratio is only a rough measure of exploitation.

Finally, value analysis can identify the essence of capitalist exploitation, distinguish it from other modes of exploitation, and facilitate empirical studies. In common with the surplus approach, value analysis implies that the workers are exploited because they work for longer than what is necessary to produce the commodities that they consume or control.[6] Marx calls *necessities* the goods appropriated by the working class. They are produced by *necessary labour*, and their value is the *value of labour power* (see section 4.2). In contrast, the capitalists appropriate the *surplus*, that is produced by *surplus labour* and whose value is the *surplus value*.

The existence of necessities and the surplus, and the division of the social labour time into necessary and surplus labour, is a consequence of exploitation in any mode of production. However, the concepts of value of labour power and surplus value, and their manifestation as wages and profits (including industrial and commercial profit, interest and rent), are essential to capitalism because in this mode of production only exploitation is mediated by value relations and the commodity form.

More generally, modes of production are distinguished from one another by the form of extraction and appropriation of the surplus. The distinction between necessities and the surplus is entirely dependent upon the existence of exploitation:

> a general surplus can exist as an objective phenomenon only if it is appropriated from the direct producer . . . Without classes, no part of society's production appears as a surplus. In such circumstances, a surplus product must be deduced on the basis of some physical (subsistence) definition of surplus, which the analyst necessarily imposes externally upon society. Thus, a general surplus product either is an objective phenomenon of exploitation, an observable, material fact of society; or it becomes arbitrarily and subjectively defined by an external observer.[7]

In contrast with pre-capitalist modes of production, capitalist exploitation does not rely upon overtly political and interpersonal relations. Therefore, it is not determined primarily at the level of the individual farm, firm, or office. Capitalist exploitation is determined at the social level and it is mediated by the market-led distribution of labour and its products.[8] However, it is not immediately obvious how exploitation is compatible with the wage workers' freedom to change jobs, and the capitalists' freedom to determine the level and composition of their own output. One of Marx's most important intellectual achievements is the explanation of how free wage workers are systematically exploited.

Under capitalism, social reproduction is guided by the law of value, or the rule of equivalent exchanges (see section 8.2). This rule of consistency operates through the price mechanism, that signals, reflects and establishes the correspondence between social needs and the social product. Two implications of the law of value are relevant at this stage. First, given equivalent exchanges commodity owners can command more valuable goods only if they increase their own value product. Alternatively, if value transfers are possible speculators, for example, can profit when buying cheap to sell dear. However, the total value is limited by the social value product, in which case those exceptional profits are not possible for every seller (one gains only at the expense of others). At this level of analysis, the law of value implies that capitalist exploitation is not based upon unequal exchanges.[9]

Second, capitalist exploitation is measured by the difference between the value produced by the workers and the value appropriated by them; in other words, total profits are both qualitatively determined and quantitatively limited by the surplus value extracted (see chapter 7). More precisely, the workers sell on the market their capacity to work or labour power, and they are paid the value of labour power (see section 4.2). This is an exchange of equivalents, because the value of labour power is presumably high enough to allow the working class to reproduce itself (and supply labour power in the next period), but too low to allow the workers, as a class, to threaten the capitalist monopoly of the means of production.

In production, the workers create new value in proportion to the length of the workday, their training and discipline, and the intensity of labour (see chapter 5). The difference between the value newly produced by the working class and the value of labour power is the surplus value. The surplus value appears as profit, the residual left after paying the production costs. In short, under capitalism the workers are exploited because they produce more value than they control or receive as wages:

> The wage-form thus extinguishes every trace of the division of the working day into necessary labour and surplus labour, into paid labour and unpaid labour. All labour appears as paid labour. Under the *corvée* system it is different. There the labour of the serf for himself, and his compulsory labour for the lord of the land, are demarcated very clearly both in space and time. In slave labour, even the part of the working day in which the slave is only replacing the value of his own means of subsistence, in which he therefore actually works for himself alone, appears as labour for his master. All his labour appears as unpaid labour. In wage-labour, on the contrary, even surplus labour, or unpaid labour, appears as paid. In the one case, the property-relation conceals the slave's labour for himself; in the other case the money-relation conceals the uncompensated labour of the wage-earner.[10]

The ratio between the surplus value (surplus labour time) and the value of labour power (necessary labour time) is the *rate of exploitation* (rate of surplus value). The rate of exploitation cannot be measured directly because it is determined by abstract rather than concrete labour. However, this concept is useful because it shows that, all else constant, capitalist exploitation can increase for at least three reasons. First, if more hours are worked.[11] Second, if labour intensity increases, for example if pliant workers replace their less subordinate fellows. Third, if the necessary labour time declines because of productivity growth in the sectors producing necessities (given the real wage). Marx calls the first two cases the production of *absolute surplus value*, while the third produces *relative surplus value*.[12] The extraction of absolute surplus value is limited because it is impossible to increase the working day or the intensity of labour indefinitely, and the workers gradually learn to resist effectively against these forms of exploitation. In contrast, relative surplus value is more flexible and harder to resist, because productivity growth can outstrip wage increases for long periods.[13]

4.2 Value of labour power

The value of labour power is usually analysed in two contrasting ways.[14] Traditionally (see section 2.1), it is given by the value of a fixed bundle of goods, the workers' consumption basket. Alternatively (see section 2.2.2), the value of labour power has been defined as the wage share of the net product. Although there is much merit in both strands of the literature, they also have severe shortcomings. This section critically reviews these approaches and outlines an alternative interpretation of the value of labour power.

The fixed bundle approach is probably the best known interpretation of the value of labour power. It claims support from Marx, for example,

> The value of labour-power is determined, as in the case of every other commodity, by the labour-time necessary for the production, and consequently also the reproduction, of this specific article . . . [T]he labour-time necessary for the production of labour-power is the same as that necessary for the production of those means of subsistence; in other words, the value of labour-power is the value of the means of subsistence necessary for the maintenance of its owner.[15]

In spite of this potential strength, and of the unambiguous determination of the physical surplus, the fixed bundle approach is inadequate for three reasons. First, it is based on a very limited interpretation of Marx's writings.[16] Second, it is unable to explain the determination of the wage bundle or the money wage, or differences between the wage levels across labour market segments. Third, this interpretation obscures the commodity aspect of labour power. It implicitly denies the monetary payment of wages and conflates the workers with the goods that they consume or, alternatively, conflates the workers' expenditures with the 'technology of production' of labour power, as if this human capacity were manufactured for profit. In either case, two fundamental distinctions collapse: on the one hand, the difference between wage workers and slaves, beasts of burden, machines or any other input and, on the other hand, the difference between the value of labour power and the value created by the workers:

If . . . we substitute the worker's means of subsistence for the actual labour-power into which the variable part of capital has been transformed, then it is clear that these means of subsistence as such are not different from the other elements of productive capital as far as the formation of value is concerned, not different for example from raw materials and from the means of subsistence of draught cattle . . . The means of subsistence cannot themselves valorize their value or add to it a surplus-value. Their value, like that of the other elements of productive capital, can reappear only in the value of the product. They cannot add more value to it than they themselves possess.[17]

Acceptance of the bundle approach has led some to conclude—as Marx anticipates above—that it is arbitrary to suppose that the workers are exploited, because this definition of value of labour power leads to identical results if corn, iron or energy are considered to be 'exploited' (see section 2.1.2).

The limitations of the fixed bundle approach, its destructive consequences for Marx's value theory, and the shift of value analysis away from physical data and towards the study of macro-monetary relations, have led many to seek alternatives. In this context, the definition of the value of labour power in the 'new interpretation', as the wage share of the net product, has gained popularity (see section 2.2.2):

The value of labor power is the claim on abstract labour time workers receive for their labor power in the form of a money wage . . . Workers in capitalist society do not bargain for, or receive, a bundle of commodities as payment for their labour power, they receive a sum of money, the money wage, which they are then free to spend as they wish . . . The usual interpretation . . . makes money disappear as a mediating element in the situation. The interpretation of the value of money as the money wage multiplied by the value of money brings the concept of money into the basic account of the capitalist system of production, where it belongs, and shows the specificity of exploitation in capitalism as an appropriation of surplus value in the form of money.[18]

This interpretation implies that the workers are paid the maximum wage that they can get, and spend it in ways that do not have to be examined. This view has important advantages, especially the recognition of the role played by distributive conflicts in the determination of the wage rate.[19]

In spite of these strengths, this approach suffers from significant drawbacks. First, Marx rejected it explicitly:

Whether [the worker's] wages are high or low is not determined by his share of the product but, on the contrary, his share of the product is determined by the amount of his wages. He actually receives a share of the value of the product. But the share he receives is determined by the value of labour [power], not conversely, the value of labour [power] by his share of the product. The value of labour [power], that is, the labour-time required by the worker for his own reproduction, is a definite magnitude; it is determined by the sale of his labour power to the capitalist. This virtually determines his share of the product as well. It does not happen the other way round, that his share of the product is determined first, and as a result, the amount or value of his wages.[20]

Second, it is analytically vacuous, because although it is trivially true *ex post* that the workers command a share of the net national income, the size of their share, and the goods which tend to be purchased, are left unexplained other than tautologically by the balance of forces between capital and labour. It is as if the economic and social reproduction of the workforce, of which the customary standard of living is one element, were irrelevant for the process of exploitation and the determination of the wage. In other words, whereas the bundle approach postulates a fixed (but unexplained) consumption basket that is later used to determine the price system, the share approach departs from given (but unexplained) prices and from (unexplained) wages in order to arrive at the value of the workers' consumption bundle (whose composition is also left unexplained).

Third, the share approach presumes that the relationship between capital and labour is symmetric, in which case the net product is shared between the two large classes primarily on the basis of their market power. This is wrong, because profits and wages are not determined simultaneously through a struggle for shares of the net product, however important distributional conflict in capitalism may be. In reality, the capitalists draw upon the value previously created by the workers to advance the value of labour power, and the capitalists retain the residual profit after the output is sold. Therefore, the relationship between profits and wages is fundamentally distinct from that between industrial profit, interest and rent, which *are* conflicting claims over the (given) mass of surplus value extracted from the workers:

> [The] struggle over the division of the net product . . . is indirect since the determination of the level of profits in response to the determination of the level of wages is mediated by the production process. In other words, it is erroneous to consider that at the end of some fictionally constructed production period there exists a given net product to be divided between capitalists and workers. To adopt such a theoretical framework is to treat capital and labour symmetrically in distributional relations, whereas the aggregate circulation of capital reveals that their roles are far from symmetrical.[21]

More generally, the relationship between capital and labour is asymmetric at several levels: (a) The wage relation is only apparently a bargain among equals, for one of the 'partners' monopolises the conditions of production, while the other needs a wage in order to survive. (b) The circuit of capital starts when the capitalists purchase labour power at a given wage (even if they pay in arrears); in contrast, profit is the residual left after the wages and the other production costs have been defrayed. In reality, there is *never* a 'fixed cake' to be divided at the end of production. (c) Having purchased labour power, the capitalists must force the workers to produce more value than the value of labour power, the difference being determined through class conflict in *production*. (d) Finally, the capitalists alone determine the level and composition of the product and future investment:

> Once the sphere of production is incorporated . . . the apparent symmetry between capital and labour, in distributional relations and in receiving profits and wages out of national income, evaporates, for the payment of wages is a precondition for the production process to begin (or, more exactly, this is true of the purchase of labour-power, whose actual payment may well come later). Profits are the result or outcome of the production process rather than the shares of the spoils after wages have been paid. Consequently, distributional relations between capital and labour are not of the 'fixed cake' variety, even if, obviously, *ceteris paribus* profits are higher if wages are lower . . . Rather, profits depend first and foremost on the ability of capitalists to extract surplus value from the production process; they need, whatever the level of wages, to coerce labour to work over and beyond the labour time required to produce those wages.[22]

Fourth, this definition of value of labour power is excessively general and it fails to contribute to the development of a theory of *value*:

> while it is perfectly true that the existence of unearned income is a fact of experience which needs no theory of value to prove it, it does not by any means follow that a *theory of distribution* can do without a theory of value. A "theory of distribution" which said only that unearned income was the fruit of the surplus labour of those employed in production would hardly qualify as a *theory* at all . . . At the best, such a "theory" could be little more than a generalised description of the appropriation by the owners of the means of production, in all types of class society, of the product of the surplus labour of the exploited classes . . . [Moreover,] how are the respective shares of the main social classes in the national income determined in . . . [capitalist] society? Unless one is content to rely on some sort of explanation in terms of "force" or "struggle" (in which case again one could only with difficulty speak of a *theory* of distribution), it is impossible to give adequate answers to these questions without basing one's account on a theory of value.[23]

In sum, it is trivially true that in every mode of production the workers command only part of the net product, and that in capitalism exploitation surfaces through the difference between the value added per hour and the wage rate. Although the share approach recognises these simple truths, it is insufficient because it cannot reach beyond one of the effects of exploitation, the inability of the workers to purchase the entire net product.

More fundamentally, the fixed bundle and the wage share approaches are inadequate because they seek to translate the value of labour power directly into a concrete outcome. However, each fails in its own way to acknowledge that the value of labour power is not appropriately attached initially either to a quantity of money or to a quantity of goods.[24] In reality, the value of labour power is neither a quantity of goods nor a sum of money, it is a quantity of *value*, the abstract labour time which the workers spend producing necessities. This value is determined at the aggregate level through the exchange between capital and labour as a whole and, subsequently, the performance of labour and exploitation in production:

> The value of wages has to be reckoned not according to the quantity of the means of subsistence received by the worker, but according to the quantity of labour which these means of subsistence cost (in fact the proportion of the working-day which he appropriates for himself), that is according to the *relative share* of the total product, or rather of the total value of this product, which the worker receives.[25]

This concept of value of labour power encompasses the two alternatives discussed previously, without being constrained by the shortcomings of either. On the one hand, it implies that the working class is exploited because part of what it produces is appropriated, through money, by the capitalists, and it acknowledges that capitalist exploitation includes an irreducibly monetary and macroeconomic aspect (rather than being encapsulated by the transhistorical inability of the workers to command the entire net product). On the other hand, it does not presume that a fixed bundle must be consumed in order to obtain specific outcomes and, consequently, it avoids the conflation between the workers and draught cattle, machines or electricity.

Wage levels, and the workers' consumption norms, are part of the conditions of reproduction of the workforce. They vary systematically across the labour markets, and have to be distinguished from one another in order to avoid 'averaging out' across the working class in spite of differences in occupation, income, gender, age, and household composition. The norm, in terms of wage or consumption levels, is more appropriately understood in a more complex way than the *ex post* average; for the levels and incidence of needs, consumption and wages are the outcome of dynamic socioeconomic processes which determine the patterns of consumption, especially the production and satisfaction of *wants*.[26] What those wants and patterns of consumption are, and how they are determined, can be very different from one commodity to another and from one section of the working class to another. Food habits, housing, entertainment, and so on, are not only differentially consumed across the working class but their patterns and levels of consumption derive from very different structures and processes of causation, including the structure of employment, the role of the state, the structure and content of housework, (changes in) skill levels, the role of trade unions and the political leverage of each section of the working class.[27]

In sum, the value of labour power cannot be legitimately conceptualised independently of the contradictory tendencies associated with the accumulation of capital for which a complex analysis ranging over the dynamic (and disaggregated) structures of consumption, employment and the distributive struggle is a precondition.[28] This analysis grinds out a determinate share of the social labour time through several mediations involving what is produced and how, the determination of needs and customs, and their reflection upon the structure of production and distribution. Short-circuiting these real processes of determination by postulating a fixed consumption bundle or an exogenously determined level of wages is insufficient to explain the social and historical meaning of the value of labour power. Moreover, they may be misleading because they pre-empt recognition of the mediations between value of labour power and the level of wages.

4.3 Conclusion

The value analysis of exploitation outlined in this chapter shows that exploitation is a class relationship with two aspects, the capitalist command over part of the output, and their exclusive control over its composition, including the investment goods and the sources of growth. Both aspects of exploitation derive from the capitalist monopoly of the means of production, the transformation of commodities into the general form of the product, and the capitalist control of the labour process (see chapter 5). Exploitation has clear implications both at the macro-monetary and the physical levels. In the latter, the existence of exploitation is revealed by the physical surplus, while in the former it appears through the profit–wage ratio.

Analyses of exploitation that focus only upon one of these aspects of exploitation are limited, and they have been criticised heavily. An alternative approach to exploitation, based upon class analysis and a value interpretation of the value of labour power, has greater explanatory power than the best known interpretations, and it avoids their shortcomings.

5   Values, prices and exploitation

Analysis of value at increasing levels of complexity includes its relationship with class and exploitation (see chapters 3 and 4), and the expression of value as price (explained below).

Commodities are produced by a co-ordinated set of concrete labours usually performed at the farm, factory or office. These labours are performed with varying degrees of efficiency, diverse skills and distinct technologies, and at different points in time. In spite of these differences, all commodities of the same kind have the same value, which appears through their price. Output values cannot be identified at the firm or sectoral levels for two reasons: first, value creation is a social process determined by the pre-dominance of specific relations of production, in which case individual production has meaning and significance only as part of the whole; second, values and prices are determined by the *abstract* labour time necessary to reproduce each type of commodity, including its inputs. In sum, the value form of the product is due to the social division of labour, values are quan-titatively determined by the collective effort and the productive potential of society, and prices are determined for the mass of commodities rather than good by good or at the level of the firm or sector in isolation.

The equalisation of labour and the determination of values and prices are the outcomes of a real process in three stages: first, individual labours are normalised across those producing the same kind of commodity; second, they are synchronised across those that have produced the same kind of commodity in the past or with distinct technologies; and, third, they are homogenised across the other types of labour as the commodity is equalised with ideal money.[1]

This chapter has four sections. The first explains the normalisation of labour, including the reduction of complex into simple labour and com-petition within branches. The second analyses the synchronisation of labour, including the determination of reproduction values, value transfers and the impact of technical change. The third explains the homogenisation of labour, including the determination of market prices when demand and supply fail to match. The fourth section summarises this chapter.

5.1 Normalisation of labour

Capitalist production is *mass production* in two senses. First, the output is generally *massive*. Even when a bewildering variety of products is available, often made to order, commodity production in its broadest sense—including finance, accounting, design, planning, logistics, hiring, training and managing the workforce, manufacturing, marketing, distribution, and so on —is a large-scale and continuous operation managed meticulously and professionally, often by large organisations. Each stage of this process is closely intertwined with the others, and with production carried out elsewhere.

Second, capitalist production employs a *massive* number of workers. Even when individual firms are small, or downsize, or spin-off independent companies, the production process remains integrated vertically into tightly-knit systems of provision or commodity chains, which employ large numbers of workers in order to produce specific commodities, including food, clothes, autos, TV shows and many others.[2] In each system of provision, the concrete labour of individual workers exists only as part of the whole, and it is performed according to the rhythm dictated by management and machinery (limited by collective resistance on the shopfloor). Therefore, wage labour performed under the control of capital is, typically, *average labour*:

> Capitalist production only really begins . . . when each individual capital simultaneously employs a comparatively large number of workers, and when, as a result, the labour-process is carried on an extensive scale, and yields relatively large quantities of products . . . This is true both historically and conceptually . . . *The labour objectified in value is labour of an average social quality, it is an expression of average labour-power* . . . The law of valorization therefore comes fully into its own for the individual producer only when he produces as a capitalist and employs a number of workers simultaneously, i.e. when from the outset he sets in motion labour of a socially average character.[3]

This averaging out of labour *in production*, rather than on the market as is the case under simple commodity production (see section 2.2.1), is due to the organised, integrated and mechanised character of capitalist production:

> each worker, or group of workers, prepares the raw material for another worker or group of workers. The result of the labour of the one is the starting-point for the labour of the other. One worker therefore directly sets the other to work . . . [T]he direct mutual interdependence of the different pieces of work, and therefore of the workers, compels each one of them to spend on his work no more than the necessary time. This creates a continuity, a uniformity, a regularity, order, and even an intensity of labour, quite different from that found in an independent handicraft or even in simple co-operation. The rule that the labour-time

expended on a commodity should not exceed the amount socially necessary to produce it is one that appears, in the production of commodities in general, to be enforced from outside by the action of competition: to put it superficially, each single producer is obliged to sell his commodity at its market price. In manufacture, on the contrary, the provision of a given quantity of the product in a given period of labour is a technical law of the process of production itself.[4]

Mass production always averages out labour. Whereas this is the exception under pre-capitalist modes of production, characterised by fragmentation and small-scale production, it is generalised under capitalism. Moreover, only under capitalism do firms compete with others producing the same goods across a range of markets, which forces them to impose strict production norms and innovate (see section 5.2) in order to survive.

These pressures arising from production and exchange *normalise* wage labour performed for capital within production. Normalisation of labour is a double process. On the one hand, it is the averaging out of labour productivity within each firm and sector, described above.[5] On the other hand, normalisation is the subsumption of the labours performed in each firm and sector under the *social* process of production of each type of commodity.

Recognition of the fact that labours are normalised across those producing the same use value has three important consequences for value analysis. First, the labour time that determines value is socially, rather than individually, determined, and commodity values express the abstract labour time necessary to produce each kind of commodity, rather than the concrete labour time required by any individual worker or firm to produce a sample of the object.[6]

Second, commodities with identical use values have the same value whatever their individual conditions of production (see section 5.2).[7] Third, during production both labour and the inputs are transformed into the output. Therefore, normalisation involves not only those labours performed in the last stage of production (e.g., assembly, packing or transport) but also the labours that produced the inputs used up. Consequently, commodity values are partly created in their own production, and partly determined by the value of the socially necessary means of production.[8]

5.1.1 Labour intensity and complexity, education and training

Suppose that the workers are identical and that the firms operating in one branch of industry are also identical, but labour is more intense in one firm than elsewhere. This difference can be analysed at two levels. From the point of view of profitability, the firm with more intensive labour is more profitable because its unit labour costs are lower than its rivals'. From the point of view of value production, this profitability difference is due to the greater value-creating capacity of intense labour:

Increased intensity of labour means increased expenditure of labour in a given time. Hence a working day of more intense labour is embodied in more products than is one of less intense labour, the length of each working day being the same . . . Here we have an increase in the number of products unaccompanied by a fall in their individual prices: as their number increases, so does the sum of their prices . . . The value created varies with the extent to which the intensity of labour diverges from its normal social level of intensity.[9]

This conclusion holds more generally: differences or changes in the intensity or complexity of labour, and differences or changes in the level of education and training of the workforce, have *identical* effects on value production:

the value of a commodity represents human labour pure and simple, the expenditure of human labour in general . . . More complex labour counts only as *intensified*, or rather *multiplied* simple labour, so that a smaller quantity of complex labour is considered equal to a larger quantity of simple labour. Experience shows that this reduction is constantly being made. A commodity may be the outcome of the most complicated labour, but through its *value* it is posited as equal to the product of simple labour, hence it represents only a specific quantity of simple labour.[10]

In sum, all else constant, more intense or complex labour, and better educated and trained workers, generally create more use values and, consequently, more value per hour. The quantitative difference depends upon the relationship between individual and social productivity in each branch, that is known precisely only *ex post*. More generally, there is no necessary or systematic relationship between these variables and possible differences or changes in wages, the value of labour power or the rate of exploitation (similarly to the absence of any fixed relationship between the value of labour power and the value produced by labour; see section 4.1).

Marx's conclusion has been criticised because the reduction coefficients (the ratio between the value-productivity of skilled and simple labour) are not specified endogenously.[11] Two alternative solutions have been proposed for this perceived problem, reduction by wages or by the indirect labour stored up in the trained worker.[12] Reduction by wages presumes that there is a fixed relationship between the productivity of trained workers and their monetary rewards or, alternatively, that the individual rates of exploitation are identical. However, there is no justification for these assumptions, for three reasons. First, labour power is not a commodity produced for sale by profit-maximising agents; alternatively, employment patterns are not primarily determined by the rate of exploitation. Second, wage discrepancies across the working class are only partly due to differences in the value-creating capacity of individual workers; to a large extent, they derive from custom, convention and deliberate attempts by management to divide the workers. Third, even if this were not the case, it is generally impossible to assess the contribution of individual workers in large-scale mechanised production.[13]

Reduction by the labour stored up assumes that the expenditure of skilled labour power counts as the simultaneous expenditure of the skilled worker's 'original' simple labour, plus a share of the worker's own past simple labour learning the skill, and a share of the direct and indirect labour of others who contributed to the training process. This view is unsustainable, because it conflates education and training with the storing up of labour in machinery and other elements of constant capital (see section 5.2); in other words, it explains the value-creating capacity of skilled labour in a different way than the value-creating capacity of simple labour. This approach presumes that, in contrast with simple labour, skilled labour has *no* value-creating capacity; its expenditure is merely a regurgitation of past labour, with no allowance for the possibility that training may *save* labour.[14] In sum, and reiterating,

> There is absolutely no suggestion . . . that the increased value-creating capacity of an hour of more intense labor bears any relationship to the amount of additional labor required to produce an hour's worth of labor-power so consumed . . . [T]he augmented value-creating capacity of skilled labour exists for the same reason. Skilled labour creates more value in equal periods of time than does unskilled labour because it is physically more productive, and there is no reason to suppose that any determinate relationship exists between this increased physical product-ivity and the physical productivity of the extra labor required to produce the skill. Hence, there is no determinate relationship between the in-creased value-creating capacity of skilled labour and the value equivalent of this training labor.[15]

5.1.2 Mechanisation, deskilling and capitalist control

Intra-sectoral competition, between firms producing the same use values, compels each firm to minimise costs in order to maximise its profit rate. Suppose that the workers are identical and that the firms producing a given commodity are also identical, but one of them produces more with the same labour input because its shopfloor design is more efficient. This simple example shows that improved technology cuts unit costs or, more precisely, increases the value-productivity of otherwise identical labour.[16] More generally, greater labour intensity increases the output (and the total value produced) because *more* simple labour is condensed in the same concrete labour time; however, it does not affect the unit value of the product (see section 5.1.1). In contrast, technical improvements *reduce* the quantity of simple labour necessary to produce a unit of the product and, consequently, tend to lower its value:

Production for value and surplus-value involves a constantly operating tendency . . . to reduce the labour-time needed to produce a commodity, i.e. to reduce the commodity's value, below the existing social average at any given time. The pressure to reduce the cost price to its minimum becomes the strongest lever for raising the social productivity of labour, though this appears here simply as a constant increase in the productivity of capital.[17]

Competition within branches compels firms to introduce new technologies in order to cut costs and, in so doing, increase the value-productivity of their employees.[18] These technical innovations will be copied or emulated elsewhere, eroding the advantage of the innovating firm while preserving the incentives for further technical progress across the economy. At the level of capital in general, this process reduces the value of all goods, including those consumed by the workers and, all else constant, it permits the extraction of relative surplus value (see section 4.1).[19]

The most important element in intra-sectoral competition is *mechanisation*, or the introduction of new technologies and new machines. For capital, mechanisation is a form of increasing profitability as well as a tool of social control. The process of mechanisation has three principal aspects. First, as was shown above, mechanisation increases the value-productivity of labour and the profit rate of the innovating capitals. Second, mechanisation facilitates the extraction of relative surplus value:

Like every other instrument for increasing the productivity of labour, machinery is intended to cheapen commodities and, by shortening the part of the working day in which the worker works for himself, to lengthen the other part, the part he gives to the capitalist for nothing. The machine is a means for producing surplus-value.[20]

Third, mechanisation is a tool of capitalist control. It reduces commodity values and allows increasingly sophisticated goods to be produced with greater investment, which can reduce the scope for competition by independent producers and their ability to survive without selling their labour power (or as subordinated contractors). Moreover, mechanisation dilutes the workers' individuality through collective labour:

Manufacture . . . has the form of a productive mechanism whose component parts are human beings. It represents a directly social form of production in the sense that the worker can work only as part of the whole. If the need for the workers to sell their labor power had initially been grounded in their propertylessness . . . it now becomes grounded in the technical nature of the labor process itself. This "technical" nature is intrinsically capitalist.[21]

More generally, underneath their seemingly neutral, scientific and pro-
ductivist guise, machines are despotic dictators of the rhythm and content of
the labour process. Historically, countless disputes over pay and working
conditions have been either triggered or resolved by mechanisation:[22]

> technology is not merely control over Nature, it also provides control
> over Man. The division of labor and the factory system provided ways
> of *controlling* the pace and quality of work, as do modern assembly-line
> methods. Technology provides for social control and discipline in the
> workplace. So the development of technology is not socially neutral; it
> will reflect class interests and sociopolitical pressures.[23]

Machines have been often deployed deliberately in order to wrestle both the
knowledge[24] and the control[25] of production away from the workers, sometimes even *at the expense of profitability*:[26]

> machinery does not just act as a superior competitor to the worker,
> always on the point of making him superfluous. It is a power inimical
> to him, and capital proclaims this fact loudly and deliberately, as well
> as making use of it. It is the most powerful weapon for suppressing
> strikes, those periodic revolts of the working class against the autocracy
> of capital . . . It would be possible to write a whole history of the
> inventions made since 1830 for the sole purpose of providing capital
> with weapons against working-class revolt.[27]

Mechanisation is closely related with *deskilling*. Deskilling is a two-fold
process. On the one hand, deskilling is a direct result of mechanisation.
It was shown above that mechanisation changes work patterns and job
descriptions, usually leading to their fragmentation into simpler operations,
that are easier to measure and control (*detail work*):

> in place of the hierarchy of specialized workers that characterizes manu-
> facture, there appears, in the automatic factory, a tendency to equalize
> and reduce to an identical level every kind of work that has to be done
> by the minders of the machines.[28]

On the other hand, deskilling is the transformation of the workers' abilities
and experience into commodities. This process includes the codification of
talents previously controlled by individual workers and their reproduction
across the working class through market mechanisms and other social
institutions, especially education and training.[29] The appropriation by
capital of the talents and abilities of individual workers increases their
versatility, or the employability of the class across the economy according to
capital's demand. One can, therefore, speak both of deskilled *jobs*, that do
not depend upon talents or abilities monopolised by individual workers, and

of deskilled *workers*, whose talents and abilities can be reproduced commercially:

> the flexibility of capital, its indifference to the particular forms of the
> labour process it acquires, is extended by capital to the worker. He is
> required to be capable of the same flexibility of *versatility* in the way he
> applies his labour-power . . . The more highly capitalist production is
> developed in a country, the greater the demand will be for *versatility* in
> labour-power, the more indifferent the worker will be towards the
> *specific content* of his work and the more fluid will be the movements of
> capital from one sphere of production to the next.[30]

The interaction between these two aspects of deskilling implies that capital
does *not* tend to transform talented craft workers into brutes who can
perform only repetitive elementary tasks in the production line, as Charles
Chaplin's character famously did in the film *Modern Times*. Even though
technical change is usually associated with unemployment and changes in
job descriptions, the remaining workers need to be trained in order to
perform different tasks and operate more complex machines.[31] Critically,
however, the training required for optimum worker performance in unskilled
jobs can be provided as and when required by capital. By the same token,
unskilled workers can be readily hired when their contribution is needed, and
dismissed when they are no longer necessary:

> Deskilling is inherent in the capitalist labour process because capital
> must aim at having labour functions that are calculable, standardised
> routines; because this labour must be performed at the maximum speed
> and with the minimum of 'porosity'; and because capital wants labour
> which is cheap and easily replaceable.[32]

Deskilling, versatility, and the decomposition of tasks into detail work,
have two important consequences. First, they increase worker alienation,
because 'the object is no longer a product in direct reference to the individual subject of labour, but only in relation to the individual capital'.[33]
Second, they increase capitalist control over the labour process, because
of mechanisation and the greater depth, flexibility and integration of the
labour markets.

These are important aspects of the transformation of goods, services,
assets, technologies and social relations into commodities. This process
results from, and reinforces, capitalism and, more specifically, capitalist
control of the workers. Control structures include, directly, foremen, managers
and consultants and, at a further remove, financial institutions and the stock
market. Capitalist control and competition are twin forces that normalise the
value-producing capacity of the workers, and subject both the output and
the labour process to social determinations.

5.2 Synchronisation of labour

The simultaneous sale, at the same price, of commodities produced in different moments shows that individual concrete labours are *synchronised* across those that have produced the same kind of commodity at other times, or with distinct technologies. Because labours are normalised and synchronised, all commodities of a kind have the same value, regardless of how, when and by whom they are produced. Normalisation explains why the labour time necessary to produce a type of commodity is socially determined, and includes that necessary to produce the inputs (see section 5.1). Synchronisation implies that this labour time is indistinguishable from and, therefore, is equivalent to living labour:

> All the labour contained in the yarn is past labour; and it is a matter of no importance that the labour expended to produce its constituent elements lies further back in the past than the labour expended on the final process, the spinning. The former stands, as it were, in the pluperfect, the latter in the perfect tense, but this does not matter. If a definite quantity of labour, say thirty days, is needed to build a house, the total amount of labour incorporated in the house is not altered by the fact that the work of the last day was done twenty-nine days later than that of the first. Therefore the labour contained in the raw material and instruments of labour can be treated just as if it were labour expended in an earlier stage of the spinning process, before the labour finally added in the form of actual spinning.[34]

The equivalence between labours producing the same commodities at different points in time or with distinct technologies is due to the fact that value is a social relation established by, and reproduced through, capitalist production, rather than a substance ahistorically embodied in the commodities by concrete labour (see section 2.1). The social reality of value implies that *only living labour creates value* or, alternatively, that Marx's value theory is based upon *social reproduction costs*. More specifically, values are determined by the current ability of society to reproduce each kind of commodity, or the *reproduction socially necessary labour time* (RSNLT). Values are not set in stone when the commodities are produced. Rather, they are socially determined continuously, and they can shift because of technical change anywhere in the economy:

> The value of any commodity . . . is determined not by the necessary labour time that it itself contains, but by the *socially* necessary labour-time required for its reproduction. This reproduction may differ from the conditions of its original production by taking place under easier or more difficult circumstances. If the changed circumstances mean that twice as much time, or alternatively only half as much, is required for

the same physical capital to be reproduced, then given an unchanged value of money, this capital, if it was previously worth £100, would now be worth £200, or alternatively £50.[35]

The value of labour power provides the clearest example of *reproduction* SNLT. It was shown in section 4.2 that the value of labour power is determined by the workers' reproduction needs, rather than the concrete labour time embodied in the workers or in the goods that they consume, or have consumed in the past:

> When Adam Smith is examining the "natural rate" of wages or the "natural price" of wages, what guides his investigation? The natural price of the means of subsistence required for the reproduction of labour-power. But by what does he determine the natural price of these means of subsistence? In so far as he determines it at all, he comes back to the correct determination of value, namely, the labour-time required for the production of these means of subsistence.[36]

Carefully sifting through Marx's works one can find passages where he seems to defend another view of value: for example, that the value of the inputs is embodied in the output and carried over through time. This has led some to defend distinct interpretations of value theory (see section 2.1), and others to complain of inconsistency.[37] However, these alleged textual discrepancies are often cited out of context, and they can be explained by the age of the texts (some older texts can seem closer to the embodied labour view), their level of abstraction (the more abstract they are, the more value resembles embodied labour) and the context of the analysis (for example, where Marx contrasts constant and variable capital).[38]

5.2.1 Value transfers

Commodity values have two parts: first, the abstract labour necessary to transform the inputs into the output, determined by RSNLT through the normalisation and synchronisation of labour (see above); second, the similarly determined value transferred from the inputs. The transfer of input values is a real process with two aspects. On the one hand, living labour *transforms* the inputs into the output; this is the basis of the normalisation of labour.[39] On the other hand, value expresses the conditions of social reproduction, including the ability of society to *re-start* production in the next period; this is the basis of synchronisation. The transfer of input values includes the circulating constant capital used up, and the physical and technical ('moral') depreciation of the fixed capital.[40] Let us deal with each of them in turn.

The value transferred by the circulating constant capital is determined, as was explained above, by the abstract labour time currently necessary to produce the inputs, while the socially necessary inputs are determined by the dominant technique of production of the output:

> The values of the means of production . . . (the cotton and the spindle) are therefore constituent parts of the value of the yarn . . . Two conditions must nevertheless be fulfilled. First, the cotton and spindle must genuinely have served to produce a use-value; they must in the present case become yarn . . . Secondly, the labour-time expended must not exceed what is necessary under the given social conditions of production. Therefore, if no more than 1 lb. of cotton is needed to spin 1 lb. of yarn, no more than this weight of cotton may be consumed in the production of 1 lb. of yarn. The same is true of the spindle. If the capitalist has a foible for using golden spindles instead of steel ones, the only labour that counts for anything in the value of the yarn remains that which would be required to produce a steel spindle, because no more is necessary under the given social conditions.[41]

Consequently, and somewhat counter-intuitively, the original value of the inputs used up, and the money-capital spent buying them, are *irrelevant* for the determination of the output value:

> the values of the material and means of labour only re-appear in the product of the labour process to the extent that they were preposited to the latter as values, i.e. they were values before they entered into the process. Their value is equal to the . . . labour time necessary to produce them under given general social conditions of production. If later on more or less labour time were to be required to manufacture these particular use values . . . their value would have risen in the first case and fallen in the second . . . Hence although they entered the labour process with a definite value, they may come out of it with a value that is larger or smaller . . . These changes in their value, however, always arise from changes in the productivity of the labour of which they are the products, and have nothing to do with the labour process into which they enter as finished products with a given value.[42]

It is similar with fixed capital. To the extent that production physically consumes the elements of fixed capital, value is added to the output such that when the machines are finally scrapped (or when new tools or buildings are necessary), enough money is available for their replacement.[43]

5.2.2 Technical change, value and crisis

Technical change in the production of the elements of fixed capital, e.g., machines, brings into existence a new generation of machines that is, in general, cheaper to run per unit of output. When new machines are introduced, the value transferred by the old machines (and the unit value of the output) declines.[44] Two important implications follow. First, technical change in different sectors of the economy can shift the value of the elements of fixed capital suddenly and unpredictably:

> According to simple value theory, capital goods unrealistically depreciate according to predetermined patterns just as they do in neoclassical production theory. Once we go beyond the analysis of semistatic, expanded reproduction, we require knowledge about future economic conditions before we can calculate the amount of abstract labour embodied in a commodity. For example, if unpredictable technical change can make a tool obsolete in the near future, how do we develop an appropriate rule to allocate the movement of value from the tool to the final product?[45]

These capital losses are potentially large, and they may be distributed unevenly because of the distinct technologies employed by each firm.[46] Firms may bear these costs in different ways, depending on their choices and relationship with the financial markets and the accounting conventions, and the costs may even be ignored temporarily. However, they cannot be avoided indefinitely because discrepancies between the technologies employed in each firm and the socially dominant techniques affect their profitability:

> When large divergences [between prices and reproduction values] become typical throughout the economy, the price system will become increasingly incapable of coordinating the economy. Malinvestment will become common . . . Eventually, forces of competition will compel prices to fall in line with reproduction values . . . Marx repeatedly explained how, over and above changes in reproduction values, value can appear to take on a more or less independent existence until a crisis brings values back in line with reproduction values . . . [I]n a real economy, actual prices tend to drift away from underlying labor values. As the linkage between prices and values becomes looser, the price system gives increasingly misleading signals, making speculation more profitable than earning profits by producing goods and services for the market.[47]

Second, the possibility of technical change introduces an unavoidable *indeterminacy* in the output values. This indeterminacy is due to the unknowable 'true' value transferred by the fixed capital, which depends upon the implications of future technical change for the current value of the machines. Moreover, the potentially different ways in which technical depreciation is incorporated by each firm (in spite of the uniformity of output values), and the impact of the bursts of spending that accompany the replacement of fixed capital, open the possibility of bankruptcy and financial crisis:[48]

Reproduction costs shift in unpredictable patterns. Because we cannot predict what future technologies will be available at any given time in the future, we have no way of knowing in advance how long a particular capital good will be used before it will be replaced . . . We cannot calculate the values of goods produced today, because knowing the appropriate values of the constant capital being transferred today is impossible without advanced knowledge of future reproduction values . . . Alternatively, we could calculate the value of goods based on capitalists' estimates of future depreciation patterns. Once we embark on the path of taking subjective estimates of future depreciation into consideration, we open a new can of worms . . . To begin with, we have no way of knowing the capitalists' subjective opinions. In addition, Marx's assertion about bankruptcies suggests that these subjective opinions are grossly mistaken.[49]

Uncertainty with respect to the output values has a knock-on effect on the calculation of surplus value, the residual left after the reproduction costs are subtracted from the output value and, consequently, upon the distribution of surplus value as profit, interest and rent. These difficulties are due to real contradictions in the process of economic reproduction, and they do not affect the meaning and significance of the concept of surplus value or the theoretical stature of value. However, they need to be accommodated into an analytical framework that is sufficiently flexible to allow them room to move, yet sufficiently robust to represent the structures of determination of reality, including the equivalence between labours performed in competing firms within each sector (normalisation), and in different firms across time or in firms employing distinct technologies (synchronisation).

5.3 Homogenisation of labour

Normalised and synchronised labours in distinct sectors of the economy generally create different quantities of value in a given time, for example in window cleaning and computer programming. The *homogenisation* of labour translates the different value-productivities of normalised and synchronised labour into distinct quantities of abstract labour (RSNLT).[50] Labours are homogenised as commodities receive a price, or when money fulfils the function of measure of value. At this level of analysis, the law of value ensures that commodity prices correspond to their RSNLT (see section 4.1).

Homogenisation has three important implications. First, value cannot appear directly as a quantity of labour-hours; it appears only as price (see sections 8.1 and 8.2).[51] In other words, the value-productivity of labours performed in distinct firms or sectors is assessed only through the (money-) value added per hour. Second, the values and prices of all commodities are determined simultaneously (see section 5.2). Third, Marx's statement that money is 'the direct incarnation of all human labour',[52] or immediately social labour, implies that the production of money is distinctive because in this sector labour is not homogenised. Rather, the value of money is the pivot of the homogenisation of labours performed in the other sectors, and it provides the benchmark for the formation of prices.

Although homogenisation is conceptually clear, the assessment of the value produced is uncertain because prices are affected by a wide range of variables at distinct levels of complexity. For example, price reductions may be due to technical progress, the possibility of capital migration (see chapter 7), excess supply, industrial, financial, tax, trade or exchange rate policies, and other variables:

> The magnitude of the value of a commodity . . . expresses a necessary relation to social labour-time that is inherent in the process by which value is created. With the transformation of the magnitude of value into the price this necessary relation . . . may express both the magnitude of value of the commodity and the greater or lesser quantity of money for which it can be sold under given circumstances. The possibility, therefore, of a quantitative incongruity between price and magnitude of value . . . is inherent in the price-form itself. This is not a defect, but, on the contrary, it makes this form the adequate one for a mode of production whose laws can only assert themselves as blindly operating averages between constant irregularities.[53]

For example, let us follow Marx's analysis of differences between supply and demand. For simplicity, suppose that the workers are identical and that the firms producing the commodity (say, linen) are also identical. Even under these circumstances, the market price of linen may be different from the direct expression of its value in terms of money. This can happen if, for example, too large or too small a share of the social labour is applied in the production of linen, given the social need for this use value:

> Let us suppose . . . that every piece of linen on the market contains nothing but socially necessary labour-time. In spite of this, all these pieces taken as a whole may contain superfluously expended labour-time. If the market cannot stomach the whole quantity at the normal price of 2 shillings a yard, this proves that too great a portion of the total social labour-time has been expended in the form of weaving. The effect is the same as if each individual weaver had expended more labour-time on his particular product than was socially necessary. As the German proverb has it: caught together, hung together. All the linen on the market counts as one single article of commerce, and each piece of linen is only an aliquot part of it.[54]

Excess supply does not imply that the commodity has lost part of its use value, that the unsold items have lost their entire use value, or that the value of each commodity has shrunk, as if value were determined by price rather than the converse (see section 2.2.1). Excess supply merely modifies the *expression* of value as price; it contracts the total price of this commodity vis-à-vis its total value (money hoards, velocity changes and credit adjust the quantity of circulating money to the demand for the product, see section 8.1):

> if the commodity in question is produced on a scale that exceeds the social need at the time, a part of the society's labour-time is wasted, and the mass of commodities in question then represents on the market a much smaller quantity of social labour than it actually contains . . . These commodities must therefore be got rid of at less than their market value, and a portion of them may even be completely unsaleable.[55]

The products of capital *are* generally commodities, and they *have* both value and use value (see section 3.1). Overinvestment, excess capacity and the accumulation of inventories and, consequently, low profitability and the devaluation of capital show that too much capital and labour have been allocated to this sector, relative to the social need; in other words, part of this labour was not socially necessary from the point of view of *exchange*. However, this does not affect either the concept of socially necessary labour in *production*, or the *fact* of exploitation:

> The total mass of commodities, the total product, must be sold . . . If this does not happen, or happens only partly, or only at prices that are less than the price of production, then *although the worker is certainly exploited*, his exploitation is not realized as such for the capitalist . . . indeed, it may even mean a partial or complete loss of his capital. The conditions for immediate exploitation and for the realization of that exploitation are not identical. Not only are they separate in time and space, they are also separate in theory. The former is restricted only by the society's productive forces, the latter by the proportionality between the different branches of production and by the society's power of consumption.[56]

The impact of economic crises is very similar. Crises may lead to market contractions and price crashes. In this case, previously created value may be redistributed or destroyed:

> When speaking of the *destruction of capital* through crises, one must distinguish between two factors . . . [Firstly, in] so far as the repro-duction process is checked and the labour-process is restricted or in some instances is completely stopped, *real* capital is destroyed . . . Secondly, however, the *destruction of capital* through crises means the depreciation of *values* which prevents them from later renewing their reproduction process as capital on the same scale. This is the ruinous

effect of the fall in the prices of commodities. It does not cause the destruction of any use-values. What one loses, the other gains . . . If the value of the commodities from whose sale a capitalist reproduces his capital was equal to £12,000, or which say £2,000 were profit, and their price falls to £6,000, then the capitalist . . . [cannot] restart his business on the former scale . . . In this way, £6,000 has been destroyed, although the buyer of these commodities, because he has acquired them at half their [price of production], can go ahead very well once business livens up again, and may even have made a profit.[57]

Value determination through RSNLT and its expression as price through normalisation, and the possibility of differences between value production and realisation because of the misallocation of social labour or economic crises, belong to distinct levels of analysis. The latter is more complex, because it includes not only the production conditions, but also the circumstances of exchange, the distribution of labour and the possibility of crisis. More generally, firms whose profit rates are lower than the average are always penalised. Within each branch, inefficient firms produce less value than their competitors, and may go bankrupt or become the target of takeover bids. These pressures can become stronger if the sector produces in excess of demand, which depresses the profit rate of all firms. Differences between individual and sectoral profit rates vis-à-vis the average are the capitalist mechanism of reallocation of labour across the economy and, simultaneously, the main lever of technical change.

5.4 Conclusion

Abstract labour, value and price are central concepts in Marx's analysis of the social form of work and the mode of exploitation under capitalism. These concepts express the dominant social relations of production, and they can be viewed at distinct levels. At a highly abstract level, value is a social relation that derives from the mode of production; therefore, labour performed within the relations of production typical of capitalism produces value regardless of the circumstances in exchange or distribution. The quantity of value produced is determined by RSNLT, and it appears initially as 'value', 'direct' or 'simple' price.[58]

The relationship between value and price can be analysed more concretely, but there is often a trade-off between conceptual detail and quantitative determinacy. For example, the transfer of the value of the means of production introduces a quantitative indeterminacy in the output value and, correspondingly, arbitrariness in the price level, because the rate of technical depreciation of the fixed capital is unknowable. By the same token, price can be seen as the mode of existence of value, as the condition of supply, or as the money that can be commanded on sale, which are, *prima facie*, unrelated to the mode of labour. In addition to these difficulties, discrepancies between supply and demand and economic crises blur the relationship between values and prices even further. In sum, shifts in the level of analysis modify the relationship between value and price and, therefore, the homogenisation of labour. In contrast, normalisation and synchronisation remain unaffected, because they are determined in production.

These limitations show that attempts to calculate values independently of prices through estimates of the vector of abstract labour are limited both conceptually and empirically, because they presume that value can appear in two different ways, both directly (as if it could be measured by concrete labour time) and through price. Simply put, the value analysis developed in this chapter does not allow the quantitative determination of long-run prices better than alternative approaches (see chapter 7). Its main advantage is theoretical: it *explains* the social relations underlying economic activity more clearly than alternative views.

6   Composition of capital

This chapter analyses Marx's concept of the composition of capital. Although this concept is essential for understanding the relationship between values and prices, technical change, and other structures and processes, it has been generally explained cursorily and understood only superficially and incorrectly in most of the literature.[1]

The argument is developed in four sections. The first briefly reviews some of the best known interpretations of the composition of capital in order to illustrate the diversity of the literature on this topic. The second follows Marx's analysis of the composition of capital in the absence of technical change. Each concept used by Marx is defined and its introduction justified. The third section discusses how the technical (TCC), organic (OCC) and value composition of capital (VCC) are affected by technical progress. It will be shown that one of Marx's aims in distinguishing the OCC from the VCC is for a focused analysis of a particular case, where the accumulation of capital occurs with technological innovation. The fourth section summarises the main findings of this chapter. The contrast between the static and dynamic cases is essential, not only to the orderly introduction of the concepts, but also to the appreciation of their contradictions, limits and shifts. Moreover, this arrangement is useful in its direct connection with the levels of analysis of the composition of capital.

6.1   Understanding the composition of capital

Widely different understandings of the composition of capital found in the literature may, at least partly, result from Marx's use of three forms of the concept, the TCC, OCC and VCC. While the content of each term is evident at times, there are moments when Marx seems to use them contradictorily; consequently, large chunks of his inquiry may look arbitrary and puzzling. A brief review of differing views of the composition of capital may give a better idea of the difficulties involved in this study.

Paul Sweezy argues that the composition of capital is the relation of constant (c) to variable capital (v) in the total capital used in production. For him, although '[s]everal ratios would serve to indicate this relation . . . the one which seems most convenient is the ratio of constant capital to total capital.'[2] Sweezy defines the OCC as $c/(c+v)$. This formulation has its roots in Bortkiewicz's work, and it is also adopted by Seton and Desai.[3] In his discussion of the transformation problem Sweezy follows Bortkiewicz's treatment and, as may be gathered from the discussion below and in chapter 7, attributes the different sectoral rates of profit to the distinct value rather than organic compositions of the invested capital, which is contrary to Marx's argument.

Michio Morishima is closer to the mark in his understanding of the TCC and the VCC, but misinterprets the OCC by defining it as the name Marx would have given to the VCC, in case the TCC underwent changes such that all relative values were left unaltered (in other words, for him OCC is the name of the VCC when the changes in the TCC are precisely reflected by changes in the VCC—as if productivity increase is identical across all sectors).[4] Morishima believes that Marx only defined the OCC to simplify his treatment of technical changes, but it will be shown below that this is insufficient.

Nobuo Okishio[5] works with the value composition of capital under the name of the organic composition in his treatment of the transformation, and he is by no means the only one to do so. Most of the current literature argues that the OCC can be defined unproblematically as c/v, as if the VCC did not exist, and they transform values into prices on the basis of this presumption.[6] However, for Marx, matters were slightly more complicated than that. In his analysis of the law of the tendency of the rate of profit to fall, Roemer also calls OCC what should really be termed VCC, and his discussion of the falling profit rate bears the mark of this fundamental misconception.[7]

In his classic paper proposing an iterative solution to the transformation problem, Shaikh calls OCC the ratio $(c+v)/v$.[8] In contrast, Sherman defines the OCC as $v/(c+v)$ while M. Smith and Wright, following Mage, call OCC the ratio $c/(v+s)$. Foley, in his outstanding textbook, defines the 'composition of capital' as $v/(c+v)$, and the 'OCC' as c/v.[9] Finally, Groll and Orzech in their detailed discussion of the composition of capital (one of whose merits is the careful distinction of the TCC, OCC and VCC from each other) argue that the OCC is a long-run value-concept while the VCC is measured in market prices and refers to the short-run, something with which Marx would probably disagree.[10]

These problems are merely a sample of the difficulties one encounters in literature on the composition of capital. In order to understand Marx's use of these concepts, this chapter reviews their development. In what follows it is shown that, while in the *Grundrisse* Marx does not yet employ the concepts which he would later call the composition of capital, in the *Theories of Surplus Value* he introduces the physical (technical) composition of capital and the organic composition of capital and, finally, in *Capital* he uses the technical composition of capital, the organic composition of capital and the value composition of capital in their most developed form. The progressive introduction of these terms reflects the increasing refinement of Marx's own perception of the matters at stake, and allows him to clarify his own arguments. It will be shown below that, although the form of Marx's arguments changes, the problems with which he deals and the results he reaches are essentially unaltered through the years.

6.2 Production and the composition of capital

The *productivity of labour* is determined by the mass of means of production that can be processed into final commodities in a given labour time or, alternatively, by the output per hour.[11] This notion is captured by the *technical composition of capital* (TCC, called earlier the physical composition of capital). The TCC is the physical ratio between the mass of material inputs (the products of past labour) and the living labour necessary to transform them into the output:

> A certain quantity of labour-power, represented by a certain number of workers, is required to produce a certain volume of products in a day, for example, and this involves putting a certain definite mass of means of production in motion and consuming them productively – machines, raw materials etc . . . This proportion constitutes the technical composition of capital, and is the actual basis of its organic composition.[12]

The TCC cannot be measured directly or compared across branches because it is the ratio between a heterogeneous bundle of use values (the material inputs) and a quantity of sectorally-specific average (normalised and synchronised) labour, rather than abstract labour (see chapter 5). For example, it is impossible to contrast directly the TCC in the construction and electronic industries, where the use value of the inputs processed per hour of labour, and the value-productivity of labour, can be very different. However, the TCC can be assessed in value terms because in capitalism all produced inputs tend to become commodities. The value-assessment of the TCC defines the *organic composition of capital* (OCC), or the value of the means of production which absorb one hour of living labour in a given firm, industry or economy:

> The organic composition can be taken to mean the following: Different ratios in which it is necessary to expend constant capital in the different spheres of production in order to absorb the same amount of labour.[13]

For Marx, the OCC is the value-reflex of the TCC, or a 'technological composition' determined in *production* and that synthesises, in value terms, the technical relations in production. The OCC relates the *total* value of the constant capital (including fixed and circulating capital) to the *total* labour time required to transform the inputs (whether paid or unpaid). Marx refers to the OCC as follows:

> The ratio between the different elements of productive capital . . . [can be] determined . . . [b]y the organic composition of productive capital. By this we mean the technological composition. With a *given productivity* of labour, which can be taken as constant so long as no change occurs, the amount of raw material and means of labour, that is, the amount of constant capital—in terms of its *material elements*— which corresponds to a definite *quantity of living labour* (paid or unpaid), that is, to the *material elements* of *variable capital*, is determined in every sphere of production.[14]

There is, however, a severe difficulty with the OCC. As the value of a bundle of means of production is the product of the values of its components by the quantities used up, it seems impossible to tell whether differences or changes in the OCC are due to differences or changes in the TCC (and, consequently, to differences or changes in the productivity of labour in *this* industry) or from differences or changes in the value of the means of production used up (that reflect the circumstances in *other* industries). However, for Marx there was no ambiguity. As the OCC is an immediate value-reflex of the TCC, it does *not* change if the TCC is kept constant, even if the value of the elements of capital changes. Having made this highly abstract claim, Marx says:

> if one assumes that the organic composition of capitals is given and likewise the differences which arise from the differences in their organic composition, then the value ratio can change although the technological composition remains the same . . . If there is any change in [e.g.] the value of variable capital independent[ly] of the organic composition, it can only occur because of a fall or a rise in the price of means of subsistence that are not produced in the sphere of production under consideration but enter into it as commodities from outside . . . The organic changes and those brought about by changes of value can have a similar effect on the rate of profit in certain circumstances. They differ however in the following way. If the latter are not due simply to fluctuations of market prices and are therefore not temporary, they are invariably caused by an organic change in the spheres that provide the elements of constant or of variable capital.[15]

Marx is clearly aware that, for a given production process, changes in the value-ratio between the (fixed and circulating) constant capital and the (paid and unpaid) quantity of labour technically required can stem from either variations in the value of the inputs *or* from technological ('organic') changes in production. Based on this definition of the OCC, and aware that technical and value changes should not be conflated, Marx planned to discuss in Chapter 2 of Part 3 of *Capital*:

1. Different organic composition of capitals, partly conditioned by the difference between variable and constant capital in so far as this arises from the *stage of production* – the absolute quantitative relations between machinery and raw materials on the one hand, and the quantity of labour which sets them in motion. These differences relate to the labour-process. The differences between fixed and circulating capital arising from the circulation process have also to be considered . . .
2. Differences in the relative value of the parts of different capitals which do not arise from their organic composition. These arise from the difference of value particularly of the raw materials, even assuming that the raw materials absorb an equal quantity of labour in two different spheres.
3. The result of those differences is diversity of the rates of profit in different spheres of capitalist production.[16]

Marx eventually realised that an adequate treatment of these problems would require a more refined distinction between the effects of the application of different technologies and the consequences of the use of inputs of distinct values. For this reason he introduces, in *Capital*, the concept of *value composition of capital* (VCC). The VCC is a concept of exchange. This is the ratio between the value of the circulating part of the constant capital (including the depreciation of fixed capital) and the variable capital required to produce a unit of the commodity.[17]

Let us follow Marx's discussion of the same problem both before and after the introduction of the VCC. This will show the place of the VCC in his analysis, and its relation to the TCC and the OCC. Marx wants to argue that if the technical and organic compositions of two capitals are equal, but the value of the means of production used up is different, the value-assessment of their TCCs from the point of view of circulation may mislead the analyst into believing that their TCCs are distinct. In the *Theories of Surplus Value* he says:

In the case of capitals of equal size . . . the *organic composition* may be *the same* in *different spheres of production*, but the *value ratio* of the primary component parts of constant and variable capital may be *different* according to the different values of the amount of instruments and raw materials used. For example, copper instead of iron, iron instead of lead, wool instead of cotton, etc.[18]

The VCC allowed Marx to become more rigorous and elegant. In *Capital*, he says:

> it is possible for the proportion [the TCC] to be the same in different branches of industry only in so far as variable capital serves simply as an *index* of labour-power, and constant capital as an *index* of the volume of means of production that labour-power sets in motion. Certain operations in copper or iron, for example, may involve the same proportion between labour-power and means of production. But because copper is dearer than iron, the value relationship between variable and constant capital will be different in each case, *and so therefore will the value composition of the two capitals taken as a whole.*[19]

These examples explain the impact of differences in the value of the means of production consumed per hour of labour in distinct sectors with equal TCCs and OCCs. For example, if copper and iron implements (or wool and cotton clothes, or silver and gold jewellery) are manufactured with identical technologies and, therefore, by capitals with the same technical and organic compositions, Marx says that their value compositions are different because of the distinct value of the material inputs.[20] In the first quote, he measures the TCCs only through the OCCs. As the OCC reflects the TCC from the point of view of production, it disregards the distinct value of the inputs used up. Marx can only point out that capitals may have equal TCCs and OCC, even though they employ means of production with distinct values. In the second example, Marx argues differently, directly claiming that if two capitals in distinct sectors have the same technical (and, therefore, organic) composition, but use means of production with different value, the equality of their TCCs and OCCs would appear distorted by their distinct VCCs.

The opposite case was also the subject of Marx's attention. If two sectors had equal VCCs, could they have different OCCs (and, therefore, distinct TCCs)? Marx's answer is in the affirmative:

> A capital of lower organic composition . . . considered simply in terms of its value composition, could evidently rise to the same level as a capital of higher organic composition, simply by an increase in the value of its constant parts . . . Capitals of the same organic composition can thus have a differing value composition, and capitals of the same percentage {value} composition can stand at varying levels of organic composition, displaying various different levels of development of the social productivity of labour.[21]

Therefore, if in two distinct production processes a given quantity of homogeneous labour power transforms different *masses* of means of production into the final product, the capitals will have different TCCs and OCCs. However, if the value of these inputs is such that the ratio between the constant and the variable capitals used up is equal, then their VCCs will be equal.[22]

These examples show that differences in the *value* of the constant and variable capital consumed in distinct industries are captured by the VCC but not the OCC; in contrast, differences in the *technologies of production* affect the OCC but they may not be accurately reflected by the VCC. The concept of OCC is important because it allows the study of technical differences (or changes, see section 6.3) in production, regardless of the corresponding value differences (or changes), while the VCC cannot distinguish between them. One final example illustrates the scope and limitations of the concept of OCC, and the role of the VCC:

> let us assume that the raw material is dearer and labour (of greater *skill*) is dearer, in the same proportion. In this case {capitalist} A employs 5 workers, where {capitalist} B employs 25, and they cost him £100—as much as the 25 workers, because their labour is dearer (their surplus labour is therefore also worth more). These 5 workers work up 100 lbs. of raw material, y, worth {£}500 and B's workers work up 1,000 lbs. of raw material, x, worth {£}500 . . . The value ratio here – £100 v to {£}500 c is the same in both cases, but the *organic composition* is different.[23]

This example is clear enough. Although capitalists A and B spend equal amounts of money on means of production and labour power—which implies that their capitals have *equal* value compositions—their organic compositions are *different* because of the distinct production technologies.

In sum, although the OCC and the VCC are value-assessments of the TCC, they are distinct concepts because of the different evaluation of the means of production and labour power. An OCC-comparison of the technologies of production adopted in two industries is independent of differences in the values of the components of capital, because the OCC is defined in production. In contrast, distinctions (or variations, see section 6.3) in the values of constant and variable capital are detected by the VCC, a concept of exchange.[24] Only in this case is it possible to apprehend Marx's definition in full:

> The composition of capital is to be understood in a two-fold sense. As value, it is determined by the proportion in which it is divided into constant capital . . . and variable capital . . . As material, as it functions in the process of production, all capital is divided into means of production and living labour-power. This latter composition is determined by the relation between the mass of the means of production employed on the one hand, and the mass of labour necessary for their employment on the other. I call the former the value-composition, the latter the technical composition of capital. There is a close correlation between the two. To express this, I call the value-composition of capital, in so far as it is determined by its technical composition and mirrors the changes in the latter, the organic composition of capital.[25]

6.3 Capital accumulation

One of the essential features of capitalism is the tendency towards the development of the production technologies (see section 5.2). Technical change is usually introduced in individual firms, raising their TCCs and, consequently, their OCCs and VCCs.[26] Because of their higher productivity, the innovating firms enjoy higher profit rates. Competition between firms in the same branch tends to generalise these technical advances, which reduces the commodity values and eliminates the advantage of the innovating firms. More generally, the technical and the organic compositions of capital in general tends to rise in every turnover and, all else constant, commodity values tend to fall.[27]

Since technical change potentially modifies the values of all commodities, whether directly or indirectly, the determination of the composition of capital in a dynamic environment is contingent upon the way changes in production affect commodity circulation. This is best analysed at the level of capital in general, where the values that exist at the beginning of the circuit ('earlier values'), at which the inputs are purchased, are higher than those at which the output is sold ('later values').[28] This conceptual distinction is essential for the analysis of accumulation:

> since the circulation process of capital is not completed in one day but extends over a fairly long period until the capital returns to its original form . . . great upheavals and changes take place in the *market* in the course of this period . . . [and] in the productivity of labour and therefore also in the *real value* of commodities, [and] it is quite clear, that between the starting-point, the prerequisite capital, and the time of its return at the end of one of these periods, great catastrophes must occur and elements of crises must have gathered and develop . . . The *comparison* of value in one period with the value of the same commodity in a later period is no scholastic illusion . . . but rather forms the fundamental principle of the circulation process of capital.[29]

Now, which values should be used in the calculation of the OCC and the VCC, the older and higher or the newer and lower? For Marx, the answer is unambiguous. The OCC reflects the TCC at the *initial* (higher) values of the component parts of capital, *before* the new technologies affect the value of the output. In contrast, the VCC reflects the TCC at the *final* (lower and synchronised) values of the elements of constant and variable capital, determined by the modified conditions of production and newly established in exchange. Therefore, changes in the social VCC capture the rise in the social TCC as well as the ensuing fall in commodity values, including those that have been used as inputs. Consequently, the VCC tends to increase more slowly than the social TCC and OCC:

> This change in the technical composition of capital . . . is reflected in its value-composition by the increase of the constant constituent of capital

at the expense of its variable constituent . . . However . . . this change in the composition of the value of the capital, provides only an approximate indication of the change in the composition of its material constituents . . . The reason is simple: with the increasing productivity of labour, the mass of the means of production consumed by labour increases, but their value in comparison with their mass diminishes. Their value therefore rises absolutely, but not in proportion to the increase in their mass.[30]

In contrast, the social OCC is measured at the 'earlier' values, and rises in tandem with the social TCC. In advanced capitalism, when technical progress is the main lever of accumulation, we may well find that the TCC and the OCC grow even faster than social capital itself:

the development of the productivity of labour . . . and the change in the organic composition of capital which results from it, are things which do not merely keep pace with the progress of accumulation, or the growth of social wealth. *They develop at a much quicker rate*, because simple accumulation, or the absolute expansion of the total social capital, is accompanied by the centralization of its individual elements, and because the change in the technical composition of the additional capital goes hand in hand with a similar change in the technical composition of the original capital.[31]

6.4 Conclusion

The OCC is distinguished from the VCC only through the comparison between contrasting situations. If one compares two capitals at the same moment of time, one would contrast the value of the constant capital productively consumed per hour of labour (which defines the VCC) with the mass of means of production processed in the same time (that determines the TCC and the OCC). This case is important theoretically, and it was through the static comparison of capitals with distinct organic compositions that Marx developed, in Part 2 of *Capital 3*, his transformation of values into prices of production (see chapter 7).

In a dynamic environment, both the OCC and VCC of a capital undergoing technical change can be calculated. It was shown above that they diverge because the OCC is an *ex ante* evaluation of the (fixed and circulating) constant capital technically required per hour of (paid and unpaid) labour, while the VCC is the *ex post* ratio between the new value of the (circulating) constant and the variable capital spent in the last phase of production. Thus, the OCC is measured at the time of production, while the VCC is determined in circulation and calculated when labours are normalised, synchronised and homogenised, new values are determined and commodities are about to enter the sphere of exchange. It was in this context that Marx presented his law of the tendency of the rate of profit to fall, in Part 3 of *Capital 3*.[32]

Marx's use of the TCC, OCC and VCC may at times look ambiguous, since both the OCC and the VCC assess the TCC in value terms. However, these concepts have very distinct meaning and significance, and the terminological changes that Marx gradually adopts almost certainly reflect his growing awareness of the importance of the composition of capital for the analysis of accumulation, the transformation of values into prices of production, the tendency of the rate of profit to fall, different types of rent and so on. However, and probably more importantly, they help to illuminate the impact of accumulation upon the reproduction of the social capital. Continuous technical change raises the TCC, the OCC and gross input values. However, output values, future input prices, and the VCC tend to fall. How the actual process of adjustment happens—especially for large blocs of fixed capital—is crucial to the process of accumulation, because the sudden devaluation of large masses of capital can lead to financial upheaval and crises.

7 Transformation of values into prices of production

Competition between capitals in different sectors introduces an important shift in the level of analysis in *Capital*. This type of competition, and the possibility of capital migration, explains the distribution of capital and labour across the economy, and transforms the expression of value as price; the latter become *prices of production*. The transformation of values (or, more precisely, 'value', 'simple' or 'direct' prices, proportional to RSNLT; see section 5.4) into prices of production is due to the distribution of surplus value according to the size of each capital, regardless of origin.

The importance of the transformation for Marx's work, and his seemingly counter-intuitive approach, have brought to this issue the attention of a vast array of writers of widely different persuasions.[1] It is often claimed that the transformation reveals fundamental flaws in Marx's method, and shows that analyses based on his value theory are doomed.[2] These claims have been rejected by a vast literature, not necessarily Marxist, that argues that the problems in Marx's transformation procedure can be rectified easily (although in different ways), or that Marx's approach is cogent and needs to be understood properly rather than corrected.[3] This chapter builds upon this tradition, but it approaches the transformation from another angle. Previous analyses usually if implicitly argue that the transformation is due to differences in the *value* composition of the advanced capitals. In contrast, it is well known that Marx attributes it to differences in their *organic* composition. These concepts were compared and contrasted in chapter 6, and their implications for the transformation are outlined below.[4]

This chapter has four sections. The first introduces the concepts of surplus value, profit, and rate of profit, and explores the role of OCC differences in the determination of profit. The second interprets Marx's transformation procedure on the basis of differences in the OCCs of the advanced capitals. The third discusses the transformation of input values and the implications of the transformation for Marx's analysis of the forms of value. Finally, the fourth section assesses the implications of this reading of Marx.

7.1 Surplus value, profit and the composition of capital

The third volume of *Capital* opens with the distinction between the concepts of surplus value (s) and profit. Surplus value is the difference between the newly produced value and the value of labour power, and profit is the difference between the value of the product and the value of the constant (c) and variable (v) capital (see section 4.1).

The rate of exploitation, e=s/v, measures the surplus value created per unit of variable capital. In contrast, the rate of profit (r) measures capital's rate of growth, in which case the distinct role in production of the means of production and labour power is immaterial. The rate of profit is:[5]

$$r = \frac{s}{c+v} = \frac{e}{(c/v)+1}$$

where c/v is the value composition of capital.[6]

Marx subsequently considers the impact on the profit rate of changes in the quantity, quality and value of the inputs, and the implications of changes in the turnover time and the rate of surplus value. In chapter 8 of *Capital 3*, Marx points out that the same factors that affect the general rate of profit may also lead to differences between the profit rates of individual capitals in distinct sectors:

> the rates of profit in different spheres of production that exist simultaneously alongside one another will differ if, other things remaining equal, either the turnover times of capitals invested differ, or the value relations between the organic components of these capitals in different branches of production. *What we previously viewed as changes that the same capital underwent in succession, we now consider as simultaneous distinctions between capital investments that exist alongside one another in different spheres of production.*[7]

This passage marks the shift in the level of analysis, or the introduction of competition between capitals in different sectors. This shift posits the need for the transformation. It may therefore come as a surprise that Marx does not immediately address this issue. Rather, in the following pages he analyses (differences between) the technical, organic and value compositions of capital (TCC, OCC and VCC; see chapter 6). It is only after this apparent detour that Marx looks into the transformation, in chapter 9 of *Capital 3*.

The profit rates of capitals invested in distinct sectors may be different because of their organic or value compositions. For example, two capitals producing steel and aluminium utensils (or cotton and wool clothing) with identical technologies have the same TCCs and OCCs. However, differences in the input values imply that their VCCs and profit rates, measured in direct prices, are different. This is how the literature has usually explained the need for the transformation. *However, Marx was interested in another problem.* Suppose, alternatively, that two identical capitals produce goods with distinct technologies, one employing relatively more machines and the other relatively more labour. In this case, regardless of the input costs (and the VCC), the capital employing more labour has a lower OCC, produces more value and surplus value and, all else constant, has a higher profit rate.

These examples are significant, because they show that the OCC connects the rate of profit with the sphere of *production*, where living labour produces value and surplus value. In contrast, the VCC links the profit rate with the sphere of *exchange*, where commodities are traded and the growth of the advanced capital is measured by the newly established values (see chapters 5 and 6). Marx describes the impact of differences or changes in the OCC and the VCC on the profit rate as follows:

> Fluctuations in the rate of profit that are independent of changes in either the capital's organic components or its absolute magnitude are possible only if the value of the capital advanced . . . rises or falls . . . If the changed circumstances mean that twice as much time, or alternatively only half as much, is required for the same physical capital to be reproduced, then given an unchanged value of money . . . the profit is also expressed accordingly in twice or only half the monetary sum. *But if it involves a change in the organic composition of the capital*, the ratio between the variable and the constant part of the capital, then, if other circumstances remain the same, *the profit rate will rise with a relatively rising share of variable capital and fall with a relatively falling share.*[8]

If Marx were primarily interested on the impact on prices of differences in the *value* of the elements of the advanced capital, or the effect on the rate of profit of the distinct *expenditure ratios* in constant and variable capital, his transformation would pivot around the VCC. Most of the literature approaches the problem from this angle, but this is not Marx's procedure. His emphasis on the OCC shows that Marx is primarily concerned with the effect on prices of the distinct (surplus) value-creating capacity of the advanced capitals, or the impact on prices of the different *quantities* of labour necessary to transform the means of production into the output, regardless of the value of the means of production.[9] This approach is intuitively obvious for a *labour* theory of value; but let us discuss this issue in further detail.

It was shown in section 6.2 that the static comparison of the TCCs and OCCs nets out differences in the value of the labour power and means of production consumed, and that only differences in the conditions of production are influential. This leads Marx to a simple yet powerful conclusion; if we abstract from the input values, the capital with the *lowest* OCC employs relatively *more* workers and produces *more* surplus value, regardless of the commodity produced.[10]

This conclusion points to two reasons why the OCC is useful for the analysis of profit creation. First, because it pins the source of surplus value and profit firmly down to *unpaid labour*. This helps Marx to substantiate his claims that machines do not create value, that surplus value and profit are not due to unequal exchange, and that industrial profit, interest and rent are merely shares of the surplus value produced (see sections 3.2 and 4.1).[11] Second, it connects the concepts of profit rate, distribution of labour, surplus value and price of production with the sphere of *production*, rather than exchange. In the sequel, Marx illustrates how the general rate of profit is formed, and how prices of production are determined, through the comparison of five capitals with distinct OCCs.

7.2 From values to prices of production

In his well-known transformation tables in chapter 9 of *Capital 3*, Marx contrasts five capitals worth £100 (including fixed and circulating capital) and states that they have different profit rates because of their distinct OCCs. From their individual profit rates he calculates an average and, from this average, Marx derives the prices of production of the output (see Table 7.1).

In spite of their importance, the reason why Marx includes capitals with the *same size*, £100, and the reason why he determines the price of production of the *entire* output of each capital, rather the unit price, have escaped the literature. They have probably been attributed to convenience or ease of exposition. However, since Marx is interested in the OCC, this procedure is *necessary*. Let us start from the equal size of the advanced capitals:

> the organic composition of capital . . . *must* be considered in percentage terms. We express the organic composition of a capital that consists of four-fifths constant and one-fifth variable capital by using the formula 80c + 20v.[12]

Marx uses the per cent form several times, in the transformation and elsewhere. He does this because this is the *only* way to assess the OCC in the static case, when it cannot be measured directly. If we assume, as Marx does, that the value-productivity of labour is the same in every firm and that the rate of surplus value is determined for the entire economy (see section 4.1), the per cent form (e.g., 60c + 40v rather than 6c + 4v or 180c + 120v; and 80c + 20v rather than 8c + 2v or 2400c + 600v) has striking consequences: variable capital becomes an *index* of the quantity of labour power purchased, labour performed, and value and surplus value produced.[13] Moreover, there is a direct relationship between the quantity of labour put in motion, the value of the output and the rate of profit. *This is what Marx wants to emphasise in the transformation*. As these relations are established in production, they involve the *organic* (rather than value) composition of capital:

Table 7.1 Marx's transformation[a]

Capitals ($M=c+v$)	Used up constant capital (c')	Cost price ($k=c'+v$)	Rate of surplus value (s/v)	Surplus value (s)	Value of the product ($M'=k+s$)	'Value' rate of profit ($r=s/M$)	Profit ($\pi=MR$)[b]	Price of production ($p=k+\pi$)	'Price' rate of profit ($r'=\pi/M$)
I. 80c+20v	50	70	100%	20	90	20%	22	92	22%
II. 70c+30v	51	81	100%	30	111	30%	22	103	22%
III. 60c+40v	51	91	100%	40	131	40%	22	113	22%
IV. 85c+15v	40	55	100%	15	70	15%	22	77	22%
V. 95c+5v	10	15	100%	5	20	5%	22	37	22%
390c+110v	202	312	100%	110	422	22%	110	422	22%

[a]The last row indicates totals or averages, where appropriate.
[b]R is the average 'value' rate of profit.

Source: Capital 3, pp. 255–256.

> Capitals of the same size, or capitals of different magnitudes reduced to percentages, operating with the same working day and the same degree of exploitation, thus produce very different amounts of surplus-value and therefore profit, and this is because their variable portions differ according to the differing organic composition of capital in different spheres of production, which means that different quantities of living labour are set in motion, and hence also different quantities of surplus labour, of the substance of surplus-value and therefore of profit, are appropriated . . . At any given level of exploitation of labour, the mass of labour set in motion by a capital of 100, and thus also the surplus labour it appropriates, depends on the size of its variable component . . . Since capitals of equal size in different spheres of production, capitals of different size considered by percentage, are unequally divided into a constant and a variable element, set in motion unequal amounts of living labour and hence produce unequal amounts of surplus-value or profit, the rate of profit, which consists precisely of the surplus-value calculated as a percentage of the total capital, is different in each case.[14]

Use of the per cent form helps to illustrate the principle that profit is created in production, and that it depends primarily upon the *quantity* of labour power put in motion, rather than the value of the means of production. For Marx, this shows that profit is a 'dividend' drawn from the social surplus value.[15] Finally, the per cent form shows clearly that total value equals total price of production, and that total surplus value equals total profit.

These aggregate equalities are essential for Marx. They should not be understood as two independent conditions or as 'testable hypotheses', as if Marx's value theory would be falsified unless they are verified empirically. For Marx, these equalities are one and the same and they necessarily hold, but they are influential at distinct levels. Total price is equal to total value *because* price is merely a form of value, or *because* total profit is equal to total surplus value. Alternatively, individual prices differ from values *because* profits differ from surplus values, due to the redistribution of surplus value in the transformation. These equalities always hold because they express the development of the same concept, social labour, across distinct levels of analysis (see section 1.1).[16]

Marx's abstraction from the transformation of the value of the inputs and the value of the money-commodity, which naturally follows from his analysis based upon the OCC, confirm that these equalities should be understood primarily *conceptually*. They express the relationship between value and surplus value with their own forms of appearance, price and profit. Prices of production are a relatively complex form of value, in which price-value differences redistribute surplus value across the economy until the average capital in each branch of industry has the same profit rate.[17]

Let us look at this relationship from another angle. Commodity values and prices can be analysed at distinct levels. At a very abstract level, value is a social relation of production or, in quantitative terms, the labour time socially necessary to reproduce each kind of commodity. It can also be seen as the monetary expression of this labour time as direct price, price of production, or market price (see chapter 5). These shifts are due to the refinement of these concepts through their reproduction at greater levels of complexity, which captures increasingly complex determinations of the price form and, therefore, of the value relation. Their detailed study comprises a large part of the body of Marx's work, and of Marxian value theory more generally.[18]

We have seen above that the per cent form is convenient, because it highlights the effect on the profit rate of differences in the OCCs of the advanced capitals. However, because it equalises all capitals to £100 regardless of their actual size, the per cent form *changes* the average rate of profit and *modifies* the quantities produced by each original capital:

> In our previous illustration of the formation of the general rate of profit, every capital in every sphere of production was taken as 100, and we did this in order to make clear the percentage differences in the rates of profit and hence also the differences in the values of the commodities that are produced by capitals of equal size. It should be understood, however, that the actual masses of surplus-value that are produced in each particular sphere of production depend on the magnitude of the capitals applied . . . [I]t is evident that the average profit per 100 units of social capital, and hence the average or general rate of profit, will vary greatly according to the respective magnitudes of the capitals invested in the various spheres.[19]

Since the values, surplus values, prices and profits calculated through the per cent form are different from their original magnitudes, it is *impossible* to calculate the price vector through Marx's transformation procedure. As the per cent form is necessary to assess the OCC, and since its use precludes the calculation of prices, it *cannot* be argued that Marx's main objective in the transformation is to devise a method for the calculation of the price vector. Although some may find this disappointing or worse, it is hardly surprising, for the transformation 'problem' is not primarily about the calculation of prices. It is essentially a *qualitative* problem: the demonstration that price of production is a more complex form of expression of social labour than value, because it reflects the distribution of labour and surplus value across the economy.[20] Analysis of the input values is irrelevant to this end, and their consideration may cloud, rather than illuminate, the essential problems at stake.

7.3 The transformation of input values

The *first* stage of the transformation, explained above, is the distribution of the surplus value newly produced by all capitals in order to equalise the profit rates across the economy. However, the transformation has *another* stage, in which the input values and the value money are transformed. This stage is analytically secondary, and it received little attention from Marx; however, this has been the source of most disputes about the meaning and significance of the transformation.

It is often argued that Marx ignores the transformation of the input values in his procedure. However, this statement is at best incomplete. Marx *abstracts* from the input values (within the limits discussed in section 6.2), for two reasons. First, the input values are *irrelevant* for his argument that prices are the form of appearance of values, and that profit is the form of appearance of surplus value. Second, the simultaneous transformation of input and output values would make *undetectable* the production and distribution of surplus value, which is the conceptual core of the transformation. If the inputs and outputs were transformed simultaneously, only two opposing and seemingly unrelated relative price systems would exist, one in values and the other in prices. Price and profit could not be assessed in the former, and value and surplus value would be absent in the latter. Their intrinsic relationship would be invisible. In contrast, if we follow Marx's procedure and abstract from the value of the means of production, this dichotomy is avoided and the change in the level of abstraction can be 'seen' through the shift of surplus value across branches of industry.

Abstraction from the value of the means of production unveils the distribution of surplus value and the ensuing determination of prices of production, regardless of the systematic modification of the exchange ratios brought about by the transformation. Moreover, it nets out the impact of the transformation of the value of the money-commodity, that would complicate further the relationship between values and prices and obscure the concepts being introduced, especially if the VCC of the money-producing sector were distinct from the social average.[21] In sum, *there are three reasons why the price vector cannot be calculated from Marx's transformation procedure*: (a) Marx works with the price of production of the mass of commodities produced per £100 advanced, rather than their unit prices; (b) he abstracts from the transformation of the input values, and (c) he abstracts from the transformation of the value of the money-commodity.[22]

In other words, the age-old objection that Marx's transformation is wrong because he failed to transform the value of the inputs is beside the point. For, if the transformation pivots around the OCC, the value of the means of production is immaterial, and their transformation cannot affect the result. The same argument can be used to dismiss the critique that Marx 'forgot' to transform the value of the money-commodity (or was mathematically incompetent to handle this problem),[23] or that he 'unwarrantedly' failed to define the problem in terms of unit values and unit prices of production. Marx's procedure is adequate for the derivation of the *concept* of price of production (although not immediately for its calculation), because it separates *cause* (the performance of labour in production and exploitation through the extraction of surplus value) from *effect* (the existence of a positive profit rate, and the forces leading to its equalisation across branches).[24]

Having introduced the concept of price of production Marx's analysis reaches a more complex level, and the second stage of the transformation may be considered. When the realm of the OCC is superseded and the prices of the means of production and labour power enter the picture, there are two reasons why commodity prices may diverge from their value:

(1) because the average profit is added to the cost price of a commodity, instead of the surplus-value contained in it;

(2) because the price of production of a commodity that diverges in this way from its value enters as an element into the cost price of other commodities, which means that a divergence from the value of the means of production consumed may already be contained in the cost price, quite apart from the divergence that may arise for average profit and surplus-value.[25]

This change in the point of view, from the *conceptual derivation of price* to the *study of the economy at the level of price*, leads to the further determination of the concept of price of production and concludes Marx's transformation procedure. Whilst the derivation of price departs from the distribution of surplus value abstracting from the value of the means of production and labour power, the calculation of the price vector involves, as is well known, the current technologies of production, the wage rate and the (price-) rate of profit.[26] In sum, as was shown in chapter 1, Marx's method involves not only the *progressive transformation of some concepts into others*, but also *gradual shifts in the meaning of each concept*, whenever this is necessary to accommodate the evolution of the analysis.[27] Having done this, Marx can now claim that his prices of production are:

the same thing that Adam Smith calls 'natural price', Ricardo 'price of production' or 'cost of production', and the Physiocrats '*prix nécessaire*', though none of these people explained the difference between price of production and value . . . We can also understand why those very economists who oppose the determination of commodity value by labour-time . . . always speak of prices of production as centres around which market prices fluctuate. They can allow themselves this because the price of production is already a completely externalized and *prima facie* irrational form of commodity value, a form that appears in competition and is therefore present in the consciousness of the vulgar capitalist and consequently also in that of the vulgar economist.[28]

At this stage,

The value of commodities appears directly only in the influence of the changing productivity of labour on the rise and fall of prices of production; on their movement, not on their final limits. Profit now appears as determined only secondarily by the direct exploitation of labour, in so far as . . . it permits the capitalist to realize a profit departing from the average.[29]

Marx's price theory is two-fold: on the one hand, it is a production cost theory similar to the classical. On the other hand, Marx's theory is distinctive because he explains the price form through the social division of labour in capitalism, analysed at increasing levels of complexity. The transformation has a four-fold impact upon the structure of *Capital*. First, it explains why market exchanges are not directly regulated by the labour time socially necessary to reproduce each commodity. Second, it shows that price is a relatively complex form of social labour. Third, it allows a more complex understanding of Marx's analysis of the forms of value (see below). Fourth, it explains the distribution of labour across the economy.[30] Even though it was left incomplete, Marx's procedure is important because it develops further his reconstruction of the capitalist economy, and substantiates the claim that *living labour alone*, and *not* the dead labour represented by the means of production, creates value and surplus value.

In contrast, approaches that argue that the input values should be taken into account from the start, and that they should be transformed together with the output values, often conflate the roles of living and dead labour in the production of value, and can hardly distinguish between workers and machines in production. The 'non-transformation of the inputs' cannot be considered a defect. Rather, it is a *feature* of Marx's method. By abstracting from (changes in) the value of the inputs and the money-commodity, Marx locates the source of profit in the performance of labour in production, and carefully builds the conditions in which circulation may be brought into the analysis and add positively to its development.

7.4 Conclusion

This chapter has shown that Marx's transformation of values into prices of production includes two stages. In the first, he abstracts from (differences in) the value of the means of production, in order to highlight the principle that value is produced by labour alone or, alternatively, that the *greater* the quantity of living labour put in motion, the *more* surplus value is produced. Distribution of the surplus value according to the size of each capital forms prices different from values. In the second stage, the economy is analysed at the level of prices of production; all commodities are sold at their prices, and the input prices are taken into account. *The role of transformation is to allow a greater determination in the form of social labour, and to explain the distribution of labour and surplus value across the economy.*

The use of the organic composition of capital is essential in order to distinguish these stages, because it helps to identify the *cause* of the transformation and to explain the *relationship* between prices and values. Moreover, it shows that Marx's interest lies in the conceptual relationship between labour, price and profit, rather than the algebraic calculation of prices or the rate of profit. Finally, it indicates that equilibrium (or simple reproduction) assumptions are unwarranted in this case. This reading of the transformation shows that the presentation in *Capital 3* is consistent with Marx's method, and is part of his reconstruction of the main categories of the capitalist economy.

Most of the literature has investigated the transformation through the VCC. Whilst this is not in itself wrong, and may lead to important theoretical developments, this approach has no bearing upon Marx's problem. The various solutions to which this approach leads can be distinguished from each other by the structures that they contemplate, the processes at the forefront, and the treatment which is given to them (in other words, the nature of the normalisation condition, the use of interactions or simultaneous equations, and so on). Most transformation procedures found in the literature are alternative to Marx's. They cannot claim to 'correct' the latter, because they address different issues and include a conception of the price-value relationship at odds with Marx's. Inadequate understanding of Marx's transformation has often led to the complaint that he unwarrantedly omitted the specification of the technologies of production or, more often, that he did not transform the value of the inputs.[31] This chapter has demonstrated that these objections are misplaced, because they emphasise issues that are not the primary object of Marx's concern in the transformation, and may obscure, rather than help to reveal, the subject of his inquiry.

8 Money, credit and inflation

This chapter summarises the value analysis developed previously, through a critical review of Marxian contributions to the theories of money, credit and inflation. It is divided into four sections. The first briefly reviews Marx's theory of money and credit, including the forms and functions of money. The second explains the relationship between money and prices of production, and develops the possibility of valueless paper currency in the Marxian system. The third critically analyses three Marxian theories of inflation, and indicates how they can be developed further. The fourth section concludes this chapter.

8.1 Labour and money

Marx's derivation of money from commodity exchange, in chapter 1 of *Capital 1*, is neither an historical explanation of the origin of money, nor a purely logical derivation of the concept of money from the commodity (see section 1.1). Marx's analysis presumes, first, that money and exchange are inseparable and, second, that exchange was marginal to pre-capitalist societies, while money also had ritual, ceremonial, and customary uses in these societies.[1] Money emerges historically out of the interaction of commodity owners with one another, especially exchange between different communities.[2] Therefore, money implies a minimum level of regularity and complexity in exchange, but it does not require either generalised barter or that most of the output is for exchange.

Marx's analysis of the forms of value, culminating with the money form, shows that money has an *essence*, to monopolise exchangeability and to be the universal equivalent. Simply put, money can be exchanged for any commodity, whereas commodities do not generally exchange for each other. In addition to this, Marx's analysis implies that the functions of money *follow* from its essence, rather than the converse as is presumed by neoclassical and post-Keynesian theory:

> Marx's approach to money implies that "what money does follows from what money is": because money monopolizes exchangeability, it also

measures value, facilitates exchange, settles debt, and so on. Seen in this way, there is order and internal cohesion to the functions of money – no arbitrariness.[3]

The social and historical determinations of money, including its essence and functions, demonstrate that money is a social relation that derives from the form of articulation between commodity producers. Commodity exchange develops fully only under capitalism, when exchange becomes generalised and impersonal and the ritual and ceremonial aspects of money are largely irrelevant.

Marx distinguishes between money as money and money as capital.[4] *Money as money* is the measure of value and the means of circulation, and it fulfils three functions, means of payment, store of value, and international money. *Money as capital* is money advanced for the production or transfer of surplus value. Money as capital is closely related to money as money, because the forms and functions of money are identical, and money may fulfil both roles simultaneously. For example, in the payment or expenditure of wages, what is C-M-C' for the workers is M-C-M' for the capitalists. Let us now look briefly into the functions and forms of money.

At the highest level of abstraction, money measures commodity values through a simple comparison of their RSNLT with its own, and expresses the result in the units of the standard of prices.[5] If, for example, the RSNLT of the monetary unit (say, the ounce of gold[6]) is thirty minutes (0.5 hours of socially necessary labour, hSNL), and £1 is its monetary name, the standard of prices is $\Omega=£1$. In this case, the monetary equivalent of labour (MEL, m) is:

$$m \equiv \frac{\Omega}{\lambda^g} = \frac{£1}{0.5hSNL} = £2/hSNL \tag{8.1}$$

This value of m implies that one hour of abstract labour creates a value of £2. It follows that the price of a commodity i produced in five hours ($\lambda^i = 5hSNL$) is:

$$p^i = m\lambda^i = £10 \tag{8.2}$$

The determination of prices does not require the actual comparison of each commodity with money; therefore, as a measure of value money is merely ideal money.[7] It was shown in section 5.3 that the price form expresses commodity values and allows differences between values and prices. There has been much controversy about the relationship between money, value and price in the labour theory of value, especially between Marxian and Ricardian interpretations (see section 2.1).[8]

A less known but equally interesting controversy involved Marx and the 'Ricardian socialist' proponents of 'labour-money', especially John Gray, John Bray, Alfred Darimon and Pierre-Joseph Proudhon.[9] This controversy illustrates the importance of properly understanding the function of measure of value.

Gray's is the best argued case for paper labour-money. His proposed monetary reform derives from the belief that labour alone bestows value and, therefore, that labour should be the measure of values. He argued that the use of valuable commodities (e.g., gold) as money was problematic for two reasons. First, Gray argues that the supply of the money commodity could never increase as rapidly as the supply of all other commodities put together. Therefore, it would be generally impossible to sell the entire output, production would be chronically below potential, and there would be unemployment and deprivation because of the defects of the monetary system.[10] This argument is clearly wrong, because Gray implicitly assumes that the velocity of circulation is always necessarily one, that turnover periods are identical for all capitals, and that hoards and credit are not available. Second, and more interestingly, the Ricardian socialists believed that money veils exchanges and allows the workers to be exploited by the capitalists, and the debtors exploited by the creditors. However, if the workers were paid in labour-money their participation in social production would be ascertained correctly, and they would be able to draw commodities with an equivalent value from the whole of that produce.[11]

Marx derided the labour-money idea in the *Grundrisse* and elsewhere, for two reasons.[12] First, if the 'just price' paid for the commodities were determined by the concrete labour time necessary to produce them, the economy would fall into disarray as the producers tried to make their commodities more 'valuable' by working less intensely. This nonsense stems from the implicit assumption that the normalisation of labours may be avoided, and that their homogenisation can be reduced into an identity between individual labour time and money (see chapter 5).

Second, if the 'just price' were based upon RSNLT, however determined, productivity growth would reduce RSNLTs and lead to the *appreciation* of the labour-money (deflation). This unwarranted outcome would benefit the cursed creditors, reduce investment and delay technical progress. Moreover,

> The time-chit, representing *average labour time*, would never correspond to or be convertible into *actual labour time*; i.e. the amount of labour time objectified in a commodity would never command a quantity of labour time equal to itself, and vice versa, but would command, rather, either more or less, just as at present every oscillation of market values expresses itself in a rise or fall of the gold or silver prices of commodities.[13]

These difficulties derive from Gray's inability to understand the necessity of synchronisation and homogenisation of labour in commodity production. When commodities are sold, money is the means of circulation (exchange).[14] Again at the highest level of abstraction, in exchanges C–M–C′ the commodity owners at all times possess the same value, alternating between the original commodity, the money commodity and the newly purchased commodity. This presumption captures the essence of simple (equivalent) exchange. However, the use of gold coins causes their wear and tear (and might encourage the clipping of coins), implying that commodities generally exchange for coins worth less than their face value. The continuity of exchanges under these circumstances shows that circulating money is merely a representative or symbol of value. Symbols of money such as inconvertible paper may, therefore, perform the same service as pure gold:

> in this process which continually makes money pass from hand to hand, it only needs to lead a symbolic existence. Its functional existence so to speak absorbs its material existence. Since it is a transiently objectified reflection of the prices of commodities, its serves only as a symbol of itself, and can therefore be replaced by another symbol. One thing is necessary, however: the symbol of money must have its own objective social validity. The paper acquires this by its forced currency.[15]

Let us now see how Marx analyses the functions of store of value, means of payment and world money.

Money functions as a store of value when it is hoarded. Hoarding is often justified in the literature because of individual preferences or uncertainty. Although these factors can play an important role in the formation of hoards, there are *structural* reasons why money hoards are formed in the course of capitalist production.[16] The most important reason is that production involves regular expenditures that are generally disconnected from the accrual of sales revenue. Producers must also accumulate reserves in order to meet unforeseen expenses, maintain and replace fixed capital, expand the output, pay dividends, offset price fluctuations and so on. These idle reserves are normally deposited in the banking system, and they form the basis of the bank reserves. Development of the credit system reduces each capitalist's hoarding needs, because the hoards of the capitalist class are available to borrow.[17] Bank loans facilitate the realisation of long-term and large-scale investment projects; however, they also facilitate speculative activity and, more broadly, increase the likelihood that localised disturbances (accumulation of inventories, price changes, technical innovations, etc.) will spread and trigger economic crises.

Money functions as means of payment when it settles transactions undertaken previously, and cancels a promise to pay. This is particularly important in commercial credit, that finances the sale of produced commodities, and banking credit, that finances new production.

Finally, the functions of money are performed in the international arena by world money, that is value in pure form and a crystallisation of abstract labour recognised across the globe. National currencies must be convertible into world money in order to allow domestic commodities to be exchanged for foreign goods, and to facilitate the inclusion of domestic labour into the international system of production.

Adjustment of the quantity of money to the needs of circulation is a complex process involving all functions of money.[18] In a simple commodity money system, it was shown above that the value of the money commodity plays an essential role in the determination of prices (see section 8.2). However, at a more complex level of analysis the quantity and velocity of money are important determinants of the expression of value as price.

Marx rejected the quantity theory of money (QTM) in the case of gold because, for him, the quantity of circulating money changes in order to realise the value produced. These changes happen primarily through hoarding and dishoarding, the output of the gold-mining sector, international bullion flows and changes in the velocity of money. For example, if the output grows the additional money necessary for its circulation will be made available through the above channels; alternatively, if the gold stock increases (with all else constant), the additional gold will be hoarded or velocity will decline. In contrast with the QTM (and Ricardo), prices remain unchanged in both cases.[19]

It is different for fiat money, which can be issued by the state potentially in arbitrary quantities through the monetisation of budget deficits or open market operations. Marx generally agrees with the QTM that, if an increasing quantity of fiat money is forced into circulation, its exchange value would decline permanently (inflation; see section 8.3). Although fiat money is a suitable means of circulation, it is unsuitable for hoarding in the same scale as gold, because its domestic (and external) exchange value is unstable. This instability derives from the absence of a direct relationship between the supply of fiat money and capital accumulation.[20]

It is different again with convertible money issued by the banks or the state, and with credit money. The value of convertible money fluctuates around the value of the gold that it replaces, temporary discrepancies occurring naturally during the cycle.[21] Inflation is possible in this system if the sphere of circulation is flooded with paper notes, but this process is limited because arbitrage makes it impossible for commodity prices to deviate permanently from their gold prices of production. However, this is likely to be neither a smooth nor a purely monetary process. Sudden disruptions of exchange, recessions, and fully-fledged monetary and economic crises, in which the money commodity plays an important role as means of payment and means of hoarding, are some of the ways in which the value of gold is made compatible with the exchange value of money.[22]

Finally, contemporary monetary systems include primarily two forms of money, inconvertible paper currency issued by the central bank (legal tender that discharges all debts) and credit money produced by the commercial banks (liabilities of private financial institutions, including deposits and banknotes, offering a potential claim on another form of money). The quantity and the exchange value of credit money are indirectly regulated by the advance and repayment of credit, that is, by the processes of production and accumulation and, at a further remove, by the central bank's influence on the operations of the financial system.[23]

Temporary discrepancies between the supply and demand for credit money are inevitable, for two reasons. First, and more generally, the empirical determinacy of the quantity and velocity of money declines as the analysis becomes more concrete. They depend on social conventions, including the property relations, the financial rules and regulations, the structure of the financial system and its relationship with production, the international relations, the degree of concentration of capital, and other variables that make 'supply' and 'demand' difficult to determine even theoretically. Second, and more specifically, even though the supply of credit money necessarily corresponds to *individual* demand (credit money is always created in response to a loan request), the *total* credit supply may not reflect the needs of the economy as a whole. This is clearly the case when speculative loans help to inflate a real estate or stock market bubble, or when banks unwittingly finance the production of unprofitable or unsaleable goods. Excess supply is likely especially when a climate of optimism is fostered by rises in the prices of financial assets, which feed upon ongoing optimism and increase it even further. In other words, excess credit, fuelled by speculation or the surge of accumulation, may lead to price increases but, barring state intervention (see section 8.3), this process is limited by the unavoidable increase in financial instability and the possibility of crisis.[24]

These mediations in the determination of the exchange value of money do not imply that it is wrong to posit, *ex post*, a monetary equivalent of labour, as in equation (8.1). However, focus upon the MEL tends to conflate levels of abstraction, and it may obscure the contradictory elements in its determination, in which case financial instability and the possibility of crisis have to be reintroduced at later stage arbitrarily and, potentially, in an impoverished manner (see section 2.2.2).

8.2 Money and prices of production

The transformation of values into prices of production (see chapter 7) has important implications not only for Marx's analysis of the forms of social labour, but also for his monetary theory. The contemporary predominance of inconvertible (valueless) paper money poses a challenge to one aspect of Marx's theory: it is not immediately clear how commodity values are measured, and expressed as price, if money has no intrinsic value.[25] This potential limitation has severe implications, because analysis of contemporary problems including the supply of credit money, inflation, and exchange rate determination, depend upon a satisfactory explanation of valueless paper money.

Some writers have refused to address this problem, either because they see inconvertible paper money as an illusion or a temporary aberration,[26] or because they postulate that money is never a commodity and is, instead, always created by the state.[27] However, the latter fails to explain how valueless money measures value. This section develops Marx's analysis of the value forms, showing that it is fully compatible with inconvertible paper money. Limited to this aim, it does not review the historical process of displacement of precious metals from circulation, or the structure of contemporary monetary systems.[28]

The explanation of valueless money departs from *equivalent exchange*. At the highest level of abstraction (see section 8.1), equivalent exchange includes commodities produced in equal RSNLTs, C–C′. The mediation of exchange by money, C–M–C′ modifies the meaning of equivalent exchange, because the commodity owners no longer necessarily hold the same value continuously, even in the case of gold money (because of abrasion). More generally, mediation of exchange by convertible paper money shows that what matters in exchange is not the intrinsic value of money but its exchange value (we ignore contingent price fluctuations).

The concept of equivalent exchange shifts again with the transformation of values into prices of production. After the transformation, equivalent exchange no longer involves commodities produced in equal RSNLT. Rather, it involves commodities whose production yields the same *profit rate*.[29] By the same token, equations (8.1) and (8.2) no longer generally hold, the MEL can be determined only *after* commodity prices (rather than before, as used to be the case), and it holds at the aggregate level, but not for every commodity. More generally, prices of production are not determined through a one-to-one ideal relationship between commodity values and the value of the money-commodity. Rather, they are determined *simultaneously* by the rate of valorisation of the advanced capitals (see sections 2.1.2 and 5.3):

$$p=(pA+wl)(1+r) \tag{8.3}$$

This equation reflects Marx's view that 'price of production is . . . in the long term . . . the condition of supply, the condition for the reproduction of commodities, in each particular sphere of production.'[30]

The shift in the price form due to the transformation implies that *no single commodity can fulfil the function of measure of value*. At this stage in the analysis, value measurement includes the assessment of the growth rate of the advanced capitals and the establishment of equivalent exchange in the relatively complex sense above, through a consistent relative price system. In other words, the money-commodity no longer measures values independently of the other commodities and production processes, as was the case previously (when absolute prices were logically determined *before* the relative prices).

After the transformation, the value of gold, its value composition, turnover time, and so on, are relevant only for the determination of the absolute price level (absolute prices are now logically determined *after* the relative prices). This is the case because, at this level of analysis, the measure of value is no longer the money-commodity but *the general profit rate*, which is the peg of the relative price system. Equation (8.3) shows that prices of production are determined by the current price of production of the inputs, marked up such that each capital draws the average rate of profit (this rate is limited by the total surplus value, see section 4.1).[31] At this stage in the analysis, gold money may be abolished, with no bearing upon the stability of the economy or our ability to understand it.

Once gold is withdrawn from circulation absolute prices can be maintained at the previous level (which is usually the case when governments decree that the currency is no longer convertible into gold), or shift to any arbitrary level (if there is a monetary reform). A developed capitalist currency is, therefore, the complex unity of a measure of value (the general profit rate) and a medium of exchange (which may take the form of gold, copper, paper, electronic impulses or whatever), and that fulfils the functions identified in section 8.1. Even under a gold money system, the analysis above shows that, under capitalism, gold is never the sole measure of value nor an adequate means of circulation. In the development of theory, however, the role of commodity money is indispensible.

8.3 Credit, money and inflation

Marxian analyses of money, credit and crises can be developed in different directions, in order to illuminate a broad range of contemporary phenomena. This section illustrates the potential usefulness of these approaches through a critical review of three theories of inflation emphasising, respectively, distributive conflicts, monopoly power and state intervention on the dynamics of credit money.[32] This is important for three main reasons. First, inflation poses an intriguing theoretical challenge.[33] Mainstream analyses, usually inspired by the QTM, have unacceptably weak foundations, including perfect competition, full employment and costless adjustment between static equilibria. In contrast, Marxian (and other political economy) contributions are promising, but remain relatively undeveloped. Second, advances in the understanding of inflation can easily be extended to the study of deflation, and both are currently important.[34] Third, inflation *and* conventional anti-inflation policies usually have high economic and social costs. They often lead to higher unemployment, lower real wages, higher rates of exploitation and shift the income distribution and the balance of social forces towards capital and, especially, financial interests. It would clearly be important to develop alternative analyses, in order to confront inflation and the consequences of conventional anti-inflation policies.

Two difficulties have frustrated attempts to develop Marxian analyses of inflation. First, inflation is a highly complex process that involves a wide range of determinants at different levels of abstraction, among them production, the supply of money, interest rates, the industrial and financial structure, external shocks, distributive conflicts, and many other variables. It is very difficult to order these influences systematically within a cogent theory. Second, it is especially difficult to explain inflation in inconvertible monetary systems, drawing on the anti-quantity theory tradition of Steuart, Tooke, Marx, Kalecki, and most post-Keynesians writers. Simply put, it is difficult to develop a theory of inflation whilst simultaneously preserving the claim that the needs of production and trade call money into circulation (endogeneity), and admitting that money may influence 'real' variables (non-neutrality). This exercise becomes even more complex when it involves different forms of money, issued by the state and by the commercial banks, each of them with a particular relationship with capital accumulation. In spite of these difficulties, this section shows that it is possible to outline the general conditions for inflation.

Conflict inflation

Non-mainstream economists of very different persuasions, including many Marxists and most post-Keynesians and neo-structuralists, argue that distributive conflicts are usually the most important cause of inflation (this approach is appealing to some Marxists because it apparently vindicates the notion of class struggle).[35]

Conflict analyses are inspired by cost-push theories, which were popular between the 1950s and the 1970s. They usually depart from equilibrium, and assume that the money supply is fully endogenous, that fiscal and monetary policies are passive, and that key agents (especially the monopoly capitalists and unionised workers) have market power and can set the price of their goods or services largely independently of demand. Inflation arises because the central bank validates incompatible demands for shares of the national income through monetary accommodation or its support for the financial system, in order to ensure financial stability and the continuity of production.[36] The inflation rate is usually a positive function of the size of the overlapping claims, the frequency of price and wage changes and the degree of capacity utilisation, and a negative function of the rate of productivity growth (the basic model can be refined endlessly by incorporating target income levels, expectations, reaction functions, and limits on the wage claims because of unemployment, or on the mark up because of competition).

The most important shortcoming of the conflict approach is the absence of a clear internal structure. This approach is compatible with widely different theories of value, production, employment, demand, income and distribution, and with different rules of determination of the target income levels. Classes are sometimes seen as partners, in which case it is relatively easy to achieve economic stability through negotiated incomes policies. Alternatively, a theory of exploitation may be used; in this case, economic stability can be achieved only through the subordination of the workers by force. This flexibility makes conflict analyses potentially appealing to a wide audience; however, it is vulnerable to the charges of arbitrariness and lack of analytical rigour. In particular, inflation generally starts from a dislocation that shifts the economy away from a Pareto-optimal equilibrium. 'Apportioning blame' is, therefore, implicitly at issue, and alternative economic policies are usually assessed in terms of their ability to make the economy return to the initial equilibrium. It is not usually explained how that equilibrium was originally determined, or why it merits return. Moreover, it was shown in sections 2.2.2 and 4.1 that capitalists and workers do not confront each other directly over the shares of the national product, firstly because the wages are *advanced*, whereas profit is the *residual* and, secondly, because disputes generally involve income levels rather than shares.

Indeterminacies such as these can be eliminated only through an organic relationship between the conflict approach and a broader economic theory. Unfortunately, many such connections are possible, and none is necessary. In other words, conflict theories, as they are usually presented, are typically 'middle range'.[37] They derive from a set of stylised empirical observations (e.g., agents exercise claims over the national product through the sale of their goods), and transform these observations into structures that are used to explain these stylised facts (e.g., distributive conflict leading to inflation). This approach conflates cause and effect, because it presumes that, since inflation has distributive *implications*, income disputes *cause* the process; and the analysis is unsound because it is not grounded by a broader structure that supports its elementary concepts and contextualises its conclusions. The lack of a theory of production implies that the state's role and policies cannot be adequately grounded either, and they usually derive from a further set of stylised facts. Consequently, the rationale for, and the power of, economic policies are left unexplained and depend heavily on the analyst's preferences.

In spite of these important limitations, the conflict approach is potentially relevant. Distributive conflicts must be part of any inflation theory, for inflation would not persist in the absence of dissatisfaction about the level and/or distribution of the national income, and the monetisation of these claims.

Monopoly capital, underconsumption and inflation

Many Marxists argue that inflation is associated with the increasing market power of large corporations and underconsumption, most clearly for the monopoly capital school.[38] This approach argues that monopolies are the most dynamic firms and the largest investors, employers, producers and exporters. In order to maximise economic growth the state supports the monopolies through purchases, cheap infrastructure, tax breaks, subsidies for research and development, and so on. More broadly, the state spends huge sums in civil servants' wages, consumables and public investment, funds health, education and defence expenditures, and makes large transfers associated with social security. These expenditures support monopoly profits directly through purchases, and indirectly through transfers to their customers. Interventionist policies of the welfare state delivered unprecedented economic stability, high employment and rapid growth, especially between the late 1940s and the late 1960s. However, they also contributed to persistent budget deficits, rising public debt and creeping inflation. In sum, inflation is the result of interventionist economic policies trying to ensure full employment and social stability, in an economy constrained by monopoly power and pricing strategies.[39]

These are important insights, but this approach is theoretically fragile. It does not include a theory of monopoly power or pricing, other than a collation of the ideas of Hilferding (for whom monopolies impose prices above the prices of production in order to reap extra profits) and Kalecki (for whom monopoly power is a stylised fact and monopolies reap extra profits because of their market power).[40] The influence of monopoly on the circuit of capital and income distribution is not explained, and the role of demand and other limits and counter-tendencies to the concentration and centralisation of capital are almost invariably ignored.

The theory of the state is also left unclear, and what is said is potentially contradictory. On the one hand, the state manages the economy relatively autonomously in order to ensure the reproduction of capital as a whole, which requires the accommodation of the interests of different fractions of capital and of the workers, and is best achieved in a democracy. On the other hand, the state is a tool of powerful (monopoly) interests, and its policies are limited by the need to obtain their consent, in which case fascism is a clear possibility. Finally, the linkages connecting monopoly power, state policies and inflation are left mostly unexplained. There is no clear theory of money, credit or finance, except for the presumption that money supply responds passively to monopoly demand or to state command, and that (largely unexplained) financial developments are contributory factors. How this leads to inflation is left unclear.[41] More generally, the causes of inflation shift between monopoly pricing decisions and excess demand induced by the state (which is, paradoxically, the result of state attempts to avoid underconsumption).[42] The distributive impact of inflation is not analysed, except to argue that monopolies benefit at the expense of the workers and other groups receiving nominally fixed revenues. It is unclear how this relates to the theory of wages or of exploitation.[43]

Extra money inflation

In the mid-1970s an alternative analysis was outlined, in which inflation is the result of a permanent increase in the relationship between commodity prices and values, caused by a discrepancy between the supply and social demand for money.[44]

The analysis departs from the circuit of capital. The productive circuit begins when capitalists draw on previously accumulated funds or borrow newly created credit money in order to finance production. Injection of these funds into the economy increases the ratio between circulating money and output value. If more output is produced and sold additional income is created, which cancels out the initial shift in the relationship between money and value. However, if the output cannot be sold at its price of production the firm suffers a loss that may be absorbed in two ways. If 'market rules' are respected, a well-defined set of agents bears the cost, usually the firm or its bank. This type of solution can be destabilising, because it may systematically lead to unemployment, capacity underutilisation, the deterioration of the working conditions, and financial fragility.

Alternatively, the loss may be socialised if the debt is refinanced or if the firm receives a state subsidy (in the extreme, it may be nationalised and 'restructured' with public funds). In either case, there is an injection of purchasing power that perpetuates the initial discrepancy between the circulating money and the output; in other words, the initial (presumably transitory) increase in the monetary equivalent of labour becomes permanent. The money injected into the economy through a violation of 'market rules' is *extra money*.[45] Extra money may also be created by central bank support to the financial institutions, by non-sterilised balance of payments surpluses, or by corporate or household dissaving or borrowing for speculative purposes.[46] Extra money typically increases the nominal income or the liquid wealth of the consolidated non-financial sector in spite of the constant value of the output, and regardless of the existence of equilibrium, currently or in the past. If the extra money induces a quantity response, the previous relationship between value and money may be restored; otherwise, the monetary expression of labour rises: this is *extra money inflation*.

Extra money inflation may be facilitated by the monetary policy stance, but the state cannot be generally 'blamed' for it because extra money is *routinely* and *necessarily* created by private decisions that are not subject to state control (including bank loans). Moreover, even if the extra money is created by the state it is impossible to know in advance whether it will have a quantity or price effect, or both (targeting is possible, but necessarily imprecise). In due course, discrepancies between the quantity of circulating money and demand will tend to be eliminated by changes in output, velocity or hoards. However, these adjustments take time, and they may create additional instability through their effects on prices, the exchange rate, the balance of payments or the interest rate. If these monetary discrepancies are continually renewed, they can lead to persistent inflation, severe balance of payments disequilibria and prolonged economic stagnation, which demonstrate the non-neutrality of money and its potential influence over the accumulation process.

Long-term inflation may derive from the attempt by the state to deliver continuous economic growth, or from the attempt to avoid deflation when growth falters. More generally, in the upswing, extra money is provided mainly by the private sector with the support of the central bank, in order to finance consumption and new investment. Therefore, growth necessarily breaches the established relationship between value and money, and it is always potentially inflationary (depending on the supply and import responses). As the economy grows, disproportions and bottlenecks inevitably develop, financial structures become more fragile and, unless cheap imports are readily available, prices (and, possibly, wages) tend to increase. At this stage, the crisis erupts either spontaneously, because of the balance of payments constraint or because contractionary policies have been adopted. If the crisis becomes acute and deflation looms, the state will usually intervene and deliberately inject (or facilitate the private creation of) extra money.[47]

In spite of their apparent similarity, the theory of extra money inflation is incompatible with the QTM. The quantity theory's assumptions that money supply is exogenous, that money is only a medium of exchange and that money is not hoarded are unacceptable from the perspective of the extra money approach. First, this approach argues that extra money is regularly and spontaneously created by the interaction between the central bank, commercial banks and firms, and that its quantity cannot be controlled, or even known precisely, by the state. In contrast, the quantity theory presumes that the banking system is always fully loaned up, and that the central bank can determine autonomously the supply of money directly (through the monetisation of government budget deficits or purchases of government securities) or indirectly (through changes in compulsory bank reserves, which should lead unproblematically to changes in the outstanding stock of loans). Other sources of changes in the supply of money are usually ignored, and the possibility that changes initiated by the central bank may be neutralised by hoarding, loan repayments or by a compensatory change in bank loans are generally neglected by the QTM.

Second, extra money is non-neutral in the short and in the long run; it may change irreversibly the level and composition of the national product and the structure of demand, depending on how it is created and how it circulates. In contrast, the QTM presumes that money is neutral in the long and, in extreme cases, even the short run. Third, the effects of extra money (whether quantity, price, or both) cannot be anticipated. All that one can say is that high capacity utilisation and activist state policies increase the probability of extra money inflation, but there is never a simple relationship between them. In contrast, for the QTM the relationship between money supply and inflation is usually straightforward. Because of the underlying assumptions of perfect competition, full employment, and money neutrality, a change in the supply of money (initiated by the central bank and automatically propagated by the commercial banks through the money multiplier) unproblematically leads to a predictable change in the price level.

The extra money approach can provide the basis for the development of a theory of inflation which incorporates the main claims of the labour theory of value, and the valuable insights of other Marxian analyses of inflation. However, this approach is still undeveloped at critical points, and it suffers from deficiencies and ambiguities that need to be addressed urgently. For example, the analysis of the supply of central bank and credit money is usually simplistic, and it would benefit from greater exposure to, and confrontation against, recent post-Keynesian developments,[48] circuitist contributions,[49] and the works of Kalecki.[50] At a more concrete level of analysis, the valuable contributions of Minsky on the financial instability of modern capitalism need to be evaluated in detail and incorporated into the analysis when this is warranted.[51]

In addition to this, much work remains to be done in order to make the structures and categories in the extra money approach fully compatible with those of Marx's theory of value. For example, the relationship between the supply of money and the monetary expression of labour is usually left unclear, the extra money approach often shifts arbitrarily between levels of analysis and leaves ambiguous the stature of competition. Finally, further work is necessary to distinguish between price increases caused by extra money and those caused by other types of money supply growth. This would help to clarify the residual ambiguity between the extra money approach and the quantity theory of money, especially with respect to the role of excess demand as the trigger of inflation.

Addressing these issues systematically will make it possible to incorporate other important phenomena into the analysis, for example financial development and financial and capital account liberalisation. It will also make it possible to analyse concrete problems such as the potentially inflationary impact of the public debt overhang, whose increasing liquidity may be synonymous with the injection of extra money into the economy.[52]

8.4 Conclusion

Marx's theory of money has often been examined exegetically, as if it were fully developed and significant only because of the succession of value forms in chapter 1 of *Capital 1*. This viewpoint is infertile. This chapter has shown that Marx's theory can be developed in important ways, including the explanation of inconvertible money and inflation. The former is important because it shows that Marx's approach is internally cogent and it does not conflict with the facts of modern capitalism. The latter is an important current problem; tackling it creatively and consistently is relevant politically, and it demonstrates the vitality of Marx's approach.

This chapter has also shown that the transformation of value into prices of production modifies money's function as measure of value, and the homogenisation of labour. It does not affect the other functions of money, or the normalisation and synchronisation of labour. Finally, this chapter has shown that the theory of inflation should focus upon the same concepts. Inflation is a macroeconomic process that affects the expression of value as price, and it influences the relationship between total output and money.

The analysis of inflation needs to be developed much further, but some of its policy implications are already clear. First, inflation can be functional, but its dysfunctional aspects gradually tend to become predominant when inflation rises. In particular, economic calculus becomes increasingly complex and capital restructuring becomes more difficult because inefficient capitals and productive processes are preserved, rather than being annihilated by 'market' processes. Second, inflation leads to financial crisis by its cumulative character, through the formation of increasingly unstable debt structures. Crises may be postponed by increasing the supply of extra money, but this may lead to hyperinflation. Third, there can be inflation purely for monetary reasons, usually associated with speculative bubbles involving housing, the stock exchange and other assets, which can harm real accumulation by draining it of funds. Fourth, permanent inflation is not inevitable, whatever the power of the banks, monopolies or the workers. However, financial deepening, the concentration of capital, the reduction of trade flows, and worker militancy increase the vulnerability of the economy to inflation, and the difficulty to reverse the process once it is under way.

Conclusion

This book analyses the relationship between labour, value, money and prices in Marx's value theory. These categories are historically determined modes of existence of capitalist social relations, and they are analysed primarily from the aggregate, or at the level of class (rather than starting at the individual level, favoured by neoclassical economics). Four important conclusions have been drawn.

First, abstract labour, value and price are essential aspects of Marx's analysis of labour and exploitation under capitalism. In spite of their importance, there is much controversy about their meaning, significance and mutual relationship, both within and outside Marxian scholarship. This book has outlined a reading of Marx's value theory that avoids the inconsistency charges often found in the literature, and it includes important pointers for further research.

Second, capitalist production necessarily involves social conflicts in production and distribution. These conflicts are unavoidable, because they spring from the relations of production that define this social system. Distributive conflicts resemble those in other class societies, for they involve disputes about how the cake (the national product) is shared among competing claims, while maintaining systemic stability. In contrast, conflicts in production derive from the class relations that distinguish capitalism from other modes of production. They are due to disputes about how much wage labour is performed and under what conditions, and their outcome plays a limiting role upon the distributive conflicts.

Third, intra-sectoral competition tends to *disperse* the individual profit rates, because more profitable capitals can invest larger sums for longer periods, select among a broader range of production techniques and hire the best workers, which reinforces their initial advantage.[1] In contrast, inter-sectoral competition leads to the *convergence* of profit rates, because capital migration redistributes the productive potential of society and increases supply in the more profitable branches, thus reducing excess profits. The financial system plays an important role in both processes. Marx's analysis of the contradictory dynamics of capital accumulation does not lead to static outcomes, either equalisation of profit rates or the relentless concentration of capital. These are rarely smooth processes, and they often generate instability and trigger economic crises, that cause hardship and can destroy livelihoods. Crises and unemployment show that capitalism is not only the most productive, but also the most *systematically destructive* mode of production in history.

Fourth, and more generally, capitalist economies are unstable because of the conflicting forces of extraction, realisation, and accumulation of surplus value under competitive conditions. This instability is *structural*, and even the best economic policies cannot avoid it completely. Competition forces every capital to strive to increase labour productivity. This generally involves technical changes that increase the degree of mechanisation, the integration between labour processes within and across firms, and the potential scale of production. Therefore, *competition socialises capitalist production*:

> production loses its private character and becomes a social process . . . For the means of production are employed as communal, social means of production and therefore not determined by the fact that they are the property of an individual, but by their relation to production, and the labour likewise is performed on a social scale.[2]

The socialisation of production is not a smooth process. It is associated with large fixed capital investment, the development of credit relations and speculation, deskilling, labour market shifts, structural unemployment, bankruptcy and crisis. These processes are often wasteful. They have led to workplace resistance and political confrontation and, historically, they have provided a powerful stimulus for social reforms and anti-capitalist revolt.

But this is not all. Capitalism changes constantly, and Marx argues that this mode of production tends to become increasingly unstable, because of its social and economic contradictions. This is essentially because *competition destroys the capitalist basis of production*:

> capital . . . increases the surplus labour time of the mass by all the means of art and science . . . It is thus, despite itself, instrumental in creating the means of social disposable time, in order to reduce labour time for the whole society to a diminishing minimum, and thus to free everyone's time for their own development. But its tendency always, on the one side, *to create disposable time, on the other, to convert it into surplus labour*. If it succeeds too well at the first, then it suffers from surplus production, and then necessary labour is interrupted, because *no surplus labour can be realised by capital*. The more this contradiction develops, the more does it become evident that the growth of the forces of production can no longer be bound up with the appropriation of alien labour but that the mass of workers must themselves appropriate their own surplus labour . . . *Labour time as the measure of value* posits wealth itself as

founded on poverty, and disposable time as existing *in and because of the antithesis to surplus labour time*; or, the positing of an individual's entire time as labour time, and his degradation therefore to mere worker, subsumption under labour. *The most developed machinery thus forces the worker to work longer than the savage does, or than he himself did with the simplest, crudest tools.*³

This extensive citation highlights two important contradictions at the heart of capitalist accumulation. First, as was shown above, competition implies the tendency towards increasing labour productivity and rising technical and organic compositions of capital. If more output can be produced with the same labour input, living standards can increase in spite of the reduction of labour time. For example, the working week of important categories of workers has declined substantially in the wealthiest countries in the world, since the mid-nineteenth century. In spite of this, living standards have improved sharply. However, reductions in the working week generally fail to keep pace with technical progress, because the capitalists tend to resist against measures that reduce the rate of exploitation. Experience shows that the success of attempts to curtail labour time depends upon the strength and political leverage of the working class, whilst the state of technology is an important, but secondary influence. Yet, the reduction of the working week is important not only for the workers. If technology improves but labour time fails to decline, the economy becomes increasingly prone to over-production crises. The contradiction between the interest of individual capitalists in extending the working week in order to extract absolute surplus value, and their collective interest in reducing it when necessary in order to help preserve economic (and political) stability with high levels of employment, makes it unlikely that maximum rates of exploitation and rapid growth can ever be compatible for long periods.

Second, and more importantly in the long term, rising labour productivity reduces the significance of living labour for the production of use values and, consequently, for the determination of value. Under capitalism, technical progress is unlikely to eliminate drudgery and long hours of work entirely. Their perpetuation is due to social, rather than technical, barriers. More specifically, technical progress facilitates the satisfaction of needs through non-market processes and it permits the reduction of labour time and the automation of repetitive, dangerous and unhealthy tasks. However, this is anathema for capitalism, because it conflicts with the valorisation of capital and the reproduction of the relations of exploitation. At some stage, Marx believes that the majority will no longer be prepared to accept these limits on the achievement of their individual and collective potential.

For Marx, the abolition of capitalism will mark the end of the prehistory of human society.⁴ However, the transition towards another mode of production, communism, is neither inexorable nor unavoidable. The social relations at the core of capitalism will change only if overwhelming pressure is applied by the majority. Failing that, capitalism may persist indefinitely, in spite of its human and environmental costs.

In the meantime, informed mass intervention is necessary in order to resolve important problems of our age, among them environmental degradation, long-term unemployment, poverty amidst plenty in rich and poor countries alike, the dissemination of curable or controllable diseases, illiteracy, cultural, ethnic and economic oppression, and other difficulties. In addressing these problems and their potential solutions, Karl Marx offers an analysis that is unencumbered by current prejudices, and that can inspire creative solutions.

Notes

Introduction

1 The evolution of Marx's economic ideas is reviewed by Oakley (1983, 1984, 1985) and Rosdolsky (1977). Basic concepts are explained clearly and concisely in Bottomore (1991). For a historical overview of Marxian political economy, see Howard and King (1989, 1991).

2 Meek (1973, p. 241). This bias is similar to that faced by other pioneers: 'Those who cavalierly reject the Theory of Evolution, as not adequately supported by facts, seem quite to forget that their own theory is supported by no facts at all. Like the majority of men who are born to a given belief, they demand the most rigorous proof of any adverse belief, but assume that theirs needs none' (Herbert Spencer, 'The Development Hypothesis', originally published in *The Leader*, 1852); I am grateful to Andrew Berry for this reference.

3 Marx's theory is often called a (or even *the*) labour theory of value. This is misleading, and a better term is the original German 'arbeitswertlehre', or theory of labour value (Diane Elson suggests 'value theory of labour', see Elson 1979b). I will, however, stick to the tradition, with thanks to Alejandro Ramos-Martínez for this insight.

4 See Lipietz (1985b, p. 83).

5 'Political economy, in the widest sense, is the science of the laws governing the production and exchange of the material means of subsistence in human society . . . The conditions under which men produce and exchange vary from country to country, and within each country again from generation to generation. Political economy, therefore, cannot be the same for all countries and for all historical epochs . . . Political economy is therefore essentially a *historical* science' (Engels 1998, pp. 185–186). For outstanding introductions to Marx's political economy, see Fine (1989), Foley (1986), D. Harvey (1999) and Weeks (1981).

6 Mohun (1991, p. 42).

7 See Fine (1980, 1982, 1989) and Weeks (1981, 1990). Other important influences in my work include Arthur (2001), Chattopadhyay (1994), Elson (1979b), Gleicher (1983), Itoh and Lapavitsas (1999), Lebowitz (1992) and Postone (1993).

8 Heller (1976, p. 22); see also Lebowitz (1992, p. 1).

9 Elson (1979b, p. 171). More broadly, Weeks (1981, pp. 8, 11) rightly claims that 'value theory is not primarily a theory of exchange or allocation, but a theory

that reveals the class relations underlying a commodity-producing society . . .
The theory of value that Marx developed provides at the same time (1) the
revelation that capitalism is merely one form of exploitative (class) society; (2)
the explanation of the historical transition from precapitalist to capitalist
society; (3) a theory of the concrete operation of a capitalist economy; and
(4) an explanation of why others would explain the workings of a capitalist
economy in an alternative theoretical framework.'

1 Materialist dialectics

1 Marx published few works in his lifetime, the most prominent being *The Poverty
of Philosophy*, the *Manifesto of the Communist Party*, the *Contribution to the
Critique of Political Economy* and *Capital 1*. Important manuscripts were edited
and published only after his death, including *Capital 2* and *3*, the *Theories of
Surplus Value* and the *Grundrisse* (see Oakley 1983).

2 *Capital 1*, p. 99.

3 See T. Smith (1990, p. 32; 1993a, p. 47).

4 *Capital 1*, p. 104. This sentence expresses Marx's approval for the publication of
the French translation of *Capital 1* as a serial.

5 Letter to Engels, December 8, 1861, quoted in Murray (1988, p. 109).

6 *Capital 1*, p.104.

7 Arthur (2000a, p. 107 n10). See also Arthur (1993a, pp. 63–64; 1997, p. 11).

8 For a detailed analysis of Marx's relationship to Hegel, see Zelený (1980, chs
12–17).

9 'Although rigorous with himself in terms of scientific methodology, Marx
submerges the methodological issues of his scientific writings' (Murray 1988, p.
109). See also Reichelt (1995).

10 Lenin (1972, p. 319).

11 The term 'materialist dialectics' is explained by Ilyenkov (1982, pp. 77, 114, 162,
278).

12 See Arthur (1998, p. 11), Carver (1980, p. xi), Ilyenkov (1982, pp. 32–33, 57, 88),
Kosik (1976, pp. 16–23), Lebowitz (1992, p. 2) and Ollman (1993, pp. 12–13).
For an excellent overview of dialectics, see Ollman (1993, ch. 1; 1998). For an
outstanding review of the history of dialectics, see Scott (1999).

13 This approach is typical of neoclassical economics. For an illuminating analysis
of its logical shortcomings, see Schotter (1990, chs 4–5).

14 Mental generalisations are also known as empiricist abstractions (Gunn 1992),
formal abstractions (Ilyenkov 1982, pp. 61–62) or general or abstract abstractions
(Murray 1988, pp. 114, 122–129). For a critical analysis, see Ilyenkov (1977,
essays 3, 5 and 10).

15 See *Grundrisse*, pp. 85–89, Gunn (1992, p. 23) and Ilyenkov (1977, p. 64; 1982,
pp. 18–19, 29–35, 48, 60–66, 78, 85).

16 See Ilyenkov (1982, pp. 21–28, 47–48, 60–61, 76, 81–86). For similar views, see
Albritton (1986, pp. 190–191), Arthur (1979, pp. 73–77; 1993a, pp. 85–86),
Aumeeruddy and Tortajada (1979, pp. 5–9), Elson (1979b, pp. 145, 164), Fine
and Harris (1979, p. 11), Gunn (1992, pp. 18–24), Himmelweit and Mohun
(1978, p. 75), Kapferer (1980, p. 77), Lebowitz (1992, pp. 39–40), Murray (1988,
pp. 114–115, 122–128), Shaikh (1982, p. 76), T. Smith (1998, p. 467) and Sohn-

Rethel (1978, pp. 20, 69–70). Marx's concept of abstraction is explained by Ollman (1993, pp. 26–33).

17 Ilyenkov (1982, p. 22). See also Brown (2001) and Ilyenkov (1977, essays 1–2).

18 Lenin (1972, pp. 360–361) claims that, in *Capital*, 'Marx first analyses the simplest, most ordinary and fundamental, most common and everyday *relation* of bourgeois (commodity) society, a relation encountered billions of times, viz. the exchange of commodities. In this very simple phenomenon (in this "cell" of bourgeois society) analysis reveals *all* the contradictions (or the germs of *all* the contradictions) of modern society. The subsequent exposition shows us the development (*both* growth *and* movement) of these contradictions and of this society in the [summation] of its individual parts, from its beginning to its end . . . Such must also be the method of exposition (or study) of dialectics in general . . . To being with what is the simplest, most ordinary, common, etc., with *any proposition* . . . Here already we have *dialectics.*'

19 Ilyenkov (1982, p. 84); see also Ilyenkov (1977, p. 369) and Zeleny (1980, pp. 31–38). For Lenin (1972, p. 152), '*law* and *essence* are concepts of the same kind (of the same order), or rather, of the same degree, expressing the deepening of man's knowledge of phenomena, the world, etc.' In what follows, essence is the 'internal law-governed structure'; this structure determines the laws of development of the concrete, which manifest themselves systematically as tendencies. The interaction between tendencies and counter-tendencies shapes the evolution of the reality (see section 1.2, Marx 1975, pp. 259–260 and Reuten 1997).

20 For Rosdolsky (1977, pp. 114–115), 'the reader should not imagine that economic categories are anything other than the reflections of real relations, or that the logical derivation of these categories could proceed independently of their historical derivation'. Similarly, Foley (1986, p. 1) rightly argues that 'Marx conceives of the social reality he is analyzing as a process that evolves in responses to its own internal contradictions. In other words, the phenomena he discusses cannot be understood independently of the history that produced them'.

21 For materialist dialectics 'the question of the universal character of a concept is transferred to another sphere, that of the study of the real *process of development*. The developmental approach becomes thereby the approach of *logic*' (Ilyenkov 1982, pp. 76–77). See also Ilyenkov (1977, pp. 354–355; 1982, pp. 83–84, 94–96).

22 '[T]he individual exists only in the connection that leads to the universal. The universal exists only in the individual and through the individual. Every individual is (in one way or another) a universal. Every universal is (a fragment or an aspect, or the essence of) an individual . . . *Here already* we have the elements, the germs, the concepts of *necessity*, of objective connection in nature, etc. Here already we have the contingent and the necessary, the phenomenon and the essence' (Lenin 1972, p.361). See also Bonefeld, Gunn and Psychopedis (1992a, pp. xv–xvi; 1992b) and Gunn (1992, pp. 20–24).

23 See Ilyenkov (1982, pp. 217–222, 232, 244). A somewhat similar approach ('historical logic') is outlined by Thompson (1978, pp. 231–238). Materialist dialectics is sharply distinct from the 'logical-historical' method of Engels (1981) and Meek (1973), see section 2.1.1.

24 Gunn (1992, p. 23).

25 See *Capital 1*, pp. 133, 283–284, 290.

26 See *Theories of Surplus Value 1*, pp. 409–410.

27 'The concrete universal expressed in the concept does not . . . comprise in itself all this wealth [of the concrete] in the sense that it comprehends all the specific instances and is applicable to them as their general name' (Ilyenkov 1982, p. 84). Foley (1986, p. 4) similarly argues that the addition of higher determinations 'may produce phenomena that appear to contradict the fundamental determinations . . . But this type of contradiction is only apparent; as long as the explanation is consistent with the structure of the theory, the fundamental determinations continue to be valid and important in the explanation and continue to operate in the more complex situation.'

28 See *Grundrisse*, pp. 460–461. For Marx, 'no phenomena, and, emphatically, no social phenomena can be understood except in their historical context. Any proposition is robbed of its sense if it is taken as an eternal verity or as a truth independent of historical circumstances' (Baumol 1983, p. 307). More specifically, 'It is one of the characteristics of Marxian analysis that theoretical work constantly touches on the facts of historical reality . . . The continuous oscillation between abstract dialectical development and concrete historical reality pervades the whole of Marx's *Capital*. At the same time . . . the Marxian analysis *detaches* itself continually from the sequence and superficialities of historical reality and expresses *in ideas* the necessary relations of that reality' (Zelený 1980, p. 36). See also Albritton (1986, p. 18), Colletti (1972, p. 3), Murray (1988, p. 113) and Thompson (1978, p. 249).

29 Marx was 'deeply suspicious of universal categories . . . He saw categories themselves as a product of a particular society and sought concepts that could serve to distinguish capitalism from other modes of production and thereby serve as a basis for dissecting capitalism's internal logic. In this manner, Marx seeks to make his materialism genuinely historical' (D. Harvey 1999, p. 6).

30 See Marx's second thesis on Feuerbach (Marx 1975, p. 422) and Moseley (1995a, pp. 93–94).

31 See chapter 2, Fine (1980, p. 123) and Ollman (1993, p. 61).

32 Böhm-Bawerk (1949, pp. 69–70).

33 For a rebuttal of Böhm-Bawerk's critique, see Glick and Ehrbar (1986–87, pp. 464–470), Hilferding (1949), and Ilyenkov (1977, essay 10, and 1982, pp. 62, 73–81).

34 'Marx did not base his concept of value on a mental construct removed from the real world and requiring all sorts of arbitrary assumptions. Rather, his argument is based upon the fact that the reduction of all types of labour to a common standard is a product of the real world itself' (Fine 1980, p. 124).

35 Value is 'a definite social mode of existence of human activity (labour)' (*Theories of Surplus Value 1*, p. 46). In other words, 'What makes labor general in capitalism is not simply the truism that it is the common [physiological] denominator of all various specific sorts of labor; rather, *it is the social function of labor that makes it general*. As a socially mediating activity, labor is abstracted from the specificity of its product, hence, from the specificity of its own concrete form. In Marx's analysis, the category of abstract labor expresses this real process of abstraction; it is not simply based on a conceptual process of abstraction' (Postone 1993, pp. 151–152). See also *Contribution*, pp. 276–277 and *Grundrisse*, pp. 296–297.

36 Marx's analysis is historical not only because of the presumably transitory existence of capitalism. In contrast with Aristotle, for example, who could only speculate about the essence of value (see *Capital 1*, pp. 151–152), Marx lived in an advanced capitalist society and he could *observe* that abstract labour is the essence of value: 'The reduction of all phenomena to "labour in general", to labour devoid of all qualitative differences, took place . . . in the reality of economic relations . . . rather than in the abstract-making heads of theoreticians. Value became that *goal* for the sake of which each thing was realised in labour; it became an "active form", a concrete universal law governing the destinies of each separate thing and each separate universal . . . [R]eduction to labour devoid of all differences appears here as an abstraction, but as a real abstraction "which is made every day in the social process of production" . . . Here labour in general, labour as such appears as a concrete universal substance, and a single individual and the single product of his labour, as *manifestations of this universal essence*' (Ilyenkov 1982, p. 97).

37 For a similar argument, see Perelman (1987, pp. 198–201), Rubin (1975, pp. 109–110; 1978, pp. 130–131) and M. Smith (1994a, p. 74). T. Smith (1998, p. 468) rightly argues that: 'As we move to progressively more complex categorizations of capital, we move to more comprehensive accounts of value as a concrete universal, subjecting ever more dimensions of social life to its imperatives . . . For Marx . . . it was not sufficient to show that value is a concrete universal in Hegel's sense. He wanted to explain *how* such an alien power could come to lord over social life. Abstract labour plays a crucial role in this explanation'.

38 Murray (1988, pp. 177–179).

39 See section 8.1, M. Smith (1994a, pp. 63–65), Thompson (1978, pp. 253–255) and, especially, Rosenthal (1999, pp. 296–300; 2000, pp. 505, 513).

40 In his analysis of capital, Marx 'distinguished (a) the conditions and presuppositions of the existence of capital, which itself creates capital by its own circulation, and (b) the conditions and presuppositions of the existence of capital which belong only to the history of the creation of capital, which are merely phases of the development of capitalism, but which disappear as soon as capital takes off on its own accord . . . As soon as capital has developed, money, functioning as money-capital in the hands of capitalists, is built up, and the real conditions for the capitalist process of value creation are no longer apprehended as a historical presupposition but as the consequence of the specific activity of capital; in that way it creates the presuppositions and conditions of its own further existence and growth' (Zelený 1980, p. 37).

41 Ilyenkov (1982, p. 282); see also *Grundrisse*, p. 776 and Arthur (2000a, p. 121). Rosenthal (1997, pp. 161–162) reaches a similar conclusion: 'Marx's justification for presenting the circuit of capital as he does lies not in the alleged necessity that value overcome its merely immediate being in the commodity . . . but rather in the more mundane fact that money actually *does* circulate in the manner described by it. Marx notes the empirical occurrence of such a circuit, and establishes that only a quantitative variation between the values represented by its extremes could motivate social activity with which it is associated (viz. buying in order to sell). He then sets himself the task of explaining how such an apparent augmentation of value through circulation (a) is possible and (b) is compatible with the basic "law of value" which governs the simple circulation of

commodities (viz. that commodities should exchange in just such quantities as their values are equal).'

42 Marx summarises his own method in *Grundrisse*, pp. 100–102, 107–108, and in *Capital 1*, pp. 99–102. Marx's understanding of 'contradiction' is discussed by Ollman (1993, pp. 15–16) and, especially, Zelený (1980, pp. 86–88, 222–223). For Ilyenkov, materialist dialectics is 'the science of development through inner contradictions' (1982, p. 278). He adds that 'The dialectical materialist method of resolution of contradictions . . . consists in tracing the process by which the movement of reality itself resolves them in a new form of expression. Expressed objectively, the goal lies in tracing, through analysis of new empirical materials, the emergence of reality in which an earlier established contradiction finds its relative resolution in a new objective form of its realisation' (pp. 262–263); see also Ilyenkov (1977, pp. 329–331).

43 For Lenin (1972, p. 196), 'The *totality of all* sides of the phenomenon, of reality and their (reciprocal) *relations*—that is what truth is composed of. The relations (= transitions = contradictions) of notions = the main content of logic, *by which* these concepts (and their relations, transitions, contradictions) are shown as reflections of the objective world. The dialectics of *things* produces the dialectics of *ideas*, and not vice versa.' More generally, he claims (pp. 92–93) that 'Logic is the science not of external forms of thought, but of the laws of development "of all material, natural and spiritual things", i.e., of the development of the entire concrete content of the world and of its cognition, i.e., the sum-total, the conclusion of the *History* of knowledge of the world.'

44 See *Grundrisse*, p. 278. For Lenin (1972, p. 183), 'The laws of logic are the reflections of the objective in the subjective consciousness of man.' Lenin adds elsewhere that 'Cognition is the eternal, endless approximation of thought to the objects. The *reflection* of nature in man's thought must be understood not "lifelessly," not "abstractly," *not devoid of movement, not without contradictions*, but in the eternal *process* of movement, the arising of contradictions and their solution' (p. 195, see also p. 182).

45 The word 'sublate' is used as the English equivalent of Hegel's 'Aufhebung' (to preserve the previous category while clearing away and substituting it). 'Supersede', 'suspend' and 'transcend' have also fulfilled a similar role in the literature; see Hegel (1991, pp. xxxv–xxxvi, 154).

46 *Capital 3*, p. 103. Groll and Orzech (1989, p. 57) rightly argue that 'Marx's concepts have a dynamic meaning in their appearances and transformations. His categories rarely have the straightforward, unequivocal meanings so familiar to, and expected by, the modern economist. On the contrary, they usually have multiple, sometimes complementary and sometimes contradictory, meanings'. See also section 7.3, especially footnotes 25–27, Aglietta (1979, p. 16), Arthur (1997, p. 22), D. Harvey (1999, pp. 1–3), Lenin (1972, p. 225) and Zelený (1980, ch. 2).

47 Arthur (1998, pp. 11–12).

48 See Fine (1982, ch. 1).

49 *Theories of Surplus Value 3*, pp. 112–113, emphasis added.

50 *Capital 3*, pp. 398–399, emphasis added.

51 This term was coined by Arthur (1993b) to describe such works as Murray (1988), Shamsavari (1991), T. Smith (1990), and others. An earlier source of inspiration is Lukács (1971). See also Albritton (1986, pp. 179, 181–186), Banaji (1979), Fraser (1997) and Reuten and Williams (1989).

52 Lenin (1972, p.180). To this daunting task, Murray (1988, p. 57) adds: 'A thorough understanding of *Capital* requires the study of Hegel's philosophy, the philosophy of the Young Hegelians, *and* Marx's critique of the entire cycle of speculative thought.' The accretion of endless philosophical prerequisites to *Capital* is regrettable because it erects barriers between readers and Marx's text (see Mattick Jr. 1993, p. 116).

53 '[I]t is precisely the lessons learned from Hegel that make *Capital* great' (Murray 1993, p. 37); '[E]lements actually incompatible with a systematic approach can also be found in *Capital*, primarily due to the fact that Marx's break from classical political economy was incomplete. The systematic dialectical reading does not incorporate the whole of the book. However, I believe that it does capture the work's unifying thread' (T. Smith 1993b, p. 25).

54 T. Smith (1990, pp. 45–46). See also Reuten and Williams (1989, pp. 19–20); for an alternative Hegelian view, see Banaji (1979).

55 See Arthur (2000a, p. 106), Reuten (1993, pp. 92–93), Reuten and Williams (1989, pp. 4, 21–22) and T. Smith (1990, p. x; 1993a, p. 115; 1993b, p. 20).

56 Reuten and Williams (1989, p. 22). See also Arthur (1993a, p. 67), Campbell (1993) and T. Smith (1990, p. 13; 1997, p. 191). T. Smith (1998, pp. 464–465) attempts to reconstruct *Capital* employing eight levels of abstraction, with mixed results.

57 Arthur (1993a, p. 67). See also Reuten and Williams (1989, pp. 5, 23).

58 For Reuten and Williams (1989, p. 34), 'although history is significant in explaining why the existent *came* into being, it cannot explain why it is "what it is", how the existent is *reproduced* as an interconnected whole'. See also Arthur (1992, p. xiii), Murray (1988, p. 182) and T. Smith (1993a, p. 102).

59 See Saad-Filho (1997c).

60 See Clarke (1991), Holloway (1994) and Lebowitz (1994).

61 'Marx's . . . modest attitude toward the concept leads him to ascribe . . . [great] importance to the "contingent". For the "contingent", while it may not have a place in the abstract conceptual analysis, still possesses a truth by virtue of its historical reality, and it must necessarily be incorporated in a full presentation of the social object in its concreteness' (Fracchia and Ryan 1992, p. 60).

62 In his analysis of the tendency of the rate of profit to fall (*Capital 3*, part 3) Marx shows that this abstract tendency does not imply the existence of trend, because several counter-tendencies, influential at different levels, also affect the rate of profit (see Fine 1989, ch.10; 1992; and Reuten 1997).

63 Thompson (1978, p. 253) criticises Althusser's work for similar reasons. For Althusser, 'once capital has emerged on the page, its self-development is determined by the innate logic inherent within the category, and the relations so entailed . . . Capital is an operative category which laws its own development, and capital*ism* is the effect, in social formations, of these laws. This mode of analysis must necessarily be anti-historical . . . This is an extraordinary mode of thought to find in a materialist, for capital has become Idea, which unfolds itself in history.' See also pp. 275–276, 290, 345, 355, Albritton (1999), Bonefeld (1992), Callari and Ruccio (1996), Holloway (1992) and Resnick and Wolff (1996).

64 In their critique of T. Smith's (1999b, p. 166) claim that there is an 'unbridgeable gulf between systematic dialectics and historical theorising', Fine, Lapavitsas and Milonakis (2000, p. 136) rightly argue that the new dialectics' neglect of

history 'grants unlimited degrees of freedom to the theorist when it comes to explaining particular historical phenomena. If it were so, any explanation could be made compatible with any general (systematic) theory referring to the same phenomenon . . . We believe that an attempt to drive a wedge between logic and history is deeply misguided. Rather, logic ought to draw upon, and to allow for, the historically specific forms in which the accumulation of capital is realised.'

65 Rosenthal (1997, p. 113).
66 Rosenthal (1997, p. 141); see also pp. 151–152, Mattick Jr. (1993) and Psychopedis (1992) and T. Smith's (1999a) subdued response to Rosenthal.
67 *Capital 1*, pp. 102–103.
68 Ibid. These criticisms repeat earlier ones, for example: 'Hegel fell into the illusion of conceiving the real as the product of thought concentrating itself, probing its own depths, and unfolding itself out of itself, by itself' (*Grundrisse*, p. 101). Or, 'The crux of the matter is that Hegel everywhere makes the Idea into the subject, while the genuine, real subject . . . is turned into the predicate' (Marx 1975, p. 65); see also pp. 61–73, 80–82, 98–100. T. Smith (1993a, pp. 47, 76–77) argues that Marx had an incorrect reading of Hegel. This claim is painstakingly disproved by Rosenthal (1997). For a scathing critique of the mystical side of Hegelian Marxism, see Bradby (1982, pp. 131–132).
69 Ilyenkov (1982, p. 82).
70 Ilyenkov (1982, p. 28). 'Hegel's logic treated the fundamental categories of thought as pure categories independent of any contingent empirical instantiation. He presented them as systematically ordered, from simple abstract ones to more complex, and hence more concrete, ones. This system of categories was said to be "self-moving" in that one category necessarily gives rise to another contrary, or more comprehensive, one, until the most comprehensive is reached—the Absolute Idea. Hegel was an absolute idealist in so far as he seems to think that he has thereby shown the necessity of such relationships arising and developing in the real world' (Arthur 2000a, pp. 107–108). See also Arthur (1993a, p. 64), Ilyenkov (1977, essays 5 and 7), Murray (1988, p. 116), Rosenthal (1997, pp. 151–152), Rubin (1975, pp. 91–92) and Zeleny (1980, p. 64).
71 Bharadwaj (1986, p. 5). See also *Grundrisse*, p. 90.
72 Marx (1989, pp. 544–545), see also p. 547.
73 'Hegel likes to think of the categories arising and dissolving out of their own instability; insofar as they are thought, it is by some "objective mind." This objectivist tendency of his logic is further strengthened because its truth is meant ontologically as much as logically. The coherence of the logic is at the same time the coherence of reality' (Arthur 1993a, pp. 67–68). See also Albritton (1999, p. 57), Colletti (1972), Fracchia and Ryan (1992, p. 59) and Lenin (1972, pp. 88–97, 146–147, 167–171, 177–180, 187, 190).
74 Scott (1999, pp. 3, 409); see also p. 61 and Mattick Jr. (1993, p. 121). In the same vein, Thompson (1978, p. 306) argues that 'We have often been told that Marx had a "method" . . . and that this constitutes the *essence* of Marxism. It is therefore strange that . . . Marx never wrote this essence down. Marx left many notebooks. Marx was nothing if not a self-conscious and responsible intellectual worker. If he had found the clue to the universe, he would have set a day or two aside to put it down. We may conclude from this that it was not written because *it could not be written*, any more than Shakespeare or Stendhal could have reduced their art to a clue. For it was not a method but a practice, and a

practice learned through practising. So that, in this sense, dialectics can never be set down, nor learned by rote.'
75 Arthur (1993a, p. 63) rightly claims that 'science must adopt the logic proper to the peculiar character of the object under investigation.'

2 Interpretations of Marx's value theory

1 See, however, Desai (1989, 1992), Dostaler and Lagueux (1985), Elson (1979a), Fine (1986a), Fine and Harris (1979), Foley (2000), Freeman and Carchedi (1996), Howard and King (1989, 1991), Saad-Filho (1997a), M. Smith (1994a) and Steedman (1981).
2 Hodgson (1981, p. 88), for example, argues that for Ricardo and Marx 'The embodied labour value of a commodity is defined such that the total embodied labour value of the gross output of a process equals the embodied labour value of all the inputs plus the amount of socially necessary living labour employed.' See also Böhm-Bawerk (1949, p.109), Garegnani (1985), Meek (1973, pp. 164–165), Morishima (1973, p. 15) and Nuti (1977).
3 See Dobb (1940, 1967), Meek (1973) and Sweezy (1968). This approach is critically reviewed by Arthur (1997), Postone (1993, ch. 2), T. Smith (1998), de Vroey (1982 and, especially, 1985) and Weeks (1981, chs 1–2). For a critique of the 'surplus approach' associated with this interpretation of Marx, see Chattopadhyay (2000), Pilling (1980, p. 57), Roberts (1987) and Roosevelt (1977).
4 Marx explains the relationship between production, circulation and distribution in *Grundrisse*, pp. 88–99 and Marx (1974, p. 348); see also Engels (1998, pp. 238–239).
5 Winternitz (1948, p. 277). See also Morishima (1974, p. 624) and Sweezy (1968, chs 2, 4, 7).
6 'The "derivation of prices from values" . . . must be regarded as a historical as well as a logical process. In "deriving prices from values" we are really reproducing in our minds, in logical and simplified form, a process which has actually happened in history. Marx began with the assumption that goods sold "at their values" under capitalism (so that profit rates in the various branches of production were often very different), not only because this appeared to be the proper starting-point from the logical point of view but also because he believed that it had "originally" been so. He proceeded on this basis to transform values into prices, not only because this course appeared to be logically necessary but also because he believed that history itself had effected such a transformation' (Meek 1956, pp. 104–105); see also pp. xxiv, 152, 180–181, 241–242, 303–305. This view draws upon Engels (1981). For a critique, see Catephores (1986) and Fine (1986b); see also Brenner (1986) and Milonakis (1990).
7 See Albritton (1986, pp. 18–19) and Reinfelder (1980, p. 13).
8 'Ricardian' interpretations of Marx are heavily criticised by, among others, Faccarello (1986), Ganssmann (1986), Gerstein (1986), Shaikh (1977, 1981, 1982) and works in Freeman and Carchedi (1996) and Mandel and Freeman (1984).
9 '[T]o regard Marx's theory of value as a proof of exploitation tends to dehistoricise value, to make it synonymous with labour-time, and to make redundant Marx's distinction between surplus labour and surplus value. To know whether or not there is exploitation, we must examine the ownership and

control of the means of production, and the process whereby the length of the working day is fixed . . . Marx's concern was with the particular *form* that exploitation took in capitalism . . . for in capitalism surplus labour could not be appropriated simply in the form of the immediate product of labour. It was necessary for that product to be sold and translated into *money* (Elson 1979b, p. 116). See also Fine (1982), Postone (1993, p. 54) and Rubin (1979, part 4).

10 See Bortkiewicz (1949, 1952), Dmitriev (1974), Hodgson (1973, 1981), Pasinetti (1977), Seton (1957), Sraffa (1960), Steedman (1977, 1981), Sweezy (1968, ch.7) and Tugan-Baranowsky (1905); see also Shibata (1933). For a critical review, see Ramos-Martínez and Rodríguez-Herrera (1996). The conclusions of Haberler (1966) and Samuelson (1957, 1971, 1973, 1974) are substantively identical to the Sraffian.

11 Early Sraffian developments were welcomed by traditional Marxists: 'I would . . . wish to urge that this enquiry should be conducted within a rather different conceptual framework—that provided by Sraffa in his *Production of Commodities by Means of Commodities* . . . I shall try to . . . show how certain basic elements of this system could conceivably be adapted and used by modern Marxists' (Meek 1973, p. xxxii); see also Dobb's (1943) expression of support for Bortkiewicz's work.

12 Hodgson (1981, p. 83), for example, states that 'Although the Sraffa system is conceptually different from a general equilibrium system of the Walrasian type, or even the von Neumann model, these all have one thing in common: they do not include money. Clower has shown that money can never be introduced into a stationary-state, general equilibrium model.'

13 For a review of these difficulties from the traditional point of view, see May (1948), Meek (1956), Seton (1957), Sweezy (1968, ch. 7) and Winternitz (1948).

14 The argument that any commodity may be 'exploited' is presented by Bródy (1974), Dmitriev (1974), Hodgson (1981), Vegara i Carrio (1978) and Wolff (1984). Dissenters within this approach have attempted to salvage the role of labour by making the system asymmetrical because of the non-commodity aspects of labour power (e.g., Bowles and Gintis 1981). For a critique, see Glick and Ehrbar (1986–87) and M. Smith (1994b).

15 See Morishima (1974); for a critique, see Mohun (2000) and Naples (1989).

16 For detailed critiques of Sraffianism, see Fine (1980), Fine and Harris (1979, ch. 2), Gleicher (1985–86), Goode (1973), Kliman and McGlone (1988), Ramos-Martínez and Rodríguez-Herrera (1996), Rowthorn (1980, ch. 1), Savran (1979, 1980, 1984), Schwartz (1977), Shaikh (1977, 1981, 1982, 1984), M. Smith (1994a, pp. 77–94) and Yaffe (1974).

17 'The point is not that no abstraction is involved in the concept of embodied labour; rather it is not a *social* abstraction corresponding to particular historical process, but it is *arbitrary*, a mental convenience: an assumption that labour is homogeneous *when it is plainly not*' (Himmelweit and Mohun 1978, p. 81). See also Weeks (1982b, p. 65).

18 Steedman (1977, p. 19), for example, assumes that all labour is simple and of equal intensity and training, 'so that each individual expenditure of labour-time is an expenditure of socially necessary labour-time.'

19 'The search for a privileged technological input in the labor process, which determines the value of the product, comes from a misunderstanding of what value is. Abstract labour is not a privileged input into production because

abstract labour is *not an input into production at all* . . . It is attached to the product (as a price tag) only because of the particular social relations in a commodity producing society' (Glick and Ehrbar 1986–87, p. 472). See also p. 465, Ilyenkov (1982, pp. 87, 284), Lipietz (1985b, p. 90), Mattick Jr. (1991–92, p. 58) and Shaikh (1981, 1982).

20 For a devastating critique along those lines, see Rowthorn (1980, ch.1).

21 Yaffe (1974, p. 31).

22 See Shaikh (1982, pp. 71–72).

23 Gleicher (1985–86, p. 465); see also Lee (1993, p. 464).

24 See Glick and Ehrbar (1986–87, pp. 473–476), Fine (1996, p. 11), D. Harvey (1999, pp. 35–36) and Yaffe (1995, p. 95).

25 Different versions of value form analysis are proposed by Backhaus (1974) de Brunhoff (1973a, 1976, 1978c), Eldred (1984), Eldred and Hanlon (1981), Lipietz (1985a), Reuten (1993), Reuten and Williams (1989) and de Vroey (1981, 1982, 1985); for a clear presentation, see N. Taylor (2000). For a critique, see Elson (1979b), Gleicher (1985), Likitkijsomboon (1995), Moseley (1997a), Saad-Filho (1997a) and Weeks (1990).

26 Althusser (1969, 1970), Backhaus (1974), de Brunhoff (1973b, 1978b, 1978c), Rubin (1975, 1978); see also Gerstein (1986), Himmelweit and Mohun (1978) and Pilling (1972).

27 Rubin (1975, p. 114, emphasis omitted). See also pp. 63–64, 92, Benetti and Cartelier (1980) and de Brunhoff (1973a, ch. 2). For Meek (1973, p. 302 n.2), '"Commodity production" in the Marxian sense means roughly the production of goods for exchange on some sort of market by individual producers or groups of producers who carry on their activities more or less separately from one another.'

28 Rubin (1975, pp. 1, 22–24, 31, 47, 62–64, 70, 85, 89–94, 114, 125, 141).

29 See Aglietta (1979, p. 278), de Brunhoff (1978c), Guttman (1994, p. 20) and de Vroey (1981, p. 185).

30 Rubin (1975, pp. 96–97, 142; 1978, pp. 118–119). See also Rubin (1975 pp. 66–71, 97–99, 120, 127–130, 141–146, 150; 1978, pp. 124–125). For de Vroey (1981, p. 176), 'Labour is first performed as private labour, initiated by an independent decision. It is transformed into social labour through, and only through, the sale of its product. When social labour is formed in this context, it is called abstract labour, the adjective referring to the operation of homogenization or abstraction achieved by exchange on the market.' Therefore, 'rather than being linked to a mere embodiment of labour—a technical process —value refers to the validation of private labour through the exchange of commodities against money . . . private labour becomes validated (ie reckoned as a fraction of social labour, serving effectively this reproduction) only in so far as its product is sold. Otherwise, private labour is a waste' (de Vroey 1982, p. 40). See also Eldred and Hanlon (1981, pp. 26, 35), Himmelweit and Mohun (1978, pp. 73–74; 1981, pp. 232–234), Mattick Jr. (1991–92, pp. 33–35), Mohun (1991), Reuten (1995), Reuten and Williams (1989, pp. 66–70), T. Smith (1990, p. 72; 1993b, p. 21) and de Vroey (1981, pp. 176, 184; 1982, p. 46; 1985, p. 47).

31 See de Brunhoff (1978b), Reuten and Williams (1989) and de Vroey (1981, pp. 184–186; 1985, pp. 45–46).

32 Rubin realised that this argument is untenable: 'Some critics say that our conception may lead to the conclusion that abstract labour originates only in

the act of exchange, from which it follows that value also originates only in exchange' (Rubin 1975, p. 147; see also 1978, p. 121). He attempts to evade this difficulty through the distinction between exchange as the social form of the process of production, and exchange as one phase of reproduction, alternating with production. Rubin (1975, pp. 95, 100–101, 144–151; 1978, pp. 122–124) claims that his argument that value is determined in exchange refers to the first meaning of the term, rather than the second. However, this distinction is invalid, and Rubin himself states that the relationship between the producers is established through the *act*, rather than the social structure, of exchange (see Rubin 1975, pp. 7–9, 61, 64, 70, 80–88, 143; 1978, p. 114).

33 See *Capital 1*, p. 482, *Theories of Surplus Value 1*, pp. 78, 409 and *Theories of Surplus Value 3*, p. 272.

34 Postone (1993, p. 155) rightly argues that the commodity is the material objectification of the double character of labour in capitalism; thus, it is both a product and a social mediation. The commodity 'is not a use value that has value but, as the materialized objectification of concrete and abstract labor, it is a use value that is a value and, therefore, has exchange value.'

35 Weeks (1990, p. 8). For Marx, 'The division of labour within manufacture presupposes a concentration of the means of production in the hands of one capitalist; the division of labour within society presupposes a dispersion of those means among many independent producers of commodities. While, within the workshop, the iron law of proportionality subjects definite numbers of workers to definite functions, in the society outside the workshop, the play of chance and caprice results in a motley pattern of distribution of the producers and their means of production among the various branches of social labour . . . The planned and regulated *a priori* system on which the division of labour is implemented within the workshop becomes, in the division of labour within society, an *a posteriori* necessity imposed by nature, controlling the unregulated caprice of the producers, and perceptible in the fluctuations of the barometer of market-prices. Division of labour within the workshop implies the undisputed authority of the capitalist over men, who are merely the members of a total mechanism which belongs to him. The division of labour within society brings into contact independent producers of commodities, who acknowledge no authority other than that of competition, of the coercion exerted by the pressure of their reciprocal interests, just as in the animal kingdom the "war of all against all" more or less preserves the conditions of existence of every species' (*Capital 1*, pp. 476–477). See also pp. 439–441, 464–465, 1019, *Capital 3*, p. 172, *Theories of Surplus Value 3*, p.378, *Contribution*, pp. 321–322 and *Grundrisse*, p. 709.

36 'Those who equate price with value and, therefore, reduce value determination to exchange are in effect considering value in the context of simple commodity production, a situation in which value has no determining role' (Weeks 1990, p. 8). See also Saad-Filho (1997a).

37 Weeks (1981, pp. 31–32, emphasis added). See also Arthur (1997, pp. 13–15), Uno (1980, p. 34) and Weeks (1990, p. 11).

38 Duménil (1980, 1983–84, 1984), Duménil and Lévy (1991), Foley (1982, 1983, 1986); see also Ehrbar (1989), Glick and Ehrbar (1987), Lipietz (1982, 1984, 1985a) and Mohun (1994). This section draws upon Fine, Lapavitsas and Saad-Filho (2000) and Saad-Filho (1996a). See also Moseley (2000a).

39 See sections 2.2.1 and 4.2, and Aglietta (1979) and Rubin (1975, 1978).

40 This is not discussed in what follows; see, however, Mohun (2000, forthcoming).

41 See Aglietta (1979, pp. 38–39, 277), Duménil (1980, pp. 13–14) and Lipietz (1982, p. 60). For Foley (1982, p. 37), the labour theory of value is 'the claim that the money value of the whole mass of net production of commodities expresses the expenditure of the total social labor in a commodity-producing economy . . . The concept of value as a property of the whole mass of the net commodity product in this approach is analytically prior to the concept of price, the amount of money a particular commodity brings on the market.' See also Foley (1986, pp. 14, 97), Glick and Ehrbar (1987, p. 303) and Mohun (1994); for a critique, see Stamatis (1998–99).

42 See Aglietta (1979, pp. 41–44), and Foley (1982). For an alternative view, focusing on the gross product, see Shaikh (1991, p. 78). Marx does not distinguish explicitly between the gross and the net product, see, for example, *Capital 1*, pp. 162–163, 297 and *Theories of Surplus Value 2*, pp. 414, 416, 538.

43 'If we assume that one hour of labor power sold yields one hour of labor time in production, the value of labor power will be a fraction between 0 and 1 and expresses the fraction of expended labor time the workers work "for themselves," or the fraction of labor expended which is "paid labor." The value of labor power is also, under the assumption that an hour of labor power yields an hour of labor time, equal to the wage share of value added' (Foley 1982, p. 40); see also Duménil (1984, p. 342) and Lipietz (1984, pp. 352–353; 1985b, p. 92).

44 The wage rate is paid per unit of simple, unskilled labour power. Three other simplifying assumptions are made: the workers are identical to one another, they are invariably productive, and they create equal value per hour of labour power sold (see Lipietz 1982, p. 62).

45 See Duménil (1980, p. 82).

46 See Duménil (1980, pp. 62–63; 1983–84, pp. 441–442).

47 Weeks (1983, p. 220).

48 In his groundbreaking paper on the NI, Foley (1982, p. 41) invites the reader to 'Suppose . . . we have a commodity-producing system in which, for one reason or another, the money prices of commodities are not proportional to labor values. One reason might be that prices deviate from labor values so that profit rates can be equalized when invested capital per worker varies over different sectors. Other reasons might be monopoly, government regulations, the exploitation of information differentials in markets by middlemen, and so on.' Collapsing categories at distinct levels of complexity in order to apply macroeconomic identities may be useful for policy analysis, but it can be unhelpful analytically because it obscures the structures of determination of the mode of production.

49 See Foley (1982, pp. 42–43; 1986, pp. 15, 41) and Lipietz (1982, p. 75).

50 Marx was heavily critical of theories of exploitation that focused primarily upon the distribution of income; see Marx (1974, pp. 344–345) and Saad-Filho (1993a).

51 See Flaschel (1984) and Szumski (1991).

3 Value and capital

1 'Interpreted on very narrow terms, social reproduction includes the processes necessary for the reproduction of the workforce, both biologically and as compliant wage-labourers. More generally, social reproduction is concerned with how society as a whole is reproduced and transformed over time' (Fine 2001, p. 32).

2 This transhistorical background is explicit in the *Grundrisse*, p. 108. See also Mattick Jr. (1991–92, pp. 32, 42), Perlman (1977) and M. Smith (1994a, p. 42).

3 'Rather than justifying the concept of value on the basis of the results to which it leads in price or distribution theory, Marx wished to demonstrate that value is a concept that has itself to be explained in terms of its correspondence to relations that exist in the real world. The relevant questions are what is value and why does it exist, for in contrast to prices, for example, values are not a simple observational fact of everyday life. Goods in a shop window have their prices displayed to the world, the same cannot and could not be true for their value. Consequently, there is a certain methodological inconsistency when prices and values are introduced simultaneously at the outset into an analysis of the relationship between them. For the two concepts have a different status, one requires justification for its existence, the other does not' (Fine 1980, p. 123).

4 Use value is a mental generalisation expressing the capacity of certain goods to satisfy specific human needs, see *Capital 1*, pp. 125–126 and Marx (1977, p. 197). D. Harvey (1999, p. 5) rightly claims that 'At the basis of Marx's conception of the world lies the notion of an appropriation of nature by human beings in order to satisfy their wants and needs. This appropriation is a material process embodied in the acts of production and consumption . . . The material side of commodities is captured in its relation to human wants and needs by the concept of *use value*.' For detailed analyses of the concept of use value, see Fine (2001, ch. 2), Fine and Leopold (1993, Part IV), Lebowitz (1992, p. 23) and Pilling (1980, p. 138).

5 *Capital 1*, p. 133. For Shaikh (1982, p. 68), 'the relation of people to nature exists only in and through definite relations of people to people; these are therefore two aspects of the same set of relations which define the mode of (re)production of social life. The production of material wealth goes hand in hand with the reproduction of social relations . . . while it is true that use-values may occasionally arise as the spontaneous fruits of nature (wild grapes, etc.), it is obvious that no society could exist for long without the *production* of use-values, that is, without labor itself.' See also *Capital 1*, pp. 137, 283–284, 287, 290, Post (1996, pp. 27–28) and Shaikh (1977, p. 114).

6 '[L]abour-power, or labour-capacity, [is] the aggregate of those mental and physical capabilities existing in the physical form, the living personality, of a human being, capabilities which he sets in motion whenever he produces a use-value of any kind' (*Capital 1*, p. 270).

7 '[A]s soon as men start to work for each other in any way, their labour also assumes a social form' (*Capital 1*, p. 164). See also p. 134, *Theories of Surplus Value 3*, pp. 168–169 and Chattopadhyay (1999, p. 1).

8 See *Capital 1*, pp. 471–472, Rowthorn (1980, p. 31) and Lapavitsas (2000d). Marx (1977, p. 198) claims that 'the mode of exchanging products is regulated by the mode of producing them'. There is exploitation if some people are

compelled to act in ways that are systematically advantageous to others: 'To exploit a person is to use them toward the exploiter's ends. Exploiter status differs qualitatively, not quantitatively, from being the one exploited' (Naples 1989, p. 149). See also Himmelweit (1991, pp. 182–184) and Schutz (1999, pp. 307–310). For a historical analysis of modes of exploitation, see Milonakis (1990, 1993–94).

 9 'What distinguishes the various economic formations of society—the distinction between for example a society based on slave-labour and a society based on wage-labour—is the form in which surplus labour is in each case extorted from the immediate producer, the worker' (*Capital 1*, p. 325). See also pp. 344–345, *Theories of Surplus Value 1*, p. 390, *Theories of Surplus Value 3*, p. 400, *Grundrisse*, pp. 525–527 and Post (1996).

10 'To Marx . . . the essence of capitalist property is the control of the productive process and therefore the control over laborers. Forced labor rather than low wages, alienation of labor rather than alienation of the product of labor are, according to Marx, the essence of capitalist exploitation' (Medio 1977, p. 384).

11 Marx (1988a, p. 68). See also Marx (1976, p. 31), J. Devine (1989), Fine (1996), Hilferding (1949, pp. 130–131) and Pilling (1980, pp. 43–47).

12 Grossman (1977, p. 46). See also *Capital 1*, pp. 473, 949–954, *Theories of Surplus Value 2*, p. 528, *Grundrisse*, pp. 102, 776 and Marx (1989, pp. 551–552).

13 See *Capital 1*, pp. 733–734, *Capital 2*, p. 461, *Theories of Surplus Value 1*, p. 406 and *Theories of Surplus Value 3*, pp. 270–272, 491.

14 See *Grundrisse*, pp. 296–297 and Ilyenkov (1982, pp. 196–197). Although commodity production requires a certain level of development of the division of labour, its existence is insufficient to define the mode of production; see Lapavitsas (2000c). For a wide-ranging study of market relations, see Polanyi (1944). Labour markets are dissected by Fine (1998).

15 'Since the production and the circulation of commodities are the general prerequisites of the capitalist mode of production, division of labour in manufacture requires that a division of labour within society should have already attained a certain degree of development. Inversely, the division of labour in manufacture reacts back upon that in society, developing it further. With the differentiation of the instruments of labour, the trades which produce these instruments themselves become more and more differentiated' (*Capital 1*, p. 473).

16 See Lapavitsas (2000d) and Shaikh (1981, p. 275). Perelman (1987, p. 142) rightly argues that 'the authority exercised within a firm is not specific to value relationships; we would expect the same sort of management rules to apply to a slaveholder, or within limits, to a feudal lord . . . What is unique is the indirect authority exercised by the market within the capitalist mode of production.'

17 Mohun (1991, p. 564). For Ilyenkov (1982, p. 34), abstract labour is the 'objective characteristic of the form which human labour assumes in developed commodity production, in capitalist production'. Shaikh (1982, p. 70) rightly argues that under capitalism, the 'labour involved in the production of commodities produces value, while exchange merely realizes it in money form.' See also *Theories of Surplus Value 3*, pp. 131, 253, *Grundrisse*, pp. 104–105, Arthur (2001), Cleaver (1979, p. 108), Cohen (1974, pp. 246–247), Colletti (1972, pp. 22–23, 80–84), Fine (1989 p. 10), Himmelweit and Mohun (1981, p. 225) and Shaikh (1981, p. 273).

18 '[C]apitalist production is commodity production as the general form of production, but it is only so, and becomes ever more so in its development, because labour itself here appears as a commodity, because the worker sells labour, i.e. the function of his labour power, and moreover, as we have assumed, at a value determined by the costs of its reproduction' (*Capital 2*, p. 196); see also *Capital 1*, p. 733.

19 *Capital 1*, pp. 475–477; see also *Theories of Surplus Value 3*, p. 378. For Cleaver (1979, p. 164), money is 'the magic wand by which new elements of the world are incorporated into capital . . . *The commodity which is set equal to some quantity of money, that is, given a price, is instantly tied into the whole world of capital.* How? By setting a price, it is affirmed that this use-value, having been produced by useful labor of some sort, is only one special product of that universal tool of capital's control: work.' See also Fine (2001, p. 33), Kliman (2000) and Shaikh (1977, p. 112).

20 *Capital 1*, p. 125; see also *Contribution*, p. 269.

21 In the first chapters of *Capital 1*, Marx often illustrates basic points of theory about commodity and monetary relations through examples of advanced capitalism, see, for example, pp. 237 n.52–53, 238 n.54, 327–329.

22 *Capital 3*, pp. 1019–1020. See also *Capital 1*, pp. 174, 274, 949–953, *Capital 2*, p. 196, *Theories of Surplus Value 3*, pp. 74, 112–113, Echeverría (1978, p. 376), Ilyenkov (1982, pp. 77, 80, 104, 200, 232), Likitkijsomboon (1995, p. 76), Postone (1993, pp. 5, 271, 285), Sekine (1975, p. 850), M. Smith (1994a, p. 48), Uno (1980, p. 34) and Weeks (1981, p. 11).

23 For a devastating critique of these concepts, see Fine (1998, 2001).

24 For the same reason, 'Theories of abstinence, waiting, or intertemporal preference depend upon the sacrifice by capitalists of present consumption as the source of profits. Nobody could deny that these "sacrifices" (usually made in luxurious comfort) are a condition of profit, but like thousands of other conditions they are not a cause of profits. People without capital could abstain, wait, and make intertemporal choices until they were blue in the face without creating profits for themselves. It is not abstinence that creates capital, but capital that requires abstinence. Waiting has existed in all societies, it is even to be found among squirrels . . . It must always be borne in mind that it is not things, abstract or otherwise, that create economic categories . . . but definite social relations between people (Fine 1989, p. 25; see also *Grundrisse*, p. 613). The thoughtless extension of the concept of capital is part of the 'economic imperialism' by which neoclassical economics has been colonising the other social sciences (see Fine 1997).

25 *Capital 1*, pp. 1005–1006. See also pp. 247, 764, 874–875, 899–900, 927–928, *Capital 2*, p. 185, *Capital 3*, pp. 953–954, 965–968, *Theories of Surplus Value 3*, p. 272, *Theories of Surplus Value 3*, p.422, *Grundrisse*, pp. 86, 512, Aglietta (1979, p. 24), Bell (1977, p. 173), Chattopadhyay (1994, p. 7, 1998, p. 233), Nell (1992, p. xiii), M. Smith (1994a, pp. 62, 66) and Zarembka (2000). Nell (1992, p. 53) rightly argues that 'capital is not a "factor of production" earning a return in virtue of its "productive contribution" at the margin. It is a social relationship; it is the way production is organized and the product appropriated. The existence of capital as self-expanding value depends upon the exploitation of wage-labor . . . so when multinational capital moves into new areas, formerly organized non-capitalistically, new institutional arrangements must be created.

A proper "climate for investment" must be established. This means a labor force, labor discipline, protection for property in the means of production, suitable finance, and so on. These can involve major upheavals and political changes.'

26 'Marx's starting point in the treatment of capital is conceiving capital as a social totality, capital representing a *class* opposed not so much to the individual laborers as to the wage laborers as a *class*' (Chattopadhyay 1994, p. 18). See also Postone (1993, p. 351).

27 'To the extent that we are considering it here, as a relation distinct from that of value and money, capital is capital in general, i.e. the incarnation of the qualities which distinguish value as capital from value as pure value or as money. Value, money, circulation, etc., prices etc., are presupposed, as is labour etc. But we are still concerned neither with a particular form of capital, nor with an individual capital as distinct from other individual capitals etc. We are present at the process of its becoming. This dialectical process of its becoming is only the ideal expression of the real movement through which capital comes into being. The later relations are to be regarded as developments coming out of this germ. But it is necessary to establish the specific form in which it is posited at a certain point. Otherwise confusion arises' (*Grundrisse*, p. 310). See also pp. 421, 449, 517, 852, *Capital 1*, p. 710 and Pilling (1980, p. 98).

28 'Industrial capital is the only mode of existence of capital in which not only the appropriation of surplus-value or surplus product, but also its creation, is a function of capital. It thus requires production to be capitalist in character; its existence includes that of the class antagonism between capitalists and wage-labourers . . . The other varieties of capital which appeared previously, within past or declining conditions of social production, are not only subordinated to it and correspondingly altered in the mechanism of their functioning, but they now move only on its basis, thus live and die, stand and fall together with this basis. Money capital and commodity capital, in so far as they appear and function as bearers of their own peculiar branches of business alongside industrial capital, are now only modes of existence of the various functional forms that industrial capital constantly assumes and discards within the circulation sphere' (*Capital 2*, pp. 135–136).

29 Interest-bearing capital (IBC), whose form is M-M', money that becomes more money (see section 8.3), does not *produce* profit, any more than money left inside a mattress begets more money simply by lying there. The expansion of IBC is due to transfers from productive capital, see Fine (1985–86; 1989, ch. 12), Itoh and Lapavitsas (1999, ch. 3) and Moseley (1997a).

30 *Capital 1*, p. 764. In other words, 'The capitalist process of production, there-fore, seen as a total, connected process, i.e. a process of reproduction, produces not only commodities, not only surplus-value, but it also produces and repro-duces the capital-relation itself; on the one hand the capitalist, on the other the wage-labourer' (*Capital 1*, p. 724). See also *Capital 2*, pp. 428–430, Fine (2001, p. 31) and Zarembka (2000).

31 This view is associated with Rosdolsky (1977, pp. 43–51), see also Moseley (1995b) and T. Smith (1999b). For a critique, see Burkett (1991), Clarke (1994), Fine (1992), Fine, Lapavitsas and Milonakis (2000) and Heinrich (1989).

32 *Grundrisse*, p. 414. See also pp. 421n, 650–652, *Capital 1*, p. 433, Bryan (1985, p. 77), Chattopadhyay (1994, p. 12), Lebowitz (1992, pp. 65–67) and Wheelock (1983).

33 See *Capital 1*, chs 12, 16, 17, 25.
34 See *Capital 3*, chs 8–15.
35 For a similar critique, see Arthur (2000b) and Fine, Lapavitsas and Milonakis (2000); see also Brenner (1986). For Marx, 'What competition within the same sphere of production brings about, is the determination of the value of the commodity in a given sphere by the average labour-time required in it, i.e., the creation of the market-value. What competition between the different spheres of production brings about is the creation of the same general rate of profit in the different spheres through the levelling out of the different market-values into market-prices, which are [prices of production] that are different from the actual market-values. Competition in this second instance by no means tends to assimilate the prices of the commodities to their values, but on the contrary, to reduce their values to [prices of production]' (*Theories of Surplus Value 2*, p. 208).
36 The 'basis for the development of capitalist production is, in general, that *labour-power*, as the *commodity* belonging to the workers, confronts the conditions of labour as commodities maintained in the form of capital and existing independently of the workers' (*Theories of Surplus Value 1*, p. 45, see also p. 78). The transformation of labour power into a commodity is the historical result of the primitive capital accumulation (see *Capital 1*, chs 26–32 and Perelman 1999). This process includes the elimination of the capacity of the workers to satisfy their own needs except through commodity exchanges, and the establishment of a pliant and reliable wage labour force.
37 *Theories of Surplus Value 3*, pp. 490–491. Nell (1992, p. 66) rightly argues that 'Exploitation is a matter of structural coercion. Circumstances are so arranged that a large mass of people must agree to do as they are told by others in order to support themselves and their families.' See also Cleaver (1979, p. 73) and Lapides (1998, p. 8).
38 The 'relation between generalized commodity production [GCP] . . . wage labor and capitalist production is one of reciprocal implication. First . . . when labor becomes wage labor . . . commodity production is generalized. On the one hand wage labor implies GCP . . . On the other hand, GCP implies wage labor . . . Marx shows . . . that capitalist production is commodity production as the general form of production while, at the same time, emphasizing that it is only on the basis of the capitalist mode of production that all or even the majority of products of labor assume commodity form . . . Finally, the relation of wage labor and capital is also one of reciprocal implication for Marx. Capital is a production relation between the immediate producers and their conditions of production which, separated from them and passing under the control of non (immediate) producers, dominate them as capital . . . [T]he rest of the features of capitalism could be seen as the necessary resultants following from any one of these essentially equivalent central categories' (Chattopadhyay 1994, pp. 17–18). See also Gleicher (1983, p. 99) and Uno (1980, p. 21).
39 'Capitalism, and hence capital, requires a lot more by way of the social than private property and the market . . . What it does depend upon is wage labour, able and willing to produce a surplus for capital. By implication, the social attached to capital takes the form of class relations. For Marxist theory, class relations in general are fundamental in distinguishing between modes of production, such as feudalism and capitalism, and, as a corollary, between different periods of history. Capital and labour confront one another as classes

with the capitalist class monopolising the means of production or access to livelihood through work. Consequently, workers can only survive by selling their capacity to work for a wage that represents less in terms of labour time than is performed for the capitalist. The surplus labour performed over and above that necessary to provide the wage gives rise to what Marx termed exploitation, and provides for the profits of the capitalists' (Fine 2001, p. 29). See also *Grundrisse*, pp. 509–510.

40 D. Harvey (1999, p. 35). For Cleaver (1979, p. 72), 'The generalized imposition of the commodity-form has meant that forced work has become the fundamental means of organizing society—of social control. It means the creation of a working class—a class of people who can survive only by selling their capacity to work to the class that controls the means of production'.

41 Leadbeater (1985, p. 617). For Fine and Harris (1979, p. 56), 'Marx's distinction between productive and unproductive labour is, in fact, one which is simple to understand. If labour directly produces surplus value it is productive; if not, it is unproductive. This criterion has the corollary that only labour which is performed under the control of capital, . . . and in the sphere of production, is productive. For detailed analyses, see *Capital 1*, pp. 643–644, 667, 734–735, 1038–1049, *Capital 2*, pp. 225–226, *Theories of Surplus Value 1*, pp. 46, 152–165, 172–173, 202, 213, 288–289, 393–406, *Grundrisse*, pp. 308, 632–633, Cullenberg (1994), Fine and Harris (1979, ch. 3), Fine and Lapavitsas (2000, p. 364), Mohun (1996, forthcoming), Moseley (1994), Rubin (1975, ch. 19), Savran and Tonak (1999) and Weeks (1984).

42 Rubin (1975, p. 269), see also *Capital 3* pp. 406–408, 413–416. Even though unproductive workers do not produce surplus value, they are exploited because they work for longer than the value represented by their wage, see Foley (1986, pp. 120–122).

43 See Clarke (1980), Nell (1992, p. 39), Roberts (1997, pp. 498–499) and, especially, Cleaver (1979).

4 Wages and exploitation

1 For simplicity, all workers are presumed productive unless stated otherwise; see section 3.2.

2 'The specific economic form in which unpaid surplus labour is pumped out of the direct producers determines the relationship of domination and servitude, as this grows directly out of production itself and reacts back on it in turn as a determinant . . . It is in each case the direct relationship of the owners of the conditions of production to the immediate producers . . . in which we find the innermost secret, the hidden basis of the entire social edifice' (*Capital 3*, p. 927).

3 There are significant difficulties for the empirical estimation of the rate of exploitation, because of the influence of the accounting conventions, taxes, savings, unproductive labour, and so on. See, however, Cockshott and Cottrell (1995), Dunne (1991), Maniatis (1996), Mohun (1996, forthcoming) and Shaikh (1998).

4 By definition, the capitalists command only investment and luxury goods, even if these goods are identical to the necessities consumed by the workers. This *ex post* distinction between luxuries and necessities is similar to the distinction between consumption and investment goods in the national accounts.

5 Weeks (1981, pp. 64, 71–72). It follows that: 'The rate of surplus value exists as a social aggregate, independently of any particular industry. This follows from the social nature of the value of labour power, so that it is incorrect to conceive of the rate of surplus value varying across industries and the aggregate to be a mere weighted average of rates in different industries' (p. 170). For a contrasting view, see Duménil (1980, pp. 76–77) and Gerstein (1986, p. 65).

6 'Surplus value presents itself (has its real existence) in a surplus-produce in excess of the quantity of products which only replace its original elements, that is, which enter into its production costs and—taking constant and variable capital together—are equal to the total capital advanced to production' (*Theories of Surplus Value 1*, p. 213). See also pp. 389–390 and *Capital 1*, pp. 978, 992.

7 Weeks (1981, p.15). This definition implies that the surplus is independent from the level and composition of the output. For Wright (1981, p. 150), 'Exploitation can thus be defined as a social relationship within which surplus labour is appropriated through the domination of labour and the appropriation of surplus products. Since labour once performed is materially embodied in the products of labour, we can speak in shorthand of exploitation as the process of appropriation of surplus labour.' See also Chattopadhyay (1994, p. 6; 2000) and Lapides (1998, p. 181).

8 Postone (1993, p. 125) rightly argues that in 'capitalism social labour is not only the object of domination and exploitation but is itself the essential ground of domination.' See also Chattopadhyay (1994, p. 14) and Milonakis (1993–94).

9 See M. Smith (1994a, pp. 52–54), Rubin (1975, pp. 67, 78, 168, 251), Shaikh (1982, p. 69) and de Vroey (1981, p. 195).

10 *Capital 1*, p. 680. Weeks (1981, p. 45) rightly argues that the 'appropriation of unpaid labor—direct and obvious in systems of slavery and serfdom—appears as the exchange of equivalents under capitalism; this façade of equality reflects a façade of private property for all, and conceals the fact that the only property of the worker is his or her capacity to labor. Further, this "property" alienable by the worker can only be sold to capitalists. The law of exchange under capitalism is as follows: capitalists exchange at value and appropriate surplus value and accumulate; workers exchange at value and surrender unpaid labor.' For Marx's own exposition of his theory of surplus value, see *Capital 1*, pp. 263–270, 300–302, 317–320, 668–672, *Capital 2*, p. 461, *Theories of Surplus Value 1*, pp. 45–46, 315 and Marx (1988b, p. 85; 1998, p. 47). See also Aglietta (1979, pp. 46–47), Chattopadhyay (1994, p. 20; 1998, p. 235), Roberts (1996, pp. 206–207) and Shaikh (1977, pp. 120–121).

11 'In their attempts at reducing the working day to its former rational dimensions, or, where they cannot enforce a legal fixation of a normal working day, at checking overwork by a rise of wages . . . working men . . . set limits to the tyrannical usurpations of capital. Time is the room of human development. A man who has no free time to dispose of, whose whole lifetime, apart from the mere physical interruptions by sleep, meals, and so forth, is absorbed by his labour for the capitalist, is less than a beast of burden. He is a mere machine for producing Foreign Wealth, broken in body and brutalised in mind. Yet the whole history of modern industry shows that capital, if not checked, will recklessly and ruthlessly work to cast down the whole working class to this utmost state of degradation' (Marx 1998, pp. 60–61).

12 See *Capital 1*, pp. 430–437, 645–646, *Theories of Surplus Value 1*, p. 216, *Theories of Surplus Value 2*, p. 266, Aglietta (1979, p. 55), Foley (1986, p. 50), and Lapides (1998, p. 192).

13 'From one standpoint the distinction between absolute and relative surplus-value appears to be illusory. Relative surplus-value is absolute, because it requires the absolute prolongation of the working day beyond the labour-time necessary to the existence of the worker himself. Absolute surplus-value is relative, because it requires a development of the productivity of labour which will allow the necessary labour-time to be restricted to a portion of the working day. But if we keep in mind the movement of surplus-value, this semblance of identity vanishes. Once the capitalist mode of production has become the established and universal mode of production, the difference between absolute and relative surplus-value makes itself felt whenever there is a question of raising the rate of surplus-value. Assuming that labour-power is paid for at its value, we are confronted with this alternative: on the one hand, if the productivity of labour and its normal degree of intensity is given, the rate of surplus-value can be raised only by prolonging the working day in absolute terms; on the other hand, if the length of the working day is given, the rate of surplus-value can be raised only by a change in the relative magnitudes of the components of the working day, i.e. necessary labour and surplus labour, and if wages are not to fall below the value of labour-power, this change presupposes a change in either the productivity or the intensity of labour' (*Capital 1*, p. 646).

14 This section draws upon Fine (1998) and Fine, Lapavitsas and Saad-Filho (2000).

15 *Capital 1*, p. 274. See pp. 275–276, 430–431, 655, *Capital 2*, pp. 290–291, 458, *Theories of Surplus Value 1*, p. 45, Marx and Engels (1998, pp. 29–30). See also Bandyopadhyay (1981), Medio (1977, p. 384) and Steedman (1977, p. 41).

16 For devastating critiques of the textual basis of this approach, see Baumol (1992), Lapides (1998) and Lebowitz (1992).

17 *Capital 2*, pp. 290–291, see also p. 245, *Theories of Surplus Value 1*, p. 315 and D. Harvey (1999, p. 47). Lebowitz (1992, p. 17) rightly claims that 'Nothing could be further from Marx than the belief in a fixed set of necessaries. From his earliest days, Marx rejected a concept of "Abstract Man" and stressed the emergence of new human needs with the development of society'.

18 Foley (1982, p. 43). See also Duménil (1980, pp. 31, 77; 1984, p. 341), Foley (1986, p. 36) and Lipietz (1982, p. 75).

19 'The wage . . . [is the] working-class power to impose its needs, and the extent of that power is only determined by the class struggle itself (Cleaver 1984, p. xxiv). See also D. Harvey (1999, pp. 52–54).

20 *Theories of Surplus Value 3*, p. 94; see also *Theories of Surplus Value 2*, p. 418.

21 Fine (1980, pp. 22–23). See also *Capital 1*, pp. 712–713, *Theories of Surplus Value 1*, p. 315, Gleicher (1989), Rowthorn (1980, pp. 38–39) and Saad-Filho (1996a).

22 Fine (1989, pp. 52–53).

23 Meek (1973, p. 215).

24 The following paragraphs draw on Fine, Lapavitsas and Saad-Filho (2000). De Brunhoff (1978a, p. 12) rightly claims that 'it is often the case that attempts to produce a theory of wages lead to two conflicting positions either by tying

the wage to the value of labour-power and seeking to produce a more or less accurate quantitative estimate of its value, or by considering the wage as an "exogenous variable", dependent upon struggles over the share of the social product. The "economism" of the bundle of goods perspective and the "sociologism" of the struggle over distribution approach can both find some basis in one or another of Marx's formulations.'

25 *Theories of Surplus Value 2*, p. 419. See also Weeks (1984).

26 '[T]he development of new needs for workers under capitalism means that . . . each new need becomes a new requirement to work, adds a new burden. *Each new need becomes a new link in the golden chain which secures workers to capital.* The creation of new needs for workers . . . "is an essential civilizing moment, and on which the historic justification, but *also the contemporary power of capital rests*" . . . *In short, the existence of unfulfilled social needs underlies the worker's need for more money, her need for a higher wage*' (Lebowitz 1992, pp. 25, 30). See also pp. 27–29, P. Harvey (1983), Lapides (1998), Ong (1980, pp. 266–267) and Rowthorn (1980, ch. 7).

27 See Fine (1998), Fine and Heasman (1997) and Fine and Leopold (1993); for an assessment, see Saad-Filho (2000b).

28 See *Capital 1*, pp. 763, 770–771, 790.

5 Values, prices and exploitation

1 See Saad-Filho (1993a, 1997a); see also Lee (1990).

2 Systems of provision are discussed by Fine and Leopold (1993); commodity chains are analysed by Gereffi and Korzeniewicz (1994).

3 *Capital 1*, pp. 439–441, emphasis added. See also pp. 442, 453, 953–954, Aumeeruddy, Lautier and Tortajada (1978, p. 54), Elson (1979b, pp. 137–138) and Thompson (1967). Lebowitz (1992, pp. 67, 69, see also p. 78) rightly argues that collective work increases the productivity of labour, and capital reaps the benefits: '*any co-operation and combination of labour in production generates a combined, social productivity of labour which exceeds the sum of individual, isolated productivities* . . . Thus, in capitalism, the productive forces of social labour—collective unity in co-operation, combination in the division of labour, the uses of the forces of nature and the sciences—appear as productive forces of capital, the mediator. What capital secures is the productive power of socially combined labour, which appears as a productive power inherent in capital.'

4 *Capital 1*, pp. 464–465. In other words, 'Every kind of capitalist production . . . has this in common . . . it is not the worker who employs the conditions of his work, but rather the reverse, the conditions of work employ the worker. However, it is only with the coming of machinery that this inversion first acquires a technical and palpable reality. Owing to its conversion into an automaton, the instrument of labour confronts the worker during the labour process in the shape of capital, dead labour, which dominates and soaks up living labour-power' (*Capital 1*, p. 548). See also pp. 468–469, 1012 and Aglietta (1979, p. 113).

5 By definition, firms within the same branch or sector produce the same use values.

6 'If we take spinning, for example, we see that it may be performed at a rate that either falls *below* or rises *above* the social average . . . But if the spinning is

carried out with a degree of intensity normal in this particular *sphere*, e.g. if the labour expended on producing a certain amount of yarn in an hour = the normal quantity of yarn that an hour's spinning will produce on average in the given social conditions, then the labour objectified in the yarn is *socially necessary labour*. As such it has a quantitatively determinate relation to the social average in general which acts as the standard, so that we can speak of the same amount or a greater or smaller one. It itself therefore expresses a *definite quantum* of average labour' (*Capital 1*, p. 1019).

7 'If our "anyone" makes a thing which has no use value for other people, his whole force does not produce an atom of value; and if he insists on producing by hand an object which a machine produces twenty times cheaper, nineteen-twentieths of the force he puts into it produces neither value in general nor any determinate magnitude of value' (Engels 1998, p. 240).

8 'The labour-time required for the production of the cotton, the raw material of the yarn, is part of the labour necessary to produce the yarn, and is therefore contained in the yarn. The same applies to the labour embodied in the spindle, without whose wear and tear the cotton could not be spun . . . Hence in determining the value of the yarn, or the labour-time required for its production, all the special processes carried on at various times and in different places which were necessary, first to produce the cotton and the wasted portion of the spindle, and then with the cotton and the spindle to spin the yarn, may together be looked on as different and successive phases of the same labour process. All the labour contained in the yarn is past labour; and it is a matter of no importance that the labour expended to produce its constituent elements lies further back in the past than the labour expended on the final process, the spinning' (*Capital 1*, p. 294).

9 *Capital 1*, pp. 660–661. See also p. 987 and *Theories of Surplus Value 3*, pp. 307–308.

10 *Capital 1*, p. 135. See also p. 306, *Contribution*, pp. 272–273, Marx (1976, p. 9), P. Harvey (1983) and Rubin (1975, pp. 156, 161).

11 See Böhm-Bawerk (1949, pp. 81–84) and Meek (1973, pp. 240–241).

12 See, respectively, Meek (1973, pp. 171–176) and Rosdolsky (1977, ch. 31); and Hilferding (1949), Roncaglia (1974) and Rowthorn (1980, ch. 8). For a critical survey, see Lee (1990). See also Attewell (1984), J. Devine (1989), Fine (1998), Gerstein (1986), Giussani (1986), D. Harvey (1999, p. 61), P. Harvey (1985), Itoh (1987), Marglin (1974) and Tortajada (1977).

13 See Attewell (1984, pp. 115–117), Fine (1998, chs 7–10) and Lapides (1998, p. 189).

14 See P. Harvey (1985, pp. 84–90).

15 P. Harvey (1985, p. 90). For Nell (1992, p. 56 n. 4), 'Concrete labor is the practical work of producing use-values; abstract labor is the condition of being exploited, measured as the amount of time in simple labor equivalents spent working in that status. A good deal of academic labor has been expended on the question of determining the reduction of skilled to simple labor. It is not clear that such labor is socially necessary; Marx regarded the reduction as exogenous to value theory.'

16 In other words, the higher profitability of firms with more advanced technology is due to the greater value-creating capacity of their own employees, rather than transfers from their competitors. For a contrasting view, see Indart (n.d.).

17 *Capital 3*, p. 1021.
18 New technologies also allow firms to introduce new goods or to improve the quality of existing goods. However, these aspects of competition are ignored here because they merely replicate the same processes across new markets.
19 'Capital therefore has an immanent drive, and a constant tendency, towards increasing the productivity of labour, in order to cheapen commodities and, by cheapening commodities, to cheapen the worker himself' (*Capital 1*, pp. 436–437).
20 *Capital 1*, p. 492.
21 Postone (1993, p. 332); see also pp. 47–48. Broadly speaking, capital controls the workers in three ways: (a) capital owns the means of production, whereas the workers must seek paid employment in order to survive; (b) having purchased the workers' labour power, capital claims the right to control the labour process in its entirety; (c) ownership of the means of production and control over the production process allow capital to influence strongly the state, economic policy, the legal system, and other social institutions. These forms of domination are invariably contested; for example, the workers constantly strive for alternatives to paid employment and subordination in the workplace, seek higher wages and better working conditions, and may engage in collective activity in order to defend their interests in the production line and elsewhere. See also Bahr (1980, p. 102), Brighton Labour Process Group (1977) and Marglin (1974).
22 'Capital's priority for automation is to attack those stages of the productive cycle which have the most space for workers to hold down their own pace of work, those sites with the most "porosity of labour" – be it clerical offices, paint, trim and assembly shops, or stock rooms. It is this selectivity which defines the threat posed to working class collective power by restructuring' (Levidow and Young 1981, p. 2). See also *Capital 1*, pp. 486, 508.
23 Nell (1992, p. 54). In other words, 'The process of industrialization, as it achieves more and more advanced levels of technological progress, coincides with a continual growth of the capitalist's *authority*. As the means of production, counterposed to the worker, grow in volume, the necessity grows for the capitalist to exercise an absolute control' (Panzieri 1980, p. 48). See also *Capital 1*, pp. 526–527, 553–554 and Uno (1980, pp. 30–31).
24 '[W]e propose to take all the important decisions and planning which vitally affect the output of the shop out of the hands of the workmen, and centralise them in a few men, each of whom is especially trained in the art of making these decisions and in seeing that they are carried out, each man having his own particular function in which he is supreme, and not interfering with the functions of other men' (Frederick W. Taylor, cited in Sohn-Rethel 1978, p.151). For a Marxian critique, see P. Taylor (1979) and Wennerlind (2000).
25 '[The industrialists aim to stop any] process which requires peculiar dexterity and steadiness of hand from the cunning workman, and put it in the charge of a mechanism so self-regulating, that a child may superintend it. The grand object therefore of the manufacturer is, through the union of capital and science, to reduce the task of his workpeople to the exercise of vigilance and dexterity [appropriate to a child]' (Andrew Ure, *Philosophy of Manufactures*, cited in Cooley 1981, p. 60).
26 'As the case studies proliferate, the evidence accumulates against a techno-logical-determinist reading of organizational history and in favor of a conflict

approach that views organizational structures as embodiying strategies for controlling workers' behavior' (Attewell 1984, p. 119). See also Bowles and Gintis (1977, p. 180), Brighton Labour Process Group (1977), Cleaver (1979, 1992), Lebowitz (1992), Marglin (1974), Naples (1989, p. 149), Postone (1993), Sohn-Rethel (1978) and Wennerlind (2000).

27 *Capital 1*, pp. 562–563, see also pp. 489–492. For modern accounts of the role of technology in social conflicts, see Levidow and Young (1981, 1985) and Slater (1980).

28 *Capital 1*, p. 545, see also pp. 470–471.

29 See Attewell (1984, p. 96) and D. Harvey (1999, pp. 59, 109).

30 *Capital 1*, pp. 1013–1014. See also pp. 1021, 1024, 1034, 1039–1040 and Gleicher (1985–86, p. 466).

31 See D. Harvey (1999, pp. 108–109).

32 Brighton Labour Process Group (1977, p. 19). See also Attewell (1984), Coombs (1985), Schwarz (1985) and Spencer (2000).

33 Bahr (1980, p. 106). See also Braverman (1974), Elger (1979) and Laibman (1976).

34 *Capital 1*, pp. 294–295; see also *Capital 2*, p. 186 and *Theories of Surplus Value 3*, p. 279.

35 *Capital 3*, p. 238. For similar statements, see *Capital 1*, pp. 129–130, 317–318, 676–677, *Capital 2*, pp. 185–188, 222–223, 366–368, *Capital 3*, p. 522, *Theories of Surplus Value 1*, pp. 232–233, *Theories of Surplus Value 2*, p. 416, *Theories of Surplus Value 3*, p.280, *Grundrisse*, pp. 135, 402, 657, and Marx's letter to Engels dated 14 September 1851 (cited in Rosdolsky 1977, p. 318 n. 3). For an exhaustive survey of Marx's texts, see Moseley (2000b). See also, *inter alia*, Gleicher (1989, p. 77), D. Harvey (1999, p. 15), Mattick Jr. (1991–92, pp. 37–38), Perelman (1993, p. 89), Reuten and Williams (1989, p. 71), Saad-Filho (1997a), Shaikh (1977, p. 113n), M. Smith (1994a, pp. 96–98; 1994b, pp. 119–122) and Wolfstetter (1973, p. 795).

36 *Theories of Surplus Value 1*, p. 96; see also Capital 2, pp. 196, 458.

37 See, for example, Cohen (1981) and Mirowski (1989).

38 See *Capital 1*, pp. 307–308 and *Theories of Surplus Value 3*, p. 167.

39 'You are altogether in the wrong track, if you think that he [the worker] loses a single moment of his working day in reproducing or replacing the values of the cotton, the machinery and so on. On the contrary, it is because his labour converts the cotton and the spindles into yarn, because he spins, that the values of the cotton and spindles go over to the yarn of their own accord. This is a result of the quality of his labour, not of its quantity' (*Capital 1*, pp. 335–336). See also Aglietta (1979, pp. 44–45, 53, 276).

40 Constant capital is the value of the machines and other material (non-labour) inputs used up in production. Circulating capital is the value of the inputs consumed in each turnover, including constant and variable capital (wage costs) and the depreciation of fixed capital. Fixed capital is the value of the material inputs that last longer than one turnover, e.g., buildings and machinery. Fixed capital depreciates in two different ways, physically, when it is used (or simply by ageing, e.g., corrosion), and technically, if new machines, etc., can produce the output at lower cost (see Perelman 1987, ch. 5 and Weeks 1981, pp. 174–186).

41 *Capital 1*, p. 295. See also pp. 312, 317–318, 957, 985–986, *Theories of Surplus Value 1*, p. 109, *Theories of Surplus Value 3*, p. 280 and de Vroey (1981, p. 180).

42 Marx (1988b, pp. 79–80).
43 See *Capital 3*, p. 374.
44 '[I]n addition to the material wear and tear, a machine also undergoes what we might call a moral depreciation. It loses exchange-value, either because machines of the same sort are being produced more cheaply than it was, or because better machines are entering into competition with it. In both cases, however young and full of life the machine may be, its value is no longer determined by the necessary labour-time actually objectified in it, but by the labour-time necessary to reproduce either it or the better machine. It has therefore been devalued to a greater or lesser extent' (*Capital 1*, p. 528). See also p. 318, *Capital 2*, pp. 185, 250, *Theories of Surplus Value 2*, p. 495 and *Theories of Surplus Value 3*, p. 154.
45 Perelman (1993, p. 88). See also Postone (1993, pp. 289–295).
46 '[A] large part of the existing capital is always being more or less devalued in the course of the reproduction process, since the value of commodities is determined not by the labour-time originally taken by their production, but rather by the labour-time that their reproduction takes, and this steadily decreases as the social productivity of labour develops. At a higher level of development of social productivity, therefore, all existing capital, instead of appearing as the result of a long process of capital accumulation, appears as the result of a relatively short reproduction period' (*Capital 3*, p. 522). See also *Capital 2*, pp. 187–188, *Capital 3*, p. 356, *Theories of Surplus Value 2*, p. 416, *Theories of Surplus Value 3*, p. 389 and de Vroey (1981, p. 182).
47 Perelman (1999, pp. 724–725).
48 See Campbell (1998, p. 141), Fine (1980, ch. 4, 1989, ch. 9) and Perelman (1990, 1993, 1996, 1999).
49 Perelman (1999, p. 723). In other words, 'the effect of competition is both to force the introduction of new methods of production and to restrict the ability of enterprises . . . to gain from technical change' (Weeks 1992, p. 20). See also Aglietta (1980).
50 There are three reduction problems in Marx's theory of value and, correspondingly, three transformation problems. First, the value-equalisation of concrete labours performed in the same sector, or normalisation. Second, the translation of technical into value differences, or synchronisation. Third, the averaging out of these averages across different branches of the economy, or homogenisation. Only the third problem has been discussed extensively in the literature (see below, chapter 7 and Reuten 1999, p. 110).
51 For Elson (1979b, pp. 136, 138), 'the labour-time that can be directly measured in capitalist economies in terms of hours, quite independent of price, is the particular labour-time of particular individuals . . . This is not the aspect objectified as value, which is its social and abstract aspect . . . The social necessity of labour in a capitalist economy cannot be determined independently of the price-form: hence values cannot be calculated or observed independently of prices . . . Thus far from entailing that the *medium* of measurement of value must be labour-time, the argument that labour-time is the (immanent) measure of value entails that labour-time *cannot* be the medium of measurement. For we cannot, in the actual labour-time we can observe, separate the abstract from the concrete aspect.' See also Gerstein (1986, p. 52) and Roberts (1996, p. 203).
52 *Capital 1*, p. 187.
53 *Capital 1*, p. 196.

54 *Capital 3*, p. 202. See also pp. 288–289, *Capital 3*, pp. 286, 774–775, *Theories of Surplus Value 1*, pp. 231–232 and Shaikh (1984, p. 266 n. 10).

55 *Capital 3*, pp. 288–289. In other words, '*Price* . . . is distinguished from *value* not only as the nominal from the real; not only by way of the denomination in gold and silver, but because the latter appears as the law of the motions which the former runs through. But the two are constantly different and never balance out, or balance only coincidentally and exceptionally. The price of a commodity constantly stands above or below the value of the commodity, and the value of the commodity itself exists only in this up-and-down movement of commodity prices. Supply and demand constantly determine the prices of commodities; never balance, or only coincidentally; but the cost of production, for its part, determines the oscillations of supply and demand . . . On the assumption that the production costs of a commodity and the production costs of gold and silver remain constant, the rise or fall of its market price means nothing more than that a commodity, = x labour time, constantly commands > or < x labour time on the market, that it stands above or beneath its average value as determined by labour time' (*Grundrisse*, pp. 137–138). See also Marx (1989, p. 537), Rosdolsky (1977, pp. 89–93), Shaikh (1981, pp. 276–278), Shamsavari 1991, p. 256), Uno (1980, p. 79) and, especially, Rubin (1975, pp. 180–185, 203–209, 224).

56 *Capital 3*, p. 352, emphasis added.

57 *Theories of Surplus Value 2*, pp. 295–296.

58 See *Capital 3*, p. 275, Shaikh (1977, pp. 106, 121; 1982, p. 72), de Vroey (1981, p. 191) and Yaffe (1974, pp. 33–34).

6 Composition of capital

1 The interpretation in this chapter derives from, and substantiates, previous work by Fine (1983) and Saad-Filho (1993b). See also Aglietta (1979, p.56), Cleaver (1992), Fine and Harris (1979, ch. 4), Fine (1989, ch. 10; 1990; 1992), Meacci (1992) and Weeks (1981, ch. 8).

2 Sweezy (1968, p.66).

3 See Bortkiewicz (1949), Desai (1989, 1992) and Seton (1957).

4 See Morishima (1973).

5 See Okishio (1974).

6 See Bortkiewicz (1952), Howard (1983), Lipietz (1982), Meek (1956; 1973, p. 313) and Winternitz (1948).

7 See Roemer (1979).

8 Shaikh (1977, p. 123); see also Shaikh (1973, p. 38).

9 See Foley (1986, p. 45), Mage (1963), M. Smith (1994a, p. 149) and Wright (1977, p. 203).

10 See Groll and Orzech (1987, 1989); see also Fine (1990).

11 See *Capital 1*, pp. 136–137, 332, 431, 773, 959 and *Capital 3*, p. 163.

12 *Capital 3*, p. 244. See also *Theories of Surplus Value 2*, pp. 455–456.

13 *Theories of Surplus Value 3*, p. 387. 'Organic' indicates the 'intrinsic' composition of capital. When analysing the general rate of profit (see chapter 7), Marx says: 'Because the rate of profit measures surplus value against the total capital . . . surplus value itself appears . . . as having arisen from the total capital, and uniformly from all parts of it at that, so that the *organic* distinction between

constant and variable capital is obliterated in the concept of profit' (*Capital 3*, p. 267, emphasis added).

14 *Theories of Surplus Value 3*, p. 382. See also *Theories of Surplus Value 2*, pp. 276, 279.

15 *Theories of Surplus Value 3*, pp. 383–386, various paragraphs; see also *Theories of Surplus Value 2*, pp. 376–377.

16 *Theories of Surplus Value 1*, pp. 415–416.

17 See D. Harvey (1999, p. 126) and Weeks (1981, pp. 197–201).

18 *Theories of Surplus Value 3*, p. 386. Alternatively, 'With capitals in *different branches of production*—with an otherwise equal physical [technical] composition—it is possible that the higher *value* of the machinery or of the material used, may bring about a difference. For instance, if the cotton, silk, linen and wool {industries} had exactly the same physical composition, the mere difference in the cost of the material used could create such a variation' (*Theories of Surplus Value 2*, p. 289).

19 *Capital 3*, p. 244, emphasis added.

20 See Fine (1989, pp. 62–63).

21 *Capital 3*, pp. 900–901.

22 '[W]e immediately see, if the price of the dearer raw material falls down to the level of that of the cheaper one, that these capitals are none the less similar in their technical composition. The value ratio between variable and constant capital would then be the same, although no change had taken place in the technical proportion between the living labour applied and the quantity and nature of the conditions of labour required' (*Capital 3*, p. 900).

23 *Theories of Surplus Value 3*, p. 387.

24 For example: 'in this part of the work we . . . assume in each case that the productivity of labour remains constant. In effect, *the value-composition* of a capital invested in a branch of industry, that is, a certain proportion between the variable and constant capital, *always expresses a definite degree of labour productivity*. As soon, therefore, as this proportion is altered by means *other* than a mere change in the value of the material elements of the constant capital, or a change in wages, the productivity of labour must likewise undergo a corresponding change' (*Capital 3*, pp. 50–51, emphasis added).

25 *Capital 1*, p. 762. Alternatively, 'The *organic* composition of capital is the name we give to its value composition, in so far as this is determined by its technical composition and reflects it' (*Capital 3*, p. 245).

26 Although the three compositions change simultaneously, in logical terms the TCC changes first, and this shift is reflected by the OCC and, subsequently, the VCC.

27 In the *Grundrisse* Marx was already aware of this, but he had not yet defined the concepts necessary to to develop the analysis of the composition of capital: 'if the total value of the capital remains the same, an increase in the productive force means that the constant part of capital (consisting of machinery and material) grows relative to the variable, i.e. to the part of capital which is exchanged for living labour and forms the wage fund. This means at the same time that a smaller quantity of labour sets a larger quantity of capital in motion' (p. 389, emphasis omitted). In p. 831 he adds: 'The fact that in the development of the productive powers of labour the objective conditions of labour, objectified labour, must grow relative to living labour . . . appears from

the standpoint of capital not in such a way that one of the moments of social activity—objective labour—becomes the ever more powerful body of the other moment, of subjective, living labour, but rather . . . that the objective conditions of labour assume an ever more colossal independence, represented by its very extent, opposite living labour, and that social wealth confronts labour in more powerful portions as an alien and dominant power' (see pp. 388–398, 443, 707 and 746–747). See also Chattopadhyay (1994, pp. 37–38), Fine (1989, pp. 60–63), D. Harvey (1999, pp. 127–128), Reuten and Williams (1989, p. 120) and Uno (1980, pp. 52–53).

28 See section 5.2, Carchedi (1984, 1991), Fine (1990, 1992), Moseley (2000b) and Weeks (1981, ch.8).
29 *Theories of Surplus Value 2*, p. 495. See also *Capital 2*, p. 185, *Theories of Surplus Value 3*, p. 154 and Bologna (1993b).
30 *Capital 1*, pp. 773–774. See also *Capital 3*, pp. 317–319, 322–323.
31 *Capital 1*, p. 781. Moreover, 'Since the demand for labour is determined not by the extent of the total capital but by its variable constituent alone, that demand falls progressively with the growth of the total capital, instead of rising in proportion to it, as was previously assumed. It falls relatively to the magnitude of the total capital, and at an accelerated rate, as this magnitude increases. With the growth of the total capital, its variable constituent, the labour incorporated in it, does admittedly increase, but in a constantly diminishing proportion' (*Capital 1*, pp. 781–82).
32 See Fine (1989, ch. 10; 1992).

7 Transformation of values into prices of production

1 The literature on the transformation is vast, and there is neither need nor space for a survey here. See, however, Desai (1989, 1992), Dostaler and Lagueux (1985), Elson (1979a), Fine and Harris (1979, ch. 2), Freeman and Carchedi (1996), Howard and King (1991, chs 12–14), Laibman (1973), Mandel and Freeman (1984), Mohun (1995), Schwartz (1977), Steedman (1981) and Sweezy (1949).
2 See, for example, Böhm-Bawerk (1949), Samuelson (1957, 1971) and Steedman (1977).
3 See chapter 2 and Arthur and Reuten (1998), Baumol (1974, 1992), Duménil (1980), Fine (1986a), Foley (1982, 1986), Kliman and McGlone (1988), Moseley (1993), Moseley and Campbell (1997), Ramos-Martínez and Rodríguez-Herrera (1996), Shaikh (1977, 1981, 1982), Wolff, Roberts and Callari (1982, 1984) and Yaffe (1974).
4 This reading develops the approach first proposed by Fine (1983); see also Fine (1980, pp. 120–121; 1989, pp. 76–77) and Saad-Filho (1997b). For similar (though not necessarily identical) views, see Albritton (1984, pp. 165–166; 1986, pp. 60–61), Likitkijsomboon (1995, pp. 95–96), Postone (1993, p.271), Reuten (1993, pp. 101–102), Rubin (1975, pp. 223, 231, 241, 247–248) and T. Smith (1990, pp. 167–168, 170–172).
5 See *Capital 3*, pp. 42, 49, 50, 247.
6 See *Capital 3*, p. 161.
7 *Capital 3*, p. 243, emphasis added. See also *Theories of Surplus Value 2*, p. 384.
8 *Capital 3*, pp. 237–238, emphasis added. Marx recognises explicitly that several factors may influence the profitability of capital. Assuming equal rates of surplus

value, 'the amount of surplus-value produced by capitals of equal size varies *firstly* according to the correlation of their organic components, i.e., of variable and constant capital; *secondly* according to their period of circulation in so far as this is determined by the ratio of fixed capital to circulating capital and also {by} the various periods of reproduction of the different sorts of fixed capital; *thirdly* according to the duration of the actual period of production as distinct from the duration of labour-time itself, which again may lead to substantial differences between the length of the production period and circulation period. (The first of these correlations, namely, that between constant and variable capital, can itself spring from a great divergency of causes; it may, for example, be purely formal so that the raw material worked up in one sphere is dearer than that worked up in another, or it may result from the varying productivity of labour, etc.)' (*Theories of Surplus Value 2*, p. 28). However, for him the *quantity* of labour in motion is analytically the most important cause of differences in profitability (see below). See also pp. 23, 28, 175–178, 198, 381–391, 426–427, *Capital 3*, pp. 142–145, 246–248, *Theories of Surplus Value 3*, p. 177, Marx (1985, pp. 22–24), Himmelweit and Mohun (1978, pp. 70, 77) and Rubin (1975, p. 231).

9 Ben Fine (1983, p. 522) was the first to point out this essential feature of Marx's transformation: 'Because Marx discusses the transformation problem in terms of the organic composition he is concerned with the following problem: what is the effect on prices of differences across sectors in the quantities of raw materials worked up into commodities irrespective of the value of those raw materials? The transformation problem as traditionally concerned would wish to take account of differences in the values of raw materials. Usually, following on from this, account is also taken of the differences in the prices of raw materials (which differ from the differing values).' Fine concludes (p. 523) that 'Marx did not get wrong the problem that *he* posed, although it differs from the one which he is presumed to have failed to solve.'

10 'When the rate of surplus-value . . . is given, the *amount* of surplus-value depends on the organic composition of the capital, that is to say, on the *number of workers* which a capital of given value, for instance £100, employs' (*Theories of Surplus Value 2*, p. 376, emphasis added).

11 See Nell (1992, p. 55).

12 *Capital 3*, p. 254, emphasis added.

13 See *Capital 3*, pp. 137, 146, 243–246, D. Harvey (1999, p. 127) and Rubin (1975, pp. 231–247).

14 *Capital 3*, pp. 248–249. Alternatively, 'As a result of the differing organic compositions of capitals applied in different branches of production, as a result therefore of the circumstance that according to the different percentage that the variable part forms in a total capital of a given size, very different amounts of labour are set in motion by capitals of equal size, so too very different amounts of surplus labour are appropriated by these capitals, or very different amounts of surplus-value are produced by them. The rates of profit prevailing in the different branches of production are accordingly originally very different' (p. 257). See also *Capital 1*, pp. 421, 757, *Capital 3*, pp. 137–138, and *Theories of Surplus Value 3*, p. 483.

15 See *Capital 3*, pp. 257–258, 298–299, 312–313, *Theories of Surplus Value 2*, pp. 29, 64–71, 190, *Theories of Surplus Value 3*, pp. 73, 87 and *Grundrisse*, pp. 435,

547, 760. In other words, differences in the profit rates between capitals in the same sector arise because they *produce* distinct quantities of value per hour, while the equalisation of profit rates of capitals in distinct branches is due to value *transfers*: 'What competition within *the same* sphere of production brings about, is the determination of the *value of the commodity in a given sphere* by the average labour-time required in it, i.e., the creation of the *market-value*. What competition between the *different* spheres of production brings about is the *creation of the same general rate of profit in the different* spheres through the levelling out of the different market-values into market-prices, which are [*prices of production*] that are different from the actual market-values. Competition in this second instance by no means tends to assimilate the prices of the commodities to their values, but on the contrary, to reduce their values to [prices of production] that differ from these values, to abolish the differences between their values and [prices of production]' (*Theories of Surplus Value 2*, p. 208). See also pp. 126, 206–207, Shaikh (1982, p. 77) and Weeks (1981, ch. 6, 1982a).

16 See *Capital 3*, p. 257, *Theories of Surplus Value 2*, p. 190, *Grundrisse*, p. 767, Duménil (1980, pp. 10–14; 1984, p. 343), Foley (1986, p. 8), Lagueux (1985, p. 121), Roberts (1987, pp. 89–90), de Vroey (1981, p. 190; 1982, p. 45), Wolff, Roberts and Callari (1984, p. 128).

17 'Values cannot be literally transformed into prices because the two play theoretical roles at different levels of explanation; for each commodity there is thus *both* a value and a price' (Mattick Jr. 1991–92, p. 40). See also Hilferding (1949, p. 159), Rubin (1975, pp. 176, 250–257), Weeks (1981, p. 171) and Yaffe (1995, p. 85). In this sense, procedures that focus upon the aggregate equalities miss the point of the transformation.

18 See Fine (1980, p. 125); for a forceful statement, see de Vroey (1982, p. 45).

19 *Capital 3*, pp. 261–262.

20 This has been recognised by the more careful interpreters of Marx. See, for example, Baumol (1974, p. 53), Schefold (1998), Shaikh (1984, p. 44) Shamsavari (1987) and Yaffe (1974, p. 46).

21 See *Capital 3*, p. 142, Foley (1983, p. 9), Mattick Jr. (1991–92, pp. 51–52) and Uno (1980, p. 95 n. 5). In the traditional approach, the value of money is determined by the conditions of production of the money commodity (gold). Differences between them and the economy's average create a discrepancy between the 'intrinsic' value of the monetary unit and its expression in exchange, that blurs the aggregate equalities. The use of fixed capital in gold production can make this form of determination of prices very difficult to handle mathematically, robbing the traditional approach of its intuitive appeal and recourse to the use of money as a neutral unit of account.

22 Lack of understanding of these features of Marx's approach is partly responsible for the results of procedures following Bortkiewicz (1949, 1952). For example, Desai (1992, p. 17) complains that Marx's 'omission to mention the physical commodities being produced by these [five] spheres still creates a problem. Thus it is not clear where the various c_i and v_i used by these spheres come from. Also when we get p_i, the production price, it is not in terms of per unit of output but in terms of hours of labour embodied in the commodity. This is not the price we see in the market-place . . . In a way, Marx "erases" the physical input-output step in going from values to prices.'

23 See Bortkiewicz (1952, p. 56), Hodgson (1973) and Samuelson (1971, p. 418).
24 'One must . . . reject the assertion that Marx thought prices had to be *deduced* from values via his transformation calculation. Marx knew very well that his 'prices of production' were the same as the 'natural values' of classical economics . . . Thus, he does *not* accuse the classical authors of having erred in deducing their price relationships without using Marxian values in the process. Rather, the charge repeatedly reasserted is that they dealt only with "this form of appearance" . . . To Marx, prices and values are . . . not the same thing. Values are not approximations to prices nor a necessary step in their calculation. Rather, one is a surface manifestation, while the latter is intended to reveal an underlying reality' Baumol (1992, p. 56). See also Duménil (1983–84, p. 434).
25 *Capital 3*, pp. 308–309. In other words, the cost price, previously the value of the inputs, is now their *price*: 'It was originally assumed that the cost price of a commodity equalled the *value* of the commodities consumed in its production. But . . . [as] the price of production of a commodity can diverge from its value, so the cost price of a commodity, in which the price of production of others commodities is involved, can also stand above or below the portion of its total value that is formed by the value of the means of production going into it. It is necessary to bear in mind this *modified significance* of the cost price, and therefore to bear in mind too that if the cost price of a commodity is equated with the value of the means of production used up in producing it, it is always possible to go wrong' (*Capital 3*, pp. 264–265, emphasis added). See also pp. 1008–1010, *Theories of Surplus Value 3*, pp. 167–168, Mattick, Jr. (1991–92, pp. 18–19, 47–51) and Yaffe (1974, p. 46). The italicised passage highlights the shift in the concept of cost price (see section 1.1).
26 See *Capital 3*, pp. 259–265, 308–309, 990–920.
27 The concepts of price of production and general rate of profit are modified again when Marx discusses commercial capital, see section 1.1 and *Capital 3*, pp. 398–399.
28 *Capital 3*, p. 300. See also p. 268, *Capital 1*, pp. 678–679 and Marx (1998, p. 38).
29 *Capital 3*, pp. 967–968.
30 'It is often claimed that aggregate surplus-value is redistributed such that capitals . . . share in it in accordance with the amounts of capital exchanged for both labour-power and the means of production; this redistribution is supposed to occur through differences between values and prices of production. But there is no real world state which exists prior to such redistribution. Of course competition distributes aggregate surplus-value according to total capital advanced, but there is no redistribution. The process of redistribution is not a real world process, but a conceptual one which is symbolic of the theoretical transition required between concepts of a different order' (Himmelweit and Mohun 1978, p. 83). See also p. 98, *Capital 3*, pp. 311, 428–429, Himmelweit and Mohun (1981, p. 248), Salama (1984, pp. 227–233) and de Vroey (1982, p. 48). For contrasting views, see Duménil (1984), Foley (1982, p. 44), Shaikh (1977, p. 126; 1991, p. 78) and Winternitz (1948, p. 277).
31 See, for example, Bortkiewicz (1949, p. 201; 1952, p. 9), Desai (1989), Dobb (1967, pp. 532–533), Duménil (1980, pp. 8, 22–23, 51), Lipietz (1982, p. 64), Meek (1956, p. 98; 1973, pp. xxi, 191), Sweezy (1949, p. xxiv; 1968, p. 115), de Vroey (1982, p. 47) and Winternitz (1948, p. 278).

8 Money, credit and inflation

1 Marx's theory of money is analysed by Arnon (1984), de Brunhoff (1976, 1978b), Campbell (1997, 1998), Fine and Lapavitsas (2000), Foley (1975, 1983), Hilferding (1981), Itoh and Lapavitsas (1999), Lapavitsas (1994, 2000a, 2000c) and Lapavitsas and Saad-Filho (2000). See also Fine (1989, pp. 70–71), Gleicher (1983, p.100), Ilyenkov (1982, pp. 189–196, 260–279), Messori (1984), Mollo (1999), Reuten and Williams (1989, pp. 65, 84–89), Rosdolsky (1977, part II), Rosenthal (1997, chs 11, 15), Saad-Filho (1993a) and Weeks (1981, ch. 4).

2 See *Capital 1*, p. 182.

3 Fine and Lapavitsas (2000, p. 370).

4 See *Capital 1*, pp. 247–257, *Capital 2*, pp. 163–164, *Capital 3*, pp. 576–577, 592, *Theories of Surplus Value 3*, pp. 475, 490, *Contribution*, pp. 304–309, Bologna (1993c, pp. 8–9), Fine (1985–86, p. 388, 1989 pp. 79–80) and Likitkijsomboon (1995, p. 101).

5 'The first main function of gold is to supply commodities with the material for the expression of their values, or to represent their values as magnitudes of the same denomination, qualitatively equal and quantitatively comparable. It thus acts as a universal measure of value, and only through performing this function does gold, the specific equivalent commodity, become money . . . Money as a measure of value is the necessary form of appearance of the measure of value which is immanent in commodities, namely labour-time' (*Capital 1*, p. 188). See also pp. 184–196, 204 and *Grundrisse*, p. 794. De Brunhoff and Ewenczyk (1979, pp. 49–50) rightly argue that as 'measure of value and standard of prices, money gives a price form to commodities; it expresses the value of commodities in quantities of the money commodity (gold), and relates at the same time these magnitudes to a fixed unitary quantity of weight of gold, that is the standard of prices. The monetary name—the price form—expresses at the same time these two functions.'

6 The convenience of metallic currencies, including ductility, durability, and high density of value, is explained in the *Contribution*, pp. 290–291 and *Grundrisse*, pp. 166, 174–186, 387; see also A. Smith (1991, I, ch. 4).

7 See *Capital 1*, pp. 189–190.

8 See Fine (1986a), Mandel and Freeman (1984) and Schwartz (1977).

9 For a detailed review, see Saad-Filho (1993a). For further details, see Bologna (1993a,b) and Cartelier (1987).

10 '[M]oney . . . must increase just exactly and precisely as fast as all other marketable commodities put together; for if it do not do this, every commodity multipliable by the exercise of human industry faster than money itself . . . will fall in money-price; and from that instant, the greatest and most important principle in Political Economy . . . – Production the cause of Demand is expelled from our commercial system' (Gray 1848, p. 69).

11 '[B]y the adoption of the plan of exchange that is here described, goods of every kind would be made to pay for each other. Selling would be merely the act of lodging property in a particular place; buying would be merely the act of taking of it back again; and money would be merely the receipt which every man would require to keep in the interim between the period of selling and that of buying' (Gray 1831, p. 86).

12 See, *inter alia, Capital 1*, pp. 181, 188, *Contribution*, pp. 320–323 and *Grundrisse*, pp. 115, 125, 135–139, 213.

13 *Grundrisse*, p. 139.

14 See *Capital 1*, pp. 211–212 and *Contribution*, pp. 324–332. Since there is no *a priori* guarantee that the value of any specific commodity will be realised, the need to sell implies the possibility of non-sale, or the formal possibility of crises (see *Theories of Surplus Value 2*, ch. 17, Bell and Cleaver 1982, Clarke 1994 and Perelman 1987).

15 *Capital 1*, p. 226. See also pp. 222–227, *Capital 3*, p. 649, *Contribution*, pp. 344–350, *Grundrisse*, pp. 209–213, de Brunhoff (1976, pp. 31–33) and Lapavitsas (2000a). More generally, 'New forms of money only appear very gradually, and are at first rarely seen as complementary to the existing forms: they appear more as "promises of money" that are a technical device to make (real) money circulate. But as this technique spreads, its use, which was initially seen as a way of economizing on money, becomes more and more difficult to distinguish from "real" monetary use. The perspective then switches round, and the instrument is soon recognized as money. The hierarchy of money forms is thus evolutionary and the limits of money somewhat blurred; some instruments may be analyzed both as means of accelerating the circulation of money and as fully-fledged monetary forms' (Lévy-Garboua and Weymuller, in Lipietz 1985a, p. 90).

16 See *Capital 3*, pp. 432–437, 670, 701–708, Campbell (1998, pp. 137–138, 148–149), Uno (1980, p. 110) and, especially, Itoh and Lapavitsas (1999, chs 1–2) and Lapavitsas (2000b).

17 'Credit . . . is the means by which the capital of the whole capitalist class is placed at the disposal of each sphere of production, not in proportion to the capital belonging to the capitalists in a given sphere but in proportion to their production requirements—whereas in competition the individual capitals appear to be independent of each other' (*Theories of Surplus Value 2*, p. 211). See also p. 482, *Capital 3*, pp. 431–436, 566–571, 626–627, 637–640, 658, 741 and Fine (1989 pp. 79–89).

18 The following paragraphs draw upon Fine, Lapavitsas and Saad-Filho (2000) and Lapavitsas (2000a). See also *Capital 1*, pp. 213–220, *Capital 3*, pp. 578–580, 663–664, 674, *Contribution*, pp. 338–342, 394–396, *Grundrisse*, pp. 813–814, 869–870, Campbell (1998, p. 145), D. Harvey (1999, p. 12) and D. Lavoie (1986). Money supply is analysed by de Brunhoff (1971, 1978b) and Lapavitsas and Saad-Filho (2000).

19 See Ricardo (1951, ch. 27; 1966) and Schumpeter (1954, part II, ch. 6 and part III, ch. 6).

20 See *Contribution*, pp. 352–356, Cottrell (1997) and Lapavitsas (2000a). De Brunhoff (1976, pp. 35–37) claims that Marx rejects the QTM entirely.

21 Marx analyses convertible money, *inter alia*, in *Capital 1*, pp. 222–227, *Capital 3*, p.649, *Contribution*, pp. 402–403 and *Grundrisse*, p. 132; see also Foley (1975, 1983, 1998).

22 See *Capital 3*, pp. 569, 572, de Brunhoff (1978a, pp. 44–45), Clarke (1994) and Lapavitsas and Saad-Filho (2000, pp. 324–326). Itoh and Lapavitsas (1999, ch. 6) identify two types of financial crisis, those that derive from and exacerbate industrial crises, and those that originate purely from the activities of the credit system.

23 Lapavitsas and Saad-Filho (2000) and Mollo (1999) show that Marx's notion of money endogeneity is broader than the better known post-Keynesian approaches outlined in Minsky (1975, 1986) and Moore (1988).
24 See *Capital 3*, pp. 418, 653–676, 685, 738, Fine (1985–86), Guttman (1994, ch. 5), D. Harvey (1999, pp. 292–293), Lianos (1987, pp. 42, 53 n. 9) and Mandel (1968, pp. 254–259).
25 Marx was fully aware of the existence of valueless forms of money, including John Law's system and the French Assignats. He does not, therefore, presume that only commodity money must exist, or that it is somehow a necessary feature of capitalism. To put it bluntly, 'money may be dirt, although dirt is not money' (*Capital 1*, p. 204). However, he does not explain how valueless money measures value.
26 'The fact that money has necessarily to be a commodity is not a matter of faith, but is based on strong theoretical foundations, laid out by Marx in the *Grundrisse* . . . if one admits that values of commodities may be measured without reference to abstract labour as a standard, one has to admit also that values of commodities are not determined by its content in abstract labour . . . Marxist authors should not let themselves be misled by the easy inductivist procedure of concluding that the money-commodity does not exist because it is not immediately visible' (Germer 1997, pp. 94, 99, 102). See also Germer (1999, p. 2), D. Harvey (1999, p. 245 n. 6), D. Lavoie (1983, p. 55, 1986, p. 155), Loranger (1982b, p. 495) and Rosdolsky (1977, pp. 83, 139).
27 See de Vroey (1985, pp. 45–46), Mattick (1978), Reuten and Williams (1989, p. 65) and Williams (1998, 2000).
28 See Saad-Filho (1996b, 1997a).
29 Labour power and other commodities not produced for profit are exceptions, see sections 2.2.1 and 4.2.
30 *Capital 3*, p. 300.
31 At a more concrete level of analysis, including distinct turnover times, the exchange value of money is influenced by the relationship between old and new values across the economy, and by the rate of technical change in each sector.
32 This section draws upon Saad-Filho (2000a); see also Howard and King (1991, ch. 16).
33 For simplicity, inflation is identified with a sustained increase of the price level accompanied by changes in relative prices. This definition is insufficient for many reasons, among them because it ignores 'hidden' inflation (when technical progress fails to reduce prices, given the quality of the goods).
34 See Moseley (1999).
35 Conflict theories are surveyed by Burdekin and Burkett (1996) and Dalziel (1990). See also Armstrong, Glyn and Harrison (1991), Boddy and Crotty (1975, 1976), Cleaver (1989), P. Devine (1974, 2000), Glyn and Sutcliffe (1972), Gordon (1981), Green and Sutcliffe (1987), Jacobi *et al.* (1975), M. Lavoie (1992, ch. 7), Marglin and Schor (1990), Morris (1973), Palley (1996), Rosenberg and Weisskopf (1981), Rowthorn (1980, chs 5–6), Sawyer (1989, pp. 359–372) and Weintraub (1981). For a critique, see de Brunhoff (1982), Fine and Murfin (1984, ch.7), Kotz (1987), Weeks (1979) and Wright (1977). Inflation can obviously induce distributive conflicts, but these will be ignored here.

36 'When unemployment . . . was reduced to a level which threatened the capitalist power of exploitation of the working class . . . inflation provided for a time . . . a substitute for the industrial reserve army as capitalism's way of maintaining its power of exploitation. Eventually, working-class reaction to the inflationary substitute for unemployment helped produce a rapid acceleration in the rate of inflation' (Morris 1973, p. 6).

37 See Fine and Leopold (1993).

38 The classic example of this synthesis is Baran and Sweezy (1966); see also Best (1972), Bryan (1985), Dollars and Sense (1978), Dowd (1976), Gamble and Walton (1976), Morris (1972), Sherman (1972, 1976a,b), Spero (1969), Sweezy and Magdoff (1979, 1983, drawing on Steindl 1952), Szymanski (1984) and Zarifian (1975). For a critique, see Aglietta (1979, pp. 26–28), Semmler (1982), Weeks (1982b) and Wright (1977). Clarke (1988) dissects the 'Keynesian state', and Bleaney (1976) critically examines theories of underconsumption.

39 For Morris (1972, pp. 18–19), rising inflation was due to the 'endless stimulation of the moribund monopoly capitalist system by ever stronger injections of monetary and fiscal anti-depressant drugs.'

40 See Hilferding (1981, ch. 15), Kalecki (1990c) and Sawyer (1985, ch. 2); for a Marxian critique, see Fine and Murfin (1984). Bleaney (1976, pp. 225–226) rightly argues that it is 'a severe problem, in writing about modern under-consumption theories, that their influence seems to have far exceeded the extent of their theoretical exposition'.

41 See, however, Mandel (1968, p. 527) and Sweezy (1974). Sweezy claims that Baran (1973) identifies the inflationary danger in Keynesian economics: government deficit financing is not sustainable in the long run because most government spending is unproductive (e.g., military expenditures). These expenditures are potentially inflationary because they increase the ratio between money and commodities (see below).

42 See Sherman (1972); for a critique, see Weisskopf *et al.* (1985). Sweezy and Magdoff (1979, p. 9) tautologically claim that 'while monopoly capital may not be the direct cause of major upward movements of prices, it is nevertheless the necessary condition for their occurrence . . . If monopoly is not the motor, it is nonetheless the *sine qua non* of the extraordinary inflation of the current decade as well as of the preceding upward spirals.'

43 The monopoly capital school has been heavily criticised by most Marxists for its use of the concept of economic surplus instead of surplus value; see section 2.1 and Weeks (1977, 1982b).

44 Aglietta (1979), Boyer (1986, ch. 10), de Brunhoff (1978a, pp. 45–48), de Brunhoff and Cartelier (1974), Ergas and Fishman (1975), Fine (1980, ch. 4), Lipietz (1985a), Loranger (1982a, 1989), Mandel (1975, ch. 13), Mattick (1978), Orléan (1982) Reuten and Williams (1989, pp. 84–87, 95–98, 148–156), de Vroey (1984) and Weeks (1981, pp. 145–148). A similar approach is outlined by Toporowski (2000), emphasising the role of capital markets. For a fuller analysis, see Saad-Filho (2000a). Many post-Keynesian writers (e.g., Moore 1988) argue that if the money supply is endogenous there cannot be excess supply of money. For a counter-argument, see Hilferding (1981, ch. 5) and Lapavitsas and Saad-Filho (2000).

45 De Vroey (1984).

46 For a similar argument, see Kalecki (1997) and Sawyer (1985, ch. 6).
47 This view is similar to Minsky's (1986), which reinforces de Vroey's (1984) argument about the potential compatibility between the extra money approach and post-Keynesian analyses.
48 For a taste of the vast literature, see Arestis and Howells (1996), Cottrell (1994) and Dow (1996); for a critique, see Lapavitsas and Saad-Filho (2000).
49 See Loranger (1982b) and Nell and Deleplace (1996).
50 See Kalecki (1990a, 1990b, 1997) and Messori (1991).
51 See Minsky (1975, 1986), Dymski and Pollin (1994) and Mollo (1999).
52 See Grou (1977), Marazzi (1977) and Mattick (1978). For an application to the Brazilian economy, see Saad-Filho and Mollo (forthcoming) and Saad-Filho and Morais (2000).

Conclusion

1 Important counter-tendencies are the diffusion of technical innovations among competing firms, the potential ability of smaller capitals to undermine the existing technologies through invention and experimentation, and foreign competition.
2 *Theories of Surplus Value 3*, p. 447, brackets omitted.
3 *Grundrisse*, pp. 708–709, see also pp. 704–706 and *Capital 3*, pp. 357–359.
4 *Contribution*, p. 264.

Bibliography

Aglietta, M. (1979) *A Theory of Capitalist Regulation, the US Experience*, London: New Left Books.

Aglietta, M. (1980) 'La Dévalorisation du Capital: Etude des Liens entre Accumulation et Inflation', *Economie Appliquée* 33, 2: 387–423.

Albritton, R. (1984) 'The Dialectic of Capital: A Japanese Contribution', *Capital & Class* 22: 157–176.

Albritton, R. (1986) *A Japanese Reconstruction of Marxist Theory*, London: Macmillan.

Albritton, R. (1999) *Dialectics and Deconstruction in Political Economy*, London: Macmillan.

Althusser, L. (1969) *For Marx*, London: New Left Books.

Althusser, L. (1970) *Reading Capital*, London: New Left Books.

Arestis, P. and Howells, P. (1996) 'Theoretical Reflections on Endogenous Money: The Problem of Convenience Lending', *Cambridge Journal of Economics* 20, 5: 539–551.

Armstrong, P., Glyn, A. and Harrison, J. (1991) *Capitalism Since 1945*, Oxford: Blackwell.

Arnon, A. (1984) 'Marx's Theory of Money, the Formative Years', *History of Political Economy* 16, 4: 555–575.

Arthur, C. (1979) 'Dialectic of the Value-Form', in D. Elson (ed.) *Value, The Representation of Labour in Capitalism*, London: CSE Books.

Arthur, C. (1992) *Marx's Capital: A Student Edition*, London: Lawrence and Wishart.

Arthur, C. (1993a) 'Hegel's "Logic" and Marx's "Capital" ', in F. Moseley (ed.) *Marx's Method in 'Capital', A Reexamination*, Atlantic Highlands, N.J.: Humanities Press.

Arthur, C. (1993b) 'Review of Ali Shamsavari's "Dialectics and Social Theory, The Logic of Capital" ', *Capital & Class* 50: 175–180.

Arthur, C. (1997) 'Against the Logical-Historical Method: Dialectical Derivation versus Linear Logic', in F. Moseley and M. Campbell (eds) *New Investigations of Marx's Method*, Atlantic Highlands, N.J.: Humanities Press.

Arthur, C. (1998) 'Engels, Logic and History', in R. Bellofiore (ed.) *Marxian Economics: a Reappraisal, Essays on Volume III of Capital*, vol. 1, London: Macmillan.

Arthur, C. (2000a) 'From the Critique of Hegel to the Critique of Capital', in T. Burns and I. Fraser (eds) *The Hegel-Marx Connection*, London: Macmillan.

Arthur, C. (2000b) *'Capital in General and Marx's "Capital"* ', unpublished manuscript.

Arthur, C. (2001) 'Value, Labour and Negativity', *Capital & Class* 73: 15–39.

Arthur, C. and Reuten, G. (eds) (1998) *The Circulation of Capital: Essays on Volume Two of Marx's Capital*, London: Macmillan.

Attewell, P.A. (1984) *Radical Political Economy, A Sociology of Knowledge Analysis*, New Brunswick, N.J.: Rutgers University Press.

Aumeeruddy, A., Lautier, B. and Tortajada, R. (1978) 'Labour Power and the State', *Capital & Class* 6: 42–66.

Aumeeruddy, A. and Tortajada, R. (1979) 'Reading Marx on Value: a Note on the Basic Texts', in in D. Elson (ed.) *Value, The Representation of Labour in Capitalism*, London: CSE Books.

Backhaus, H.-G. (1974) 'Dialectique de la Forme Valeur', *Critiques de l'Economie Politique* 18: 5–33.

Bahr, H.-D. (1980) 'The Class Structure of Machinery: Notes on the Value Form', in P. Slater (ed.) *Outlines of a Critique of Technology*, Atlantic Highlands, N.J.: Humanities Press.

Banaji, J. (1979) 'From the Commodity to Capital, Hegel's Dialectic in Marx's "Capital" ', in D. Elson (ed.) *Value, The Representation of Labour in Capitalism*, London: CSE Books.

Bandyopadhyay, P. (1981) 'In Defence of a Post-Sraffian Approach', in I. Steedman (ed.) *The Value Controversy*, London: Verso.

Baran, P. (1973) *The Political Economy of Growth*, Harmondsworth: Penguin.

Baran, P. and Sweezy, P.M. (1966) *Monopoly Capital*, New York: Monthly Review Press.

Baumol, W.J. (1974) 'The Transformation of Values. What Marx "Really" Meant (An Interpretation)', *Journal of Economic Literature* 12, 1: 51–62.

Baumol, W.J. (1983) 'Marx and the Iron Law of Wages', *American Economic Review* 73, 2: 303–308.

Baumol, W.J. (1992) 'Wages, Virtue and Value. What Marx Really Said', in G.A. Caravale (ed.) *Marx and Modern Economic Analysis*, Aldershot: Edward Elgar.

Bell, P. (1977) 'Marxist Theory, Class Struggle, and the Crisis of Capitalism' in J.G. Schwartz (ed.) *The Subtle Anatomy of Capitalism*, Santa Monica, Calif.: Goodyear.

Bell, P. and Cleaver, H. (1982) 'Marx's Crisis Theory as a Theory of Class Struggle', *Research in Political Economy* 5, 5: 189–261.

Benetti, C. and Cartelier, J. (1980) *Marchands, Salariat et Capitalistes*, Paris: Maspéro.

Best, M. (1972) 'Notes on Inflation', *Review of Radical Political Economics* 4, 4: 85–112.

Bharadwaj, K. (1986) *Classical Political Economics and Rise to Dominance of Supply and Demand Theories*, Hyderabad: Universities Press (India).

Bleaney, M. (1976) *Underconsumption Theories: A History and Critical Analysis*, London: Lawrence and Wishart.

Boddy, R. and Crotty, J. (1975), 'Class Conflict and Macro-Policy: The Political Business Cycle', *Review of Radical Political Economics* 7: 1–19.

Boddy, R. and Crotty, J. (1976), 'Wage-Push and Working-Class Power: A Reply to Howard Sherman', *Monthly Review* 27, 10: 35–43.

Böhm-Bawerk, E. von (1949) 'Karl Marx and the Close of His System', in P.M. Sweezy (ed.) *Karl Marx and the Close of His System*, Clifton, N.J.: A.M. Kelley.

Bologna, S. (1993a,b) 'Money and Crisis, Marx as Correspondent of the New York Daily Tribune, 1856–57', Parts 1 and 2, *Common Sense* 13: 29–53 and 14: 63–89.

Bologna, S. (1993c) 'La Ricerca del Gruppo di "Primo Maggio" ', in L. Berti and A. Fumagalli (eds) *L'Antieuropa delle Monete*, Rome: Manifestolibri.

Bonefeld, W. (1992) 'Social Constitution and the Form of the Capitalist State', in W. Bonefeld, R. Gunn and K. Psychopedis (eds) *Open Marxism*, London: Pluto Press.

Bonefeld, W., Gunn, R. and Psychopedis, K. (1992a,b) 'Introduction', in *Open Marxism*, 2 vols., London: Pluto Press.

Bortkiewicz, L. von (1949) 'On the Correction of Marx's Fundamental Theoretical Construction on the Third Volume of Capital', in P.M. Sweezy (ed.) *Karl Marx and the Close of His System*, Clifton, N.J.: A.M. Kelley.

Bortkiewicz, L. von (1952) 'Values and Prices in the Marxian System', *International Economic Papers* 2: 5–60.

Bottomore, T. (ed.) (1991) *A Dictionary of Marxist Thought*, 2nd edn, Oxford: Blackwell.

Bowles, S. and Gintis, H. (1977) 'The Marxian Theory of Value and Heterogeneous Labour, Critique and Reformulation', *Cambridge Journal of Economics* 1, 2: 173–192.

Bowles, S. and Gintis, H. (1981) 'Labour Heterogeneity and the Labour Theory of Value, A Reply', *Cambridge Journal of Economics* 5, 3: 285–288.

Boyer, R. (1986) *La Théorie de la Régulation: Une Analyse Critique*, Paris: La Découverte.

Bradby, B. (1982) 'The Remystification of Value', *Capital & Class* 17: 114–133.

Braverman, H. (1974) *Labour and Monopoly Capital*, New York: Monthly Review Press.

Bray, J. (1931) *Labour's Wrongs and Labour's Remedy; Or, the Age of Might and the Age of Right*, London: LSE Reprints.

Brenner, R. (1986) 'The Social Basis of Economic Development', in J. Roemer (ed.) *Analytical Marxism*, Cambridge: Cambridge University Press.

Brighton Labour Process Group (1977) 'The Capitalist Labour Process', *Capital & Class* 1: 3–26.

Brödy, A. (1974) *Proportions, Prices and Planning: A Mathematical Restatement of the Labour Theory of Value*, Amsterdam: North Holland.

Brown, A. (2001) 'Methodological and Theoretical Perspectives on Economic Growth and Crises', PhD thesis, University of Middlesex.

Brunhoff, S. de (1971) *L'Offre de Monnaie: Critique d'un Concept*, Paris: Maspéro.

Brunhoff, S. de (1973a) *La Politique Monétaire, Un Essai d'Intérpretation Marxiste*, Paris: Presses Universitaires de France.

Brunhoff, S. de (1973b) 'Marx as an a-Ricardian, Value, Money and Price at the Beginning of "Capital" ', *Economy & Society* 2, 3: 412–430.

Brunhoff, S. de (1974–75) 'Controversies in the Theory of Surplus Value, A Reply to John Eatwell', *Science & Society* 38, 4: 478–482.

Brunhoff, S. de (1976) *Marx on Money*, New York: Urizen Books.

Brunhoff, S. de (1978a) *The State, Capital and Economic Policy*, London: Pluto Press.

Brunhoff, S. de (1978b) 'La Monnaie, Puissance Sociale, Puissance Privée', *Economies et Sociétés* 1: 2163–2186.

Brunhoff, S. de (1978c) 'L'Equilibre ou la Monnaie', *Economie Appliquée* 31, 1–2: 35–59.

Brunhoff, S. de (1982) 'Questioning Monetarism', *Cambridge Journal of Economics* 6: 285–294.

Brunhoff, S. de and Cartelier, J. (1974), 'Une Analyse Marxiste de l'Inflation', *Critique Sociale de France* 4, reprinted in S. de Brunhoff (ed.) (1979) *Les Rapports d'Argent*, Grenoble: Presses Universitaires de Grenoble.

Brunhoff, S. de and Ewenczyk, P. (1979) 'La Pensée Monétaire de K. Marx au XIXè et au XXè Siècles', in S. de Brunhoff (ed.) *Les Rapports d'Argent*, Grenoble: Presses Universitaires de Grenoble.

Bryan, R. (1985) 'Monopoly in Marxist Method', *Capital & Class* 26: 72–92.

Burdekin, R. and Burkett, P. (1996) *Distributional Conflict and Inflation: Theoretical and Historical Perspectives*, London: Macmillan.

Burkett, P. (1991) 'Some Comments on "Capital in General and the Structure of Marx's Capital" ', *Capital & Class* 44: 49–72.

Callari, A. and Ruccio D. (eds) (1996) *Postmodern Materialism and the Future of Marxist Theory: Essays in the Althusserian Tradition*, Hanover: Wesleyan University Press.

Campbell, M. (1993) 'Marx's Concept of Economic Relations and the Method of "Capital" ', in F. Moseley (ed.) *Marx's Method in 'Capital', A Reexamination*, Atlantic Highlands, N.J.: Humanities Press.

Campbell, M. (1997) 'Marx's Theory of Money: A Defense', in F. Moseley and M. Campbell (eds) *New Investigations of Marx's Method*, Atlantic Highlands, N.J.: Humanities Press.

Campbell, M. (1998) 'Money in the Circulation of Capital', in C. Arthur and G. Reuten (eds) *The Circulation of Capital: Essays on Volume Two of Marx's Capital*, London: Macmillan.

Carchedi, G. (1984) 'The Logic of Prices as Values', *Economy & Society* 13, 4: 431–455.

Carchedi, G. (1991) *Frontiers of Political Economy*, London: Verso.

Cartelier, J. (1987) 'Mesure de la Valeur et Système Monétaire, La Tentative de Gray (1848) Textes et Commentaire', *Cahiers d'Economie Politique* 13: 191–208.

Carver, T. (1980) 'Translator's Foreword', in J. Zeleny (1980) *The Logic of Marx*, Oxford: Basil Blackwell.

Catephores, G. (1986) 'The Historical Transformation Problem, A Reply', in B. Fine (ed.) *The Value Dimension*, London: Routledge & Kegan Paul.

Chattopadhyay, P. (1994) *The Marxian Concept of Capital and the Soviet Experience: Essay in the Critique of Political Economy*, Westport, Conn.: Praeger.

Chattopadhyay, P. (1998) 'Value and Exploitation: Marx's Problem and Skillman's Solution', *Science & Society* 62, 2: 218–240.

Chattopadhyay, P. (1999) 'On Some Aspects of the Dialectic of Labour in the Critique of Political Economy', unpublished manuscript.

Chattopadhyay, P. (2000) 'Surplus School and Marx: On Garegnani's Marx Reading', unpublished manuscript.

Clarke, S. (1980) 'The Value of Value', *Capital & Class* 10: 1–17.

Clarke, S. (1988) *Keynesianism Monetarism and the Crisis of the State*, Aldershot: Edward Elgar.

Clarke, S. (ed.) (1991) *The State Debate*, London: CSE/Macmillan.

Clarke, S. (1994) *Marx's Theory of Crisis*, London: Macmillan.

Cleaver, H. (1979) *Reading 'Capital' Politically*, Brighton, The Harvester Press.

Cleaver, H. (1984) 'Translator's Introduction', in A. Negri, *Marx Beyond Marx, Lessons on the Grundrisse*, South Hadley, Mass.: Bergin and Garvey.

Cleaver, H. (1989) 'Close the IMF, Abolish Debt and End Development: A Class Analysis of the International Debt Crisis', *Capital & Class* 39: 17–50.

Cleaver, H. (1992) 'The Inversion of Class Perspective in Marxian Theory: From Valorisation to Self-Valorisation', in W. Bonefeld, R. Gunn and K. Psychopedis (eds) *Open Marxism*, London: Pluto Press.

Cockshott, P. and Cottrell, A. (1995) 'Testing Marx: Some New Results from UK Data', *Capital & Class* 55: 103–129.

Cohen, G.A. (1974) 'Marx's Dialectic of Labor', *Philosophy and Public Affairs* 3, 3: 235–261.

Cohen, G.A. (1981) 'The Labour Theory of Value and the Concept of Exploitation', in I. Steedman (ed.) *The Value Controversy*, London: Verso.

Colletti, L. (1972) *From Rousseau to Lenin*, London: New Left Books.

Cooley, M. (1981) 'The Taylorisation of Intellectual Work', in L. Levidow and B. Young (eds.) *Science, Techology and the Labour Process*, vol. 1, Atlantic Highlands, N.J.: Humanities Press.

Coombs, R. (1985) 'Labour and Monopoly Capital', in L. Levidow and B. Young (eds) *Science, Techology and the Labour Process*, vol. 2, Atlantic Highlands, N.J.: Humanities Press.

Cottrell, A. (1994) 'Post-Keynesian Monetary Economics', *Cambridge Journal of Economics* 18: 587–605.

Cottrell, A. (1997) 'Monetary Endogeneity and the Quantity Theory: the Case of Commodity Money', unpublished manuscript.

Cullenberg, S. (1994) 'Unproductive Labour and the Contradictory Movement of the Rate of Profit: A Comment on Moseley', *Review of Radical Political Economics* 26, 2: 111–128.

Dalziel, P. (1990) 'Market Power, Inflation, and Incomes Policies', *Journal of Post-Keynesian Economics* 12: 424–438.

Desai, M. (1989) 'The Transformation Problem', *Journal of Economic Surveys* 2, 4: 295–333.

Desai, M. (1992) 'The Transformation Problem', in G.A. Caravale (ed.) *Marx and Modern Economic Analysis*, Aldershot: Edward Elgar.

Devine, J. (1989) 'What is "Simple Labour"? A Re-examination of the Value-Creating Capacity of Skilled Labour', *Capital & Class* 39: 113–131.

Devine, P. (1974) 'Inflation and Marxist Theory', *Marxism Today* (March): 79–92.

Devine, P. (2000) 'The "Conflict Theory of Inflation" Revisited', in J. Toporowski (ed.) *Political Economy and the New Capitalism: Essays in Honour of Sam Aaronovitch*, London: Routledge.

Dmitriev, V. (1974) *Economic Essays on Value, Competition and Utility*, Cambridge: Cambridge University Press.

Dobb, M. (1940) *Political Economy and Capitalism*, London: Routledge and Kegan Paul.

Dobb, M. (1943) 'Review of *Theory of Capitalist Development*, by Paul M. Sweezy', *Science & Society* 7: 270–275.

Dobb, M. (1967) 'Marx's "Capital" and its Place in Economic Thought', *Science & Society* 31, 4: 527–540.

Dollars and Sense (1978) 'Monopolies and Inflation', in Union for Radical Political Economics (ed.) *US Capitalism in Crisis*, New York: URPE.

Dostaler, G. and Lagueux, M. (eds) (1985) *Un Echiquier Centenaire, Théorie de la Valeur et Formation des Prix*, Paris: La Découverte.

Dow, S. (1996) 'Horizontalism: A Critique', *Cambridge Journal of Economics* 20: 497–508.

Dowd, D.F. (1976) 'Stagflation and the Political Economy of Decadent Monopoly Capitalism', *Monthly Review* 28, 5: 14–29.

Duménil, G. (1980) *De la Valeur aux Prix de Production*, Paris: Economica.

Duménil, G. (1983–84). 'Beyond the Transformation Riddle: A Labor Theory of Value', *Science and Society* 33, 4: 427–450.

Duménil, G. (1984) 'The So-Called "Transformation Problem" Revisited, A Brief Comment', *Journal of Economic Theory* 33: 340–348.

Duménil, G. and Lévy, D. (1991) 'Szumski's Validation of the Labour Theory of Value, A Comment', *Cambridge Journal of Economics* 15, 3: 359–364.

Dunne, P. (ed.) (1991) *Quantitative Marxism*, Cambridge: Polity Press.

Dymski, G. and Pollin, R. (1994) *New Perspectives in Monetary Macroeconomics: Explorations in the Tradition of Hyman P. Minsky*, Ann Arbor: University of Michigan Press.

Echeverría, R. (1978) 'A Critique of Marx's 1857 Introduction', *Economy & Society* 7, 4: 333–366.

Ehrbar, H. (1989) 'Mathematics and the Labor Theory of Value', *Review of Radical Political Economics* 21, 3: 7–12.

Eldred, M. (1984) 'A Reply to Gleicher', *Capital & Class* 23: 135–137.

Eldred, M. and Hanlon, M. (1981) 'Reconstructing Value-Form Analysis', *Capital & Class* 13: 24–60.

Elger, T. (1979) 'Valorisation and "Deskilling": a Critique of Braverman', *Capital & Class* 7: 58–99.

Elson, D (ed.) (1979a) *Value, The Representation of Labour in Capitalism*, London: CSE Books.

Elson, D. (1979b) 'The Value Theory of Labour', in D. Elson (ed.) *Value, The Representation of Labour in Capitalism*, London: CSE Books.

Engels, F. (1981) 'Supplement', in K. Marx, *Capital 3*, Harmondsworth: Penguin.

Engels, F. (1998) *Anti-Dühring*, in K. Marx and F. Engels, *Classics in Politics* (CD-Rom), London: The Electric Book Company.

Ergas, H. and Fishman, D (1975) 'The Marxian Theory of Money and the Crisis of Capital', *Bulletin of the Conference of Socialist Economists* IV, 2, 11.

Faccarello, G. (1986) 'Sraffa versus Ricardo, The Historical Irrelevance of the "Corn-Profit" Model', in B. Fine (ed.) *The Value Dimension*, London: Routledge & Kegan Paul.

Fine, B. (1980) *Economic Theory and Ideology*, London: Edward Arnold.

Fine, B. (1982) *Theories of the Capitalist Economy*, London: Edward Arnold.

Fine, B. (1983) 'A Dissenting Note on the Transformation Problem', *Economy & Society* 12, 4: 520–525.

Fine, B. (1985–86) 'Banking Capital and the Theory of Interest', *Science & Society* 49, 4: 387–413.

Fine, B. (ed.) (1986a) *The Value Dimension, Marx versus Ricardo and Sraffa*, London: Routledge & Kegan Paul.

Fine, B. (1986b) 'On the Historical Transformation Problem', in *The Value Dimension*, London: Routledge & Kegan Paul.

Fine, B. (1989) *Marx's Capital* (3rd edn), Basingstoke, Macmillan.

Fine, B. (1990) 'On the Composition of Capital, A Comment on Groll and Orzech', *History of Political Economy* 22, 1: 149–155.

Fine, B. (1992) 'On the Falling Rate of Profit', in G.A. Caravale (ed.) *Marx and Modern Economic Analysis*, Aldershot: Edward Elgar.

Fine, B. (1996) 'The Continuing Imperative of Value Theory: A Personal Account', unpublished manuscript.

Fine, B. (1997) 'The New Revolution in Economics', *Capital & Class* 61: 143–148.

Fine, B. (1998) *Labour Market Theory: A Constructive Reassessment*, London: Routledge.

Fine, B. (2001) *Social Capital versus Social Theory*, London: Routledge.

Fine, B. and Harris, L. (1979) *Rereading Capital*, London: Macmillan.

Fine, B. and Heasman, M. (1997) *Consumption in the Age of Affluence*, London: Routledge.

Fine, B. and Lapavitsas, C. (2000) 'Markets and Money in Social Theory: What Role for Economics?', *Economy and Society* 29, 3: 357–382.

Fine, B. and Leopold, E. (1993) *The World of Consumption*, London: Routledge.

Fine, B. and Murfin, A. (1984) *Macroeconomics and Monopoly Capitalism*. Brighton: Wheatsheaf.

Fine, B., Lapavitsas, C. and Milonakis, D. (2000) 'Dialectics and Crisis Theory: A Response to Tony Smith', *Historical Materialism* 6: 133–137.

Fine, B., Lapavitsas, C. and Saad-Filho, A. (2000) 'Transforming the Transformation Problem: Why the "New Solution" is a Wrong Turning', unpublished manuscript.

Flaschel, P. (1984) 'The So-Called "Transformation Problem" Revisited, A Comment', *Journal of Economic Theory* 33: 349–351.

Foley, D. (1975) *Towards a Marxist Theory of Money*, Technical report no.181, Stanford University.

Foley, D. (1982) 'The Value of Money, the Value of Labour Power and the Marxian Transformation Problem', *Review of Radical Political Economics* 14, 2: 37–47.

Foley, D. (1983) 'On Marx's Theory of Money', *Social Concept* 1, 1: 5–19.

Foley, D. (1986) *Understanding Capital, Marx's Economic Theory*, Cambridge, Mass.: Harvard University Press.

Foley, D. (1998) 'Asset Speculation in Marx's Theory of Money', in R. Bellofiore (ed.) *Marxian Economics: a Reappraisal, Essays on Volume III of Capital*, vol. 2, London: Macmillan.

Foley, D. (2000) 'Recent Developments in the Labor Theory of Value', *Review of Radical Political Economics* 32, 1: 1–39.

Fracchia, J. and Ryan, C. (1992) 'Historical-Materialist Science, Crisis and Commitment', in W. Bonefeld, R. Gunn and K. Psychopedis (eds) *Open Marxism*, vol. 2, London: Pluto Press.

Fraser, I. (1997) 'Two of a Kind: Hegel, Marx, Dialectic and Form', *Capital & Class* 61: 81–106.

Freeman, A. and Carchedi, G. (eds) (1996) *Marx and Non-Equilibrium Economics*, Aldershot: Edward Elgar.

Gamble, A. and Walton, P. (1976) *Capitalism in Crisis: Inflation and the State*, London: Macmillan.

Ganssmann, H. (1983) 'Marx Without the Labour Theory of Value', *Social Research* 50, 2: 278–304.

Ganssmann, H. (1986) 'Transformation of Physical Conditions of Production, Steedman's Economic Metaphysics', in B. Fine (ed.) *The Value Dimension*, London: Routledge & Kegan Paul.

Garegnani, P. (1985) 'La Théorie Classique de la Répartition et le Problème dit de la "Transformation" chez Marx', in G. Dostaler and M. Lagueux (eds) *Un Echiquier Centenaire, Théorie de la Valeur et Formation des Prix*, Paris: La Découverte.

Gereffi, G. and Korzeniewicz, M. (eds) (1994) *Commodity Chains and Global Capitalism*, Westport, Conn.: Praeger.

Germer, C.M. (1997) 'How Capital Rules Money—Marx's Theory of Money in Capitalism', unpublished manuscript.

Germer, C.M. (1999) 'O Conceito de 'Padrão-Ouro e os Equívocos da Economia Política', unpublished manuscript.

Gerstein, I. (1986) 'Production, Circulation and Value, The Significance of the "Transformation Problem" in Marx's Critique of Political Economy', in B. Fine (ed.) *The Value Dimension*, London: Routledge & Kegan Paul.

Giussani, P. (1986) 'Value and Labour, Simple and Complex Labour in the Labour Theory of Value', *Working Paper* no. 7, Centre for Political Science, Vrije Universiteit Brussel, Brussels.

Gleicher, D. (1983) 'A Historical Approach to the Question of Abstract Labour', *Capital & Class* 21: 97–122.

Gleicher, D. (1985) 'Note: A Rejoinder to Eldred', *Capital & Class* 24: 147–155.

Gleicher, D. (1985–86) 'The Ontology of Labour Values', *Science & Society* 49, 4:463–471.

Gleicher, D. (1989) 'Labor Specialization and the Transformation Problem', *Review of Radical Political Economics* 21, 1–2: 75–95.

Glick, M. and Ehrbar, H. (1986–87) 'The Labour Theory of Value and Its Critics', *Science & Society* 50, 4: 464–478.

Glick, M. and Ehrbar, H. (1987) 'The Transformation Problem, An Obituary', *Australian Economic Papers* 26, 49: 294–317.

Glyn, A. and Sutcliffe, B. (1972) *Workers, British Capitalism and the Profit Squeeze*, Harmondsworth: Penguin.

Goode, P. (1973) 'The Law of Value and Marx's Method', *Bulletin of the Conference of Socialist Economists* 2, 6: 65–69.

Gordon, D.M. (1981) 'Capital-Labor Conflict and the Productivity Slowdown', *American Economic Review* 71, 2: 30–35.

Gray, J. (1831) *The Social System*, Edinburgh.

Gray, J. (1848) *Lectures on the Nature and Use of Money*, Edinburgh.

Green, F. and Sutcliffe, B. (1987) *The Profit System*, Harmondsworth: Penguin.

Groll, S. and Orzech, Z. (1987) 'Technological Progress and Values in Marx's Theory of the Decline in the Rate of Profit, an Exegetical Approach', *History of Political Economy* 19, 4: 591–613.

Groll, S. and Orzech, Z. (1989) 'Stages in the Development of a Marxian Concept, the Composition of Capital', *History of Political Economy* 21, 1: 57–76.

Grossman, H. (1977) 'Marx, Classical Political Economy, and the Problem of Dynamics', *Capital & Class* 2: 32–55.

Grou, P. (1977) *Monnaie, Crise Economique*, Paris: Maspéro.

Gunn, R. (1992) 'Against Historical Materialism, Marxism as a First-Order Discourse', in W. Bonefeld, R. Gunn and K. Psychopedis (eds) *Open Marxism*, vol.2, London: Pluto Press.

Guttman, R. (1994) *How Credit-Money Shapes the Economy: The United States in a Global System*, Armonk, N.Y.: M.E. Sharpe.

Haberler, G. (1966) 'Marxian Economics in Retrospect and Prospect', *Zeitschrift für Nationalokönomie* 26: 69–82.

Harvey, D. (1999) *The Limits to Capital*, London: Verso.

Harvey, P. (1983) 'Marx's Theory of the Value of Labour Power, An Assessment', *Social Research* 50, 2: 305–344.

Harvey, P. (1985) 'The Value-Creating Capacity of Skilled Labor in Marxian Economics', *Review of Radical Political Economics* 17, 1–2: 83–102.

Hegel, G.W.F. (1991) *The Encyclopedia Logic*, Indianapolis: Hackett Publishing, Inc.

Heinrich, M. (1989) 'Marx's Theory of Capital', *Capital & Class* 38: 63–79.

Heller, A. (1976) *The Theory of Need in Marx*, London: Allison & Busby.

Hilferding, R. (1949) 'Bohm-Bawerk's Criticism of Marx', in P.M. Sweezy (ed.) *Karl Marx and the Close of His System*, Clifton, N.J.: A.M. Kelley.

Hilferding, R. (1981) *Finance Capital*, London: Routledge & Kegan Paul.

Himmelweit, S. (1991) 'Exploitation', in T. Bottomore (ed.) *A Dictionary of Marxist Thought*, 2nd edn, Oxford: Blackwell.

Himmelweit, S. and Mohun, S. (1978) 'The Anomalies of Capital', *Capital & Class* 6: 67–105.

Himmelweit, S. and Mohun, S. (1981) 'Real Abstractions and Anomalous Assumptions', in I. Steedman (ed.) *The Value Controversy*, London: Verso.

Hodgson, G. (1973) 'Marxian Epistemology and the Transformation Problem', *Economy & Society* 3, 4: 357–392.

Hodgson, G. (1981) 'Money and the Sraffa System', *Australian Economic History Review* 20, 36: 83–95.

Holloway, J. (1992) 'Crisis, Fetishism and Class Composition', in W. Bonefeld, R. Gunn and K. Psychopedis (eds) *Open Marxism*, vol. 2, London: Pluto Press.

Holloway, J. (1994) 'Global Capital and the National State', *Capital & Class* 52: 23–50.

Howard, M. (1983) *Profits in Economic Theory*, London: Macmillan.

Howard, M.C. and King, J.E. (1989, 1991) *A History of Marxian Economics*, 2 vols, London: Macmillan.

Ilyenkov, E.V. (1977) *Dialectical Logic: Essays on Its History and Theory*, Moscow: Progress Publishers.

Ilyenkov, E.V. (1982) *The Dialectics of the Abstract and the Concrete in Marx's 'Capital'*, Moscow: Progress Publishers.

Indart, G. (n.d.) 'The Microeconomic Foundation of the Theory of Market Value Determination', unpublished manuscript.

Itoh, M. (1987) 'Skilled Labour in Value Theory', *Capital & Class* 31: 39–58.

Itoh, M. and Lapavitsas, C. (1999) *Political Economy of Money and Finance*. London: Macmillan.

Jacobi, O. Bergmann, J. and Mueller-Jentsch, W. (1975) 'Problems in Marxist Theories of Inflation', *Kapitalistate* 3: 107–25.

Kalecki, M. (1990a) 'Political Aspects of Full Employment', in *Collected Works*, vol.1, Oxford: Clarendon Press.

Kalecki, M. (1990b) 'The Business Cycle and Inflation', in *Collected Works*, vol.1. Oxford: Clarendon Press.

Kalecki, M. (1990c) 'Essays in the Theory of Economic Fluctuations', in *Collected Works*, vol.1, Oxford: Clarendon Press.

Kalecki, M. (1997) 'Introductory Remarks on Inflationary and Deflationary Processes', in *Collected Works*, vol.7, Oxford: Clarendon Press.

Kapferer, N. (1980) 'Commodity, Science and Technology: A Critique of Sohn-Rethel', in P. Slater (ed.) *Outlines of a Critique of Technology*, Atlantic Highlands, N.J.: Humanities Press.

Kliman, A. (2000) 'Marx's Concept of Intrinsic Value', *Historical Materialism* 6: 89–113.

Kliman, A. and McGlone, T. (1988) 'The Transformation non-Problem and the non-Transformation Problem', *Capital & Class* 35: 56–83.

Kosik, K. (1976) *Dialectics of the Concrete, A Study on Problems of Man and World*, Dordrecht and Boston: D. Reidel Publishing Company.

Kotz, D.M. (1987) 'Radical Theories of Inflation', in URPE (ed.) *The Imperiled Economy. Book 1: Macroeconomics from a Left Perspective*, New York: URPE.

Lagueux, M. (1985) 'Le Principe de la Conservation de la Valeur et le Problème de la Transformation', in G. Dostaler and M. Lagueux (eds) *Un Echiquier Centenaire, Théorie de la Valeur et Formation des Prix*, Paris: La Découverte.

Laibman, D. (1973) 'Values and Price of Production, the Political Economy of the Transformation Problem', *Science & Society* 37, 4: 404–436.

Laibman, D. (1976). 'The Marxian Labor-Saving Bias, A Formalization', *Quarterly Review of Economics and Business* 16, 3: 25–44.

Lapavitsas, C. (1994) 'The Banking School and the Monetary Thought of Karl Marx', *Cambridge Journal of Economics* 18: 447–461.

Lapavitsas, C. (2000a) 'Money and the Analysis of Capitalism: The Significance of Commodity Money', *Review of Radical Political Economics* 32, 4: 631–656.

Lapavitsas, C. (2000b) On Marx's Analysis of Money Hoarding in the Turnover of Capital, *Review of Political Economy* 12, 2: 219–235.

Lapavitsas, C. (2000c) 'On the Origin of Money in the Relations of Commodity Owners with Each Other', unpublished manuscript.

Lapavitsas, C. (2000d) 'Distinguishing between Commodity and Gift', unpublished manuscript.

Lapavitsas, C. and Saad-Filho, A. (2000) 'The Supply of Credit Money and Capital Accumulation: a Critical View of Post-Keynesian Analysis', *Research in Political Economy* 18: 309–334.

Lapides, K. (1998) *Marx's Wage Theory in Historical Perspective: Its Origins, Development and Interpretation*, Westport, Conn.: Praeger.

Lavoie, D. (1983) 'Some Strengths in Marx's Disequilibrium Theory of Money', *Cambridge Journal of Economics* 7: 55–68.

Lavoie, D. (1986) 'Marx, the Quantity Theory, and the Theory of Value', *History of Political Economy* 18, 1: 155–170.

Lavoie, M. (1992) *Foundations of Post-Keynesian Economic Analysis*, Aldershot: Edward Elgar.

Leadbeater, D. (1985) 'The Consistency of Marx's Categories of Productive and Unproductive Labour', *History of Political Economy* 17, 4: 591–618.

Lebowitz, M. (1992) *Beyond Capital, Marx's Political Economy of the Working Class*, London: Macmillan

Lebowitz, M. (1994) 'The Theory of the Capitalist State', unpublished manuscript.

Lee, C.-O. (1990) 'On the Three Problems of Abstraction, Reduction and Transformation in Marx's Labour Theory of Value', PhD Thesis, University of London.

Lee, C.-O. (1993) 'Marx's Labour Theory of Value Revisited', *Cambridge Journal of Economics* 17, 4: 463–478.

Lenin, V.I. (1972) *Philosophical Notebooks, Collected Works*, vol. 38, London: Lawrence and Wishart.

Levidow, L. and Young, B. (1981, 1985) *Science, Technology and the Labour Process, Marxist Studies*, 2 vols., London: Free Association Books.

Lianos, T. (1987). 'Marx on the Rate of Interest', *Review of Radical Political Economics* 19, 3: 34–55.

Lipietz, A. (1982) 'The So-Called "Transformation Problem" Revisited', *Journal of Economic Theory* 26, 1: 59–88.

Lipietz, A. (1984) 'The So-Called "Transformation Problem" Revisited, A Brief Reply to Brief Comments', *Journal of Economic Theory* 33, 2: 352–355.

Lipietz, A. (1985a) *The Enchanted World: Inflation, Credit and the World Crises*, London: Verso.

Lipietz, A. (1985b) 'Le Débat sur la Valeur: Bilan Partiel et Perspectives Partiales', in G. Dostaler and M. Lagueux (eds) *Un Echiquier Centenaire, Théorie de la Valeur et Formation des Prix*, Paris: La Découverte.

Likitkijsomboon, P. (1995) 'Marxian Theories of Value-Form', *Review of Radical Political Economics* 27, 2: 73–105.

Loranger, J.-G. (1982a) 'Le Rapport entre la Pseudo-Monnaie et la Monnaie: de la Possibilité à la Réalité des Crises', *Critiques de l'Economie Politique* 18: 114–132.

Loranger, J.-G. (1982b) 'Pseudo-Validation du Crédit et Etalon Variable de Valeur', *Economie Appliquée* 35, 3: 485–499.

Loranger, J.-G. (1989) 'Circuit of Capital: a New Look at Inflation', *Review of Radical Political Economics* 21, 1–2: 97–112.

Lukács, G. (1971) *History and Class Consciousness*, London: Merlin Press.

Mage, S. (1963) 'The Law of the Falling Tendency of the Rate of Profit, Its Place in the Marxian System and Relevance to the US Economy', PhD Thesis, Columbia University.

Mandel, E. (1968), *Marxist Economic Theory*. London: Merlin Press.

Mandel, E. (1975) *Late Capitalism*, London: New Left Books.

Mandel, E. and Freeman, A. (eds) (1984) *Ricardo, Marx, Sraffa*, London: Verso.

Maniatis, T. (1996) 'Testing Marx: A Note', *Capital & Class* 59: 37–54.

Marazzi, C. (1977) 'Money in the World Crisis: The New Basis of Capitalist Power', *Zerowork* 2: 91–111.

Marglin, S. (1974) 'What Do Bosses Do?', *Review of Radical Political Economics* 6, 2: 60–112.

Marglin, S. and Schor, J. (eds) (1990) *The Golden Age of Capitalism: Reinterpreting the Postwar Experience*, Oxford: Clarendon Press.

Marx, K. (1974) 'Critique of the Gotha Programme', in *The First International and After*, Harmondsworth: Penguin.

Marx, K. (1975) *Early Writings*, Harmondsworth: Penguin.

Marx, K. (1976) *Value: Studies by Marx*, in A. Dragstedt (ed.), London: New Park.

Marx, K. (1977) 'The Poverty of Philosophy', in D. McLellan (ed.) *Karl Marx: Selected Writings*, Oxford: Oxford University Press.

Marx, K. (1978a, 1969, 1972) *Theories of Surplus Value*, 3 vols., London: Lawrence and Wishart.

Marx, K. (1981a) *Grundrisse*, Harmondsworth: Penguin.

Marx, K. (1976, 1978b, 1981b) *Capital*, 3 vols., Harmondsworth: Penguin.

Marx, K. (1985) *Collected Works*, vol. 41, London: Lawrence and Wishart.

Marx, K. (1987) *A Contribution to the Critique of Political Economy, Collected Works*, vol. 29, London: Lawrence and Wishart.

Marx, K. (1988a) *Letter to Kugelmann, July 11, 1868, Collected Works*, vol. 43, London: Lawrence and Wishart.

Marx, K. (1988b) *Collected Works*, vol. 30, London: Lawrence and Wishart.

Marx, K. (1989) *Marginal Notes on Adolph Wagner's 'Lehrbuch der Politischen Ökonomie', Collected Works*, vol. 24, London: Lawrence and Wishart.

Marx, K. (1998) *Value, Price and Profit*, in K. Marx and F. Engels, *Classics in Politics* (CD-Rom), London: The Electric Book Company.

Marx, K. and Engels, F. (1998) *The Communist Manifesto*, in K. Marx and F. Engels, *Classics in Politics* (CD-Rom), London: The Electric Book Company.

Mattick, P. (1978) *Economics, Politics, and the Age of Inflation*, White Plains, N.Y.: M.E. Sharpe.

Mattick, P. Jr. (1991–92) 'Some Aspects of the Value-Price Problem', *International Journal of Political Economy* 21, 4: 9–66.

Mattick, P. Jr. (1993) 'Marx's Dialectic', in F. Moseley (ed.) *Marx's Method in 'Capital', A Reexamination*, Atlantic Highlands, N.J.: Humanities Press.

Mattick, P. Jr. (1997) 'Theory as Critique, On the Argument in *Capital*', in F. Moseley and M. Campbell (eds) *New Investigations of Marx's Method*, Atlantic Highlands, N.J.: Humanities Press.

May, K. (1948) 'Value and Price of Production, A Note on Winternitz's Solution', *Economic Journal* 58: 596–599.

Meacci, F. (1992) 'The Organic Composition of Capital and the Falling Rate of Profit', in G.A. Caravale (ed.) *Marx and Modern Economic Analysis*, Aldershot: Edward Elgar.

Medio, A. (1977) 'Neoclassicals, Neo-Ricardians, and Marx', in J.G. Schwartz (ed.) *The Subtle Anatomy of Capitalism*, Santa Monica, Calif.: Goodyear.

Meek, R.L. (1956) 'Some Notes on the "Transformation Problem"', *Economic Journal* 66: 94–107.

Meek, R.L. (1973) *Studies in the Labour Theory of Value*, London: Lawrence and Wishart.

Messori, M. (1984) 'Teoria del Valore Senza Merce-Denaro? Considerazioni Preliminari Sull'Analisi Monetaria di Marx', *Quaderni di Storia dell'Economia Política* 2, 1–2: 185–232.

Messori, M. (1991) 'Financing in Kalecki's Theory', *Cambridge Journal of Economics* 15: 301–313.

Milonakis, D. (1990) 'Historical Aspects of the Law of Value and the Transition to Capitalism', PhD Thesis, University of London.

Milonakis, D. (1993–94) 'Prelude to the Genesis of Capitalism: The Dynamics of the Feudal Mode of Production', *Science & Society* 57, 4: 390–419.

Minsky, H.P. (1975) *John Maynard Keynes*, New York: Columbia University Press.

Minsky, H.P. (1986) *Stabilizing an Unstable Economy*, New Haven: Yale University Press.

Mirowski, P. (1989) *More Heat than Light, Economics as Social Physics; Physics as Nature's Economics*, Cambridge: Cambridge University Press.

Mohun, S. (1991) 'Value', in in T. Bottomore (ed.) *A Dictionary of Marxist Thought*, 2nd edn, Oxford: Blackwell.

Mohun, S. (1994) 'A Re(in)statement of the Labour Theory of Value', *Cambridge Journal of Economics* 18: 391–412.

Mohun, S. (ed.) (1995) *Debates in Value Theory*, London: Macmillan.

Mohun, S. (1996) 'Productive and Unproductive Labor in the Labor Theory of Value', *Review of Radical Political Economics* 28, 4: 30–54.

Mohun, S. (2000) 'New Solution or Re(in)statement? A Reply', *Cambridge Journal of Economics* 24, 1: 113–117.

Mohun, S. (forthcoming) 'Productive and Unproductive Labor: A Reply to Houston and Laibman', *Review of Radical Political Economics*.

Mollo, M.L.R. (1999) 'Money Endogeneity: Post-Keynesian and Marxian Views Compared', *Research in Political Economy* 17: 3–25.

Moore, B. (1988) *Horizontalists and Verticalists: The Macroeconomics of Credit Money*, Cambridge: Cambridge University Press.

Morishima, M. (1973) *Marx's Economics—A Dual Theory of Value and Growth*, Cambridge: Cambridge University Press.

Morishima, M. (1974) 'Marx in the Light of Modern Economic Theory', *Econometrica* 42, 4: 611–632.

Morris, J. (1972) 'The Monetary Crisis of World Capitalism', *Monthly Review* 23, 8: 17–27.

Morris, J. (1973) 'The Crisis of Inflation', *Monthly Review* 25, 4: 1–22.

Moseley, F. (ed.) (1993) *Marx's Method in 'Capital', A Reexamination*, Atlantic Highlands, N.J., Humanities Press.

Moseley, F. (1994) 'Unproductive Labor and the Rate of Profit, A Reply to Cullenberg's Comment', *Review of Radical Political Economics* 26, 2: 121–128.

Moseley, F. (1995a) 'Marx's Economic Theory: True or False? A Marxian Response to Blaug's Appraisal', in *Heterodox Economic Theories: True or False?*, Aldershot: Edward Elgar.

Moseley, F. (1995b) 'Capital in General and Marx's Logical Method: A Response to Heinrich's Critique', *Capital & Class* 56: 15–48.

Moseley, F. (1997a) 'The Development of Marx's Theory of the Distribution of Surplus Value', in F. Moseley and M. Campbell (eds) *New Investigations of Marx's Method*, Atlantic Highlands, N.J.: Humanities Press.

Moseley, F. (1997b) 'Abstract Labor: Substance or Form? A Critique of the Value-Form Interpretation of Marx's Theory', unpublished manuscript.

Moseley, F. (1999) 'The United States Economy at the Turn of the Century: Entering a New Era of Prosperity?' *Capital & Class* 67: 25–46.

Moseley, F. (2000a) 'The "New Solution" to the Transformation Problem: A Sympathetic Critique', *Review of Radical Political Economics* 32, 2: 282–316.

Moseley, F. (2000b) 'The Determination of Constant Capital in the Case of a Change in the Value of the Means of Production', unpublished manuscript.

Moseley, F. and Campbell, M. (eds) (1997) *New Investigations of Marx's Method*, Atlantic Highlands, N.J.: Humanities Press.

Murray, P. (1988) *Marx's Theory of Scientific Knowledge*, Atlantic Highlands, N.J.: Humanities Press.

Murray, P. (1993) 'The Necessity of Money: How Hegel Helped Marx Surpass Ricardo's Theory of Value', in F. Moseley (ed.) *Marx's Method in 'Capital', A Reexamination*, Atlantic Highlands, N.J.: Humanities Press.

Naples, M. (1989) 'A Radical Economic Revision of the Transformation Problem', *Review of Radical Political Economics* 21, 1–2: 137–158.

Nell, E.J. (1992) *Transformational Growth and Effective Demand*, New York: New York University Press.

Nell, E.J. and Deleplace, G. (eds) (1996) *Money in Motion: The Circulation and Post Keynesian Approaches*, London: Macmillan.

Nuti, D.M. (1977) 'The Transformation of Labor Values into Production Prices and the Marxian Theory of Exploitation', in J.G. Schwartz (ed.) *The Subtle Anatomy of Capitalism*, Santa Monica, Calif. Goodyear.

Oakley, A. (1983) *The Making of Marx's Critical Theory*, London: Routledge & Kegan Paul.

Oakley, A. (1984, 1985) *Marx's Critique of Political Economy, Intellectual Sources and Evolution*, 2 Vols., London: Routledge & Kegan Paul.

Okishio, N. (1974) 'Value and Production Price', *Kobe University Economic Review* 20: 1–19.

Ollman, B. (1993) *Dialectical Investigations*, London: Routledge.

Ong, N.-P. (1980) 'Marx's Classical and Post-Classical Conceptions of the Wage', *Australian Economic Papers* 19, 35: 264–277.

Orléan, A. (1982) 'Inflation et Souveraineté Monétaire', *Critiques de l'Economie Politique* 18: 93–113.

Palley, T. (1996) *Post Keynesian Economics: Debt, Distribution and the Macro Economy*, London: Macmillan.

Panzieri, R. (1980) 'The Capitalist Use of Machinery: Marx versus the "Objectivists"', in P. Slater (ed.) *Outlines of a Critique of Technology*, Atlantic Highlands, N.J.: Humanities Press.

Pasinetti, L. (1977) *Lectures on the Theory of Production*, New York: Columbia University Press.

Perelman, M. (1987) *Marx's Crises Theory: Scarcity, Labor, and Finance*, Westport, Conn.: Praeger.

Perelman, M. (1990) 'The Phenomenology of Constant Capital and Fictitious Capital', *Review of Radical Political Economics* 22, 2–3: 66–91.

Perelman, M. (1993) 'The Qualitative Side of Marx's Value Theory', *Rethinking Marxism* 6, 1: 82–95.

Perelman, M. (1996) *The Pathology of the US Economy*. London: Macmillan.

Perelman, M. (1999) 'Marx, Devalorisation, and the Theory of Value', *Cambridge Journal of Economics* 23, 6: 719–728.

Perlman, F. (1977) 'The Reproduction of Daily Life', in J.G. Schwartz (ed.) *The Subtle Anatomy of Capitalism*, Santa Monica, Calif.: Goodyear.

Pilling, G. (1972) 'The Law of Value in Ricardo and Marx', *Economy & Society* 1, 3: 281–307.

Pilling, G. (1980) *Marx's 'Capital', Philosophy and Political Economy*, London: Routledge & Kegan Paul.

Polanyi, K. (1944) *The Great Transformation, The Political and Economic Origins of Our Time*, Beacon Hill: Beacon Press.

Post, K. (1996) *Regaining Marxism*, London: Macmillan.

Postone, M. (1993) *Time, Labour and Social Domination, A Re-examination of Marx's Critical Theory*, Cambridge: Cambridge University Press.

Psychopedis, K. (1992) 'Dialectical Theory: Problems of Reconstruction', in W. Bonefeld, R. Gunn and K. Psychopedis (eds) *Open Marxism*, vol. 1, London: Pluto Press.

Ramos-Martínez, A. and Rodríguez-Herrera, A. (1996). 'The Transformation of Values into Prices of Production: A Different Reading of Marx's Text', in A. Freeman and G. Carchedi (eds) *Marx and Non-Equilibrium*, Aldershot: Edward Elgar.

Reichelt, H. (1995) 'Why did Marx Conceal his Dialectical Method?', in W. Bonefeld, R. Gunn, J. Holloway and K. Psychopedis (eds) *Emancipating Marx*, London: Pluto.

Reinfelder, M. (1980) 'Breaking the Spell of Technicism', in P. Slater (ed.) *Outlines of a Critique of Technology*, Atlantic Highlands: Humanities Press.

Resnick, S. and Wolff, R. (1996) 'The New Marxian Political Economy and the Contribution of Althusser', in A. Callari and D. Ruccio (eds) *Postmodern Marxism and the Future of Marxist Theory: Essays in the Althusserian Tradition*, Hanover, Penn.: Wesleyan University Press.

Reuten, G. (1993) 'The Difficult Labor of a Theory of Social Value, Metaphors and Systematic Dialectics at the Beginning of Marx's "Capital"', in F. Moseley (ed.) *Marx's Method in 'Capital', A Reexamination*, Atlantic Highlands, N.J.: Humanities Press.

Reuten, G. (1995) 'Conceptual Collapses: A Note on Value-Form Theory', *Review of Radical Political Economics* 27, 3: 104–110.

Reuten, G. (1997) 'The Notion of Tendency in Marx's 1894 Law of Profit', in F. Moseley and M. Campbell (eds) *New Investigations of Marx's Method*, Atlantic Highlands, N.J.: Humanities Press.

Reuten, G. (1999) 'The Source versus Measure Obstacle in Value Theory', *Rivista di Política Econômica* 89, 4–5: 87–115.

Reuten, G. and Williams, M. (1989) *Value-Form and the State, The Tendencies of Accumulation and the Determination of Economic Policy in Capitalist Society*, London: Routledge.

Ricardo, D. (1951) *On the Principles of Political Economy and Taxation*, Cambridge: Cambridge University Press.

Ricardo, D. (1966) *The High Price of Bullion, a Proof of the Depreciation of Bank Notes*, in *Collected Works*, vol. 3, Cambridge: Cambridge University Press.

Roberts, B. (1987) 'Marx After Steedman, Separating Marxism from "Surplus Theory"', *Capital & Class* 32: 84–103.

Roberts, B. (1996) 'The Visible and the Measurable: Althusser and the Marxian Theory of Value', in A. Callari and D. Ruccio (eds) *Postmodern Marxism and the Future of Marxist Theory: Essays in the Althusserian Tradition*, Hanover, Penn.: Wesleyan University Press.

Roberts, B. (1997) 'Embodied Labour and Competitive Prices: A Physical Quantities Approach', *Cambridge Journal of Economics* 21: 483–502.

Roemer, J.E. (1979) 'Continuing Controversy on the Falling Rate of Profit, Fixed Capital and Other Issues', *Cambridge Journal of Economics* 3: 379–398.

Roncaglia, A. (1974) 'The Reduction of Complex Labour to Simple Labour', *Bulletin of the Conference of Socialist Economists* 9.

Roosevelt, F. (1977) 'Cambridge Economics as Commodity Fetishism', in J.G. Schwartz (ed.) *The Subtle Anatomy of Capitalism*, Santa Monica, Calif.: Goodyear.

Rosdolsky, R. (1977) *The Making of Marx's 'Capital'*, London: Pluto Press.

Rosenberg, S. and Weisskopf, T. (1981) 'A Conflict Theory Approach to Inflation in the Postwar U.S. Economy', *American Economic Review* 71, 2: 42–47.

Rosenthal, J. (1997) *The Myth of Dialectics: Reinterpreting the Marx-Hegel Relation*, London: Macmillan.

Rosenthal, J. (1999) 'The Escape from Hegel', *Science & Society* 63, 3: 283–309.

Rosenthal, J. (2000) 'The Escape from Hegelians: Rejoinder', *Science & Society* 64, 4: 502–517.

Rowthorn, B. (1980) *Capitalism, Conflict and Inflation*, London: Lawrence and Wishart.

Rubin, I.I. (1975) *Essays on Marx's Theory of Value*, Montréal: Black Rose Books.

Rubin, I.I. (1978) 'Abstract Labour and Value in Marx's System', *Capital & Class* 5: 107–140.

Rubin, I.I. (1979) *A History of Economic Thought*, London: Pluto Press.

Saad-Filho, A. (1993a) 'Labour, Money and "Labour-Money", A Review of Marx's Critique of John Gray's Monetary Analysis', *History of Political Economy* 25, 1: 65–84.

Saad-Filho, A. (1993b) 'A Note on Marx's Analysis of the Composition of Capital', *Capital & Class* 50: 127–146.

Saad-Filho, A. (1996a) 'The Value of Money, the Value of Labour Power and the Net Product, An Appraisal of the "New Approach" to the Transformation Problem', in A. Freeman and G. Carchedi (eds) *Marx and Non-Equilibrium Economics*, Aldershot: Edward Elgar.

Saad-Filho, A. (1996b) 'Inconvertible Paper Money and the Labour Theory of Value', discussion paper E96/07, University of Leeds.

Saad-Filho, A. (1997a) 'Concrete and Abstract Labour in Marx's Theory of Value', *Review of Political Economy* 9, 4: 457–477.

Saad-Filho, A. (1997b) 'An Alternative Reading of the Transformation of Values into Prices of Production', *Capital & Class* 63: 115–136.

Saad-Filho, A. (1997c) 'Re-Reading both Hegel and Marx: The "New Dialectics" and the Method of "Capital"', *Revista de Economia Política-Brazilian Journal of Political Economy* 17, 1: 107–120.

Saad-Filho, A. (2000a) 'Inflation Theory: A Critical Literature Review and a New Research Agenda', *Research in Political Economy* 18: 335–362.

Saad-Filho, A. (2000b) ' "Vertical" versus "Horizontal" Economics: Systems of Provision, Consumption Norms and Labour Market Structures', *Capital & Class* 72: 209–214.

Saad-Filho, A. and Mollo, M.L.R. (forthcoming) 'Inflation and Stabilization in Brazil: A Political Economy Analysis', *Review of Radical Political Economics*.

Saad-Filho, A. and Morais, L. (2000) 'The Costs of Neomonetarism: The Brazilian Economy in the 1990s', *International Papers in Political Economy* 7, 3.

Salama, P. (1984) 'Value and Price of Production, A Differential Approach', in E. Mandel and A. Freeman (eds) *Ricardo, Marx, Sraffa*, London: Verso.

Samuelson, P.M. (1957) 'Wages and Interest, A Modern Dissection of Marxian Economic Models', *American Economic Review* 47, 6: 884–912.

Samuelson, P.M. (1971) 'Understanding the Marxian Notion of Exploitation, A Summary of the So-Called Transformation Problem Between Marxian Values and Competitive Prices', *Journal of Economic Literature* 9, 2: 399–431.

Samuelson, P.M. (1973) 'Reply on Marxian Matters', *Journal of Economic Literature* 11, 1: 64–68.

Samuelson, P.M. (1974) 'Insight and Detour in the Theory of Exploitation, A Reply to Baumol', *Journal of Economic Literature* 12, 1: 62–70.

Savran, S. (1979) 'On The Theoretical Consistency of Sraffa's Economics', *Capital & Class* 7: 131–140.

Savran, S. (1980) 'On Confusions Concerning Sraffa (and Marx), Reply to Critics', *Capital & Class* 12: 85–98.

Savran, S. (1984) 'The Negation of Negative Values', in E. Mandel and A. Freeman (eds) *Ricardo, Marx, Sraffa*, London: Verso.

Savran, S. and Tonak, A. (1999) 'Productive and Unproductive Labour: An Attempt at Clarification and Classification' *Capital & Class* 68: 113–152.

Sawyer, M.C. (1985) *The Economics of Michal Kalecki*, London: Macmillan.

Sawyer, M.C. (1989) *The Challenge of Radical Political Economy*, Aldershot: Edward Elgar.

Schefold, B. (1998) 'The Relationship between the Rate of Profit and the Rate of Interest: A Reassessment after the Publication of Marx's Manuscript of the Third Volume of *Das Kapital*', in R. Bellofiore (ed.) *Marxian Economics: A Reappraisal, Essays on Volume III of Capital*, vol. 2, London: Macmillan.

Schotter, A. (1990) *Free Market Economics*, Oxford: Blackwell.

Schutz, E. (1999) 'Exploitation', in P. O'Hara (ed.) *Encyclopedia of Political Economy*, vol. 1, London: Routledge.

Schumpeter, J.A. (1954) *History of Economic Analysis*, London: Allen & Unwin.

Schwartz, J.G. (ed.) (1977) *The Subtle Anatomy of Capitalism*, Santa Monica, Calif.: Goodyear.

Schwarz, B. (1985) 'Re-Assessing Braverman: Socialisation and Dispossession in the History of Technology', in L. Levidow and B. Young (eds) *Science, Techology and the Labour Process*, vol. 2, Atlantic Highlands, N.J.: Humanities Press.

Scott, S. (1999) 'Thought and Social Struggle: A History of Dialectics', PhD Thesis, University of Bradford.

Sekine, T. (1975) 'Uno-Riron, A Japanese Contribution to Marxian Political Economy', *Journal of Economic Literature* 13, 3: 847–877.

Semmler, W. (1982) 'Theories of Competition and Monopoly', *Capital & Class* 18: 91–116.

Seton, F. (1957) 'The "Transformation Problem"', *Review of Economic Studies* 24: 149–160.

Shaikh, A. (1973) 'Theories of Value and Theories of Distribution', PhD Thesis, Columbia University.

Shaikh, A. (1977) 'Marx's Theory of Value and the "Transformation Problem"', in J.G. Schwartz (ed.) *The Subtle Anatomy of Capitalism*, Santa Monica, Calif.: Goodyear.

Shaikh, A. (1981) 'The Poverty of Algebra', in I. Steedman (ed.) *The Value Controversy*, London: Verso.

Shaikh, A. (1982) 'Neo-Ricardian Economics, A Wealth of Algebra, a Poverty of Theory', *Review of Radical Political Economics* 14, 2: 67–83.

Shaikh, A. (1984) 'The Transformation from Marx to Sraffa', in E. Mandel and A. Freeman (eds) *Ricardo, Marx, Sraffa*, London: Verso.

Shaikh, A. (1991) 'Values and Value Transfers: A Comment on Itoh', in B. Roberts and S. Feiner (eds.) *Radical Economics*, Boston: Kluwer.

Shaikh, A. (1998) 'The Empirical Strength of the Labour Theory of Value', in R. Bellofiore (ed.) *Marxian Economics: A Reappraisal, Essays on Volume III of Capital*, vol. 1, London: Macmillan.

Shamsavari, A. (1987) *A Critique of the Transformation Problem*, London: Kingston Polytechnic Discussion Papers in Political Economy, no. 58.

Shamsavari, A. (1991) *Dialectic and Social Theory, The Logic of 'Capital'*, Braunton, Devon: Merlin Books.

Sherman, H. (1972) 'Inflation, Profits and the New Economic Policy', *Review of Radical Political Economics* 4, 4: 113–121.

Sherman, H. (1976a), *Stagflation: A Radical Theory of Unemployment and Inflation*, New York: Harper and Row.

Sherman, H. (1976b) 'Inflation, Unemployment, and Monopoly Capital', *Monthly Review* 27, 10: 25–35.

Shibata, K. (1933) 'The Meaning of the Theory of Value in Theoretical Economics', *Kyoto University Economic Review* 8, 2: 49–68.

Slater, P. (ed.) (1980) *Outlines of a Critique of Technology*, Atlantic Highlands, N.J.: Humanities Press.

Smith, A. (1991) *The Wealth of Nations*, London: Everyman.

Smith, M. (1994a) *Invisible Leviathan: The Marxist Critique of Market Despotism beyond Postmodernism*, Toronto: University of Toronto Press.

Smith, M. (1994b) 'Alienation, Exploitation and Abstract Labor: A Humanist Defense of Marx's Theory of Value', *Review of Radical Political Economics* 26, 1: 110–133.

Smith, T. (1990) *The Logic of Marx's 'Capital', Reply to Hegelian Criticisms*, Albany, N.Y.: State of New York Press.

Smith, T. (1993a) *Dialectical Social Theory and Its Critics*, Albany: State University of New York Press.

Smith, T. (1993b) 'Marx's "Capital" and Hegelian Dialectical Logic', in F. Moseley (ed.) *Marx's Method in 'Capital', A Reexamination*, Atlantic Highlands, N.J.: Humanities Press.

Smith, T. (1997) 'Marx's Theory of Social Forms and Lakatos's Methodology of Scientific Research Programs', in F. Moseley and M. Campbell (eds) *New Investigations of Marx's Method*, Atlantic Highlands, N.J.: Humanities Press.

Smith, T. (1998) 'Value Theory and Dialectics', *Science & Society* 62, 3: 460–470.

Smith, T. (1999a) 'The Relevance of Systematic Dialectics to Marxian Thought: Reply to Rosenthal', *Historical Materialism* 4: 215–240.

Smith, T (1999b). 'Brenner and Crisis Theory: Issues in Systematic and Historical Dialectics', *Historical Materialism* 5: 145–178.

Sohn-Rethel, A. (1978) *Intellectual and Manual Labour: A Critique of Epistemology*, London: Macmillan.

Spencer, D. (2000) 'Braverman and the Contribution of Labour Process Analysis to the Critique of Capitalist Production—Twenty Five Years On', *Work, Employment and Society* 14, 2: 223–243.

Spero, N. (1969) 'Notes on the Current Inflation', *Monthly Review* 21, 2: 29–32.

Sraffa, P. (1960) *Production of Commodities By Means Of Commodities: Prelude to a Critique of Economic Theory*, Cambridge: Cambridge University Press.

Stamatis, G. (1998–99) 'On the "New Solution"', *International Journal of Political Economy* 28, 4: 23–46.

Steedman, I. (1977) *Marx after Sraffa*, London: New Left Books.

Steedman, I. (ed.) (1981) *The Value Controversy*, London: Verso.

Steindl, J. (1952) *Maturity and Stagnation in American Capitalism*, Oxford: Blackwell.

Sweezy, P. (1949) 'Introduction', in *Karl Marx and the Close of His System*, Clifton: N.J.: A.M. Kelley.

Sweezy, P. (1968) *The Theory of Capitalist Development*, New York: Monthly Review Press.

Sweezy, P. (1974) 'Baran and the Danger of Inflation', *Monthly Review* 27, 7: 11–14.

Sweezy, P. and Magdoff, H. (1979) 'Inflation without End?' *Monthly Review* 31, 6: 1–10.

Sweezy, P. and Magdoff, H. (1983) 'Supply-side Theory and Capital Investment', *Monthly Review* 34: 1–9.

Szymanski, A. (1984) 'Productivity Growth and Capitalist Stagnation', *Science and Society* 48, 3: 295–322.

Szumski, J. (1991) 'On Duménil and Lévy's Denial of The Existence of The So-Called Transformation Problem, A Reply', *Cambridge Journal of Economics* 15, 3: 365–371.

Taylor, N. (2000) 'Abstract Labour and Social Mediation in Marxian Value Theory', Bachelor of Economics (Honours) dissertation, Murdoch University.

Taylor, P. (1979) 'Labour Time, Work Measurement and the Commensuration of Labour', *Capital & Class* 9: 23–37.

Thompson, E.P. (1967) 'Time, Work-Discipline, and Industrial Capitalism', *Past and Present* 38: 56–97.

Thompson, E.P. (1978) *The Poverty of Theory*, London: Merlin Press.

Toporowski, J. (2000) *The End of Finance*, London: Routledge.

Tortajada, R. (1977) 'A Note on the Reduction of Complex Labour to Simple Labour', *Capital & Class* 1: 106–116.

Tugan-Baranowsky, M.I. (1905) *Theoretische Grundlagen des Marxismus*, Leipzig: Doucker und Humboldt.

Uno, K. (1980) *Principles of Political Economy: Theory of a Purely Capitalist Society*, Brighton: Harvester Press.

Vegara i Carrio, J. (1978) *Economía Política y Modelos Multisectoriales*, Madrid: Editorial Tecnos.

Vroey, M. de (1981) 'Value, Production and Exchange', in I. Steedman (ed.) *The Value Controversy*, London: Verso.

Vroey, M. de (1982) 'On the Obsolescence of the Marxian Theory of Value, A Critical Review', *Capital & Class* 17: 34–59.

Vroey, M. de (1984) 'Inflation, A Non-Monetarist Monetary Interpretation', *Cambridge Journal of Economics* 8: 381–399.

Vroey, M. de (1985) 'La Théorie Marxiste de la Valeur, Version Travail Abstrait, Un Bilan Critique', in G. Dostaler and M. Lagueux (eds) *Un Echiquier Centenaire, Théorie de la Valeur et Formation des Prix*, Paris: La Découverte.

Weeks, J. (1977) 'The Sphere of Production and the Analysis of Crisis in Capitalism', *Science and Society* 41: 281–302.

Weeks, J. (1979) 'The Process of Accumulation and the Profit Squeeze Hypothesis', *Science and Society* 43: 259–280.

Weeks, J. (1981) *Capital and Exploitation*, Princeton: Princeton University Press.

Weeks, J. (1982a) 'Equilibrium, Uneven Development and the Tendency of the Rate of Profit to Fall' *Capital & Class* 16: 62–77.

Weeks, J. (1982b) 'A Note on Underconsumptionist Theory and the Labor Theory of Value', *Science & Society* 46, 1: 60–76.

Weeks, J. (1983) 'On the Issue of Capitalist Circulation and the Concepts Appropriate to Its Analysis', *Science & Society* 48, 2: 214–225.

Weeks, J. (1984) 'Theory, Ideology and Idolatry', *Economic and Political Weekly* 19, 48: 2054–2056.

Weeks, J. (1990) 'Abstract Labor and Commodity Production', *Research in Political Economy* 12: 3–19.

Weeks, J. (1992) 'Competition and Technical Change in an Aggregate Circulation Framework', unpublished manuscript.

Weintraub, S. (1981) 'An Eclectic Theory of Income Shares', *Journal of Post Keynesian Economics* 4, 1: 10–24.

Weisskopf, T., Bowles, S. and Gordon, D. (1985) 'Two Views of Capitalist Stagnation: Underconsumption and Challenges to Capitalist Control', *Science and Society* 49, 3: 259–286.

Wennerlind, C. (2000) 'The Labor Theory of Value and the Strategic Nature of Alienation', unpublished manuscript.

Wheelock, J. (1983) 'Competition in the Marxist Tradition', *Capital & Class* 21: 18–47.

Williams, M. (1998) 'Money and Labour-Power: Marx after Hegel, or Smith plus Sraffa?' *Cambridge Journal of Economics* 22: 187–198.

Williams, M. (2000) 'Why Marx neither has nor Needs a Commodity Theory of Money', *Review of Political Economy* 12, 4: 435–451.

Winternitz, J. (1948) 'Values and Prices, A Solution to the So-Called Transformation Problem', *Economic Journal* 58, 2: 276–280.

Wolff, R. (1984) *Understanding Marx: A Reconstruction and Critique of 'Capital'*, Princeton: Princeton University Press.

Wolff, R., Roberts, B. and Callari, A. (1982) 'Marx's (not Ricardo's) Transformation Problem, A Radical Reconceptualization', *History of Political Economy* 14, 4: 564–582.

Wolff, R., Roberts, B. and Callari, A. (1984) 'A Marxian Alternative to the Traditional "Transformation Problem"', *Review of Radical Political Economics* 16, 2–3: 115–135.

Wolfstetter, E. (1973) 'Surplus Labour, Synchronised Labour Costs and Marx's Labour Theory of Value, *Economic Journal* 83: 787–809.

Wright, E.O. (1977) 'Alternative Perspectives in Marxist Theory of Accumulation and Crisis', in J.G. Schwartz (ed.) *The Subtle Anatomy of Capitalism*, Santa Monica, Calif.: Goodyear.

Wright, E.O. (1981) 'The Value Controversy and Social Research', in I. Steedman (ed.) *The Value Controversy*, London: Verso.

Yaffe, D. (1974) 'Value and Price in Marx's "Capital"', *Revolutionary Communist* 1: 31–49.

Yaffe, D. (1995) 'Value, Price and the Neo-Ricardians: An Introductory Note', in S. Mohun (ed.) *Debates in Value Theory*, London: Macmillan.

Zarembka, P. (2000) 'Accumulation of Capital, its Definition: A Century after Lenin and Luxemburg', *Research in Political Economy* 18: 183–225.

Zarifian, P. (1975) *Inflation et Crise Monétaire*, Paris: Editions Sociales.

Zelený, J. (1980) *The Logic of Marx*, Oxford: Basil Blackwell.

Index

value 19, 22–4, 27–9, 33, 35–7, 43, 56, 63, 68–9, 107, 109, 115, 119, 122, 133; added 31; analysis 12, 22, 27, 46, 54; as capital 127; concept 19; creation or production 47, 54, 57–8, 84, 90, 115, 122, 125; definition 114; destruction 28, 68–9; essence 115; form 22–3, 26, 36, 43, 90, 92, 98, 105; indeterminacy 65; inputs 63, 75, 87–8, 90, 119, 135; machines 84; magnitude 23; market 128; 'natural' 142; new 83; and price 45, 66–7, 81, 88–9, 91, 93, 105, 122, 137; realisation 28, 125; redistribution 68; relations 12, 21, 27, 32, 36, 46, 87; reproduction (RSNLT) 54, 62–3, 65–6, 69, 81, 87, 90, 93–4, 98, 136; substance 10, 12, 22–3, 25, 29; tendency to fall 78, 177; symbol 95; transfer 54, 63, 65–6, 141; uncertainty 65–6; vector 23–5, 27; *see also* exchange value; labour; Marx's value theory; price; valorisation; value productivity
value-form theory 23, 26, 29; *see also* Rubin tradition
Vegara i Carrio, J. 120
versatility 60–1; *see also* labour
Vroey, M. de 119, 121, 130, 135–7, 141–2, 145–7.

wage 45, 48–9, 57, 93, 101, 129–32, 138; exploitation 44; rate 24, 49, 52, 89;

relation 3–4, 28, 50; theory 102; *see also* capital; exploitation
wage workers 27, 29, 36, 38; militancy 106; resistance 55; subordination 29; *see also* class
Walton, P. 146
wants 52, 124; *see also* needs; poverty
wealth 124, 139
Weeks, J. 3, 111, 119–23, 126, 129, 130, 132, 135–9, 141, 143, 145
Weintraub, S. 145
Weisskopf, T. 145–6
Wennerlind, C. 134–5
Wheelock, J. 127
Williams, M. 116–17, 121, 135, 139, 143, 145–6
Winternitz, J. 119–20, 137, 142
Wolff, R. 117, 120, 139, 141
Wolfstetter, E. 135
work: collective 132; forced 129; *see also* labour
workers: discipline 47, 127; training 25, 47, 56–7, 60, 120; *see also* labour
working day 47–8, 120, 130–2; *see also* labour
Wright, E.O. 72, 130, 137, 145

Yaffe, D. 120–1, 137, 139, 141–2
Young, B. 134–5

Zarembka, P. 126–7
Zarifian, P. 146
Zelený, J. 112–16, 118

Printed in the United States
93314LV00001B/128/A

9 780415 459266